Made *for* (

Christian Nothhaft

Made *for* China

Success Strategies
From China's Business
Icons

Copernicus Books is a brand of Springer

Christian Nothhaft
Shatin, Hong Kong

ISBN 978-3-319-61583-7   ISBN 978-3-319-61584-4   (eBook)
DOI 10.1007/978-3-319-61584-4

Library of Congress Control Number: 2017950081

This Springer imprint is published by Springer Nature
The registered company is Springer International Publishing AG
The registered company address is: Gewerbestrasse 11, 6330 Cham, Switzerland

Why I Wrote This Book

In 1997, I decided to break ties with my home country, Germany, and move to Asia.

The reason for this major move emerged in 1996 while I was working for a chain-store restaurant company as global development director. I was determined to prove my board members—who had allowed me to consider business in Asia but were not prepared to fund it with major company money—wrong. So, I raised money from business partners in Asia to develop restaurant chains in five Asian countries. Many of my friends thought I was crazy to go there and start a business. But when the businesses opened in that year, we were surprised by—despite an Asian crises—how many customers flocked to our restaurants, in some cases spending 2 days' worth of salary on a meal with friends. So with "Asia rising" in my head, at the age of 30 I decided to say "goodbye" to my fiancé (to the initial horror of my family) and my friends and set up an office in Hong Kong. Though developing business across Asia from Hong Kong was fun and exciting, the "big elephant" in the room was always the massive potential consumer market in China.

In 1996, I made several visits to China, especially Shanghai, at a time when Pudong looked more like a swamp than a Global Finance District. Though still in the early days, the place was bustling. I wondered: How long would it take before China "happened?"

In 1999, I decided to move to China in search of the answer and found myself in a city in the middle of nowhere, initially producing food for the export market but increasingly for urban Chinese who were getting used to what we in the West call "supermarkets." But this was still in its infancy back then, and business life was a seemingly never-ending cycle of navigating the so-called planned economy. When I returned to Hong Kong around 2002 to raise money to buy a coffee house chain and go to China with it (then the number two player after Starbucks), the fundraising round mostly involved convincing investors that Chinese people would one day drink coffee. I found it challenging to bring the message of global trends across. More often than not, I was turned down with the argument: "Chinese people drink tea—that will never change." Looking back, it was an interesting learning experience, given the fact that Starbucks now has 2300 stores in China and opens an average of 300 new stores every year.

So, essentially by accident, in 2003 I found myself in Hong Kong working for Asia's (then) richest man, trying to figure out how to sell wine and electronic products to young consumers. Back then, wine was a staple for Westerners, but not yet for young Chinese locals, as they didn't understand the product, nor were they familiar with electronic products that constantly changed, including the appearance of the iPhone. During those days, I noticed a major shift in how business was being done in China. Importers and state-owned monopolies became less prominent, and retailers rose to reflect customers who were increasingly confident enough to demand choices and better products. This caught my attention!

In 2007, I asked our company to move me to China to see what we could do with a 200-store retail chain that we owned there. Having finally recognized the market potential, I happily decided to move (together with my family), offering my Hong Kong-born children (then aged 4 and 5) the perfect opportunity to prepare them for the future new world order—a world that would speak both English and Mandarin.

Nine years later, that 200-store retail chain in China has grown to over 3000 stores in 450 cities, with nearly half of its sales coming from products it either makes itself or sells exclusively. From 2009, as we began entering the Digital Age, our business evolved into consumer data collection, and today, we have over 60 million customer connections in our rapidly growing digital ecosystem. Riding the first wave of the consumer market, and focusing on female consumers, the company grew rapidly by evolving along with its consumers. Despite the slowdown in the Chinese economy, we are still opening 500 new stores a year, while our Internet business has nearly doubled in size year-on-year. Meanwhile, our China company has evolved from selling products to creating its own product brands—with many of them outperforming international competitors in terms of sales and growth. In some product categories, it's the leader in its market, with the next largest competitor being about a fifth of its size.

In 2014, I began to reflect upon whether we were an exception. I decided to investigate other leading Chinese companies to better understand how they have grown, what opportunities they see, and how they implement their strategies for success. I was also keen to discover the biggest success stories in the consumer market and identify trends worth investing in and developing as a consumer business like ours in China. In this book, I attempt to summarize them as four consumer Mega Stories: face (customer individuality), family, food, and fun. In fact, I have structured the book accordingly.

The Internet and mobile space currently continue to grab the headlines. However, it is my conviction that the next phase of the consumer market in China belongs to the product makers. So—for this book—I was particularly interested in interviewing product makers, brand owners, and physical retailers with a presence throughout China, to hear and learn from their stories. Given the insular nature of traditional companies, and especially their founders, I feared this would be extremely difficult to achieve. But it was also an intriguing challenge, especially since more Chinese companies had become engaged in mergers overseas, and I wanted to understand what the objectives behind such bold and sometimes puzzling moves were.

To put the stories of how Chinese companies came to be leaders in their respective markets in perspective, we first need to understand how the Chinese consumer market got to where it is today. This book, therefore, first describes some of the key drivers challenging the entrepreneurs interviewed for this book (and for myself in the market); it then explores the evolution of the consumer generations in China over such a short period of time, and the competition to keep up with ever-changing consumer demands, as well as the disruptive emergence of e-commerce, which is breaking up traditional distribution channels, fueling competition and enabling smaller companies to compete with bigger players.

Before we "get going" with our stories, first and foremost, I need to thank the interviewees for making time in their busy schedules and for being both straightforward and open-minded in our often-lengthy conversations. To those interviewees who I have known more closely for several years, a big thank you for also being my competitors and teachers on how to run things well in China. Besides the interviewees themselves, many people who I cherish were involved in setting up the interviews. I would like to thank my personal network, my friends, including Yue Sai Kan and Danxia Chen, for helping with introductions and explaining the sincerity and value of this project in their business networks. Also to Catherine Yang who worked for me in a freelance capacity, which included helping to write some chapters, thus keeping my mind free to run the company, while not drowning in this "weekend project." Also a special thank you to Matthew Crabbe of Mintel, an expert with a 30-year business record in China and vast experience with Chinese consumer market numbers (and a truly up-to-date trend expert), and to Yuhan Shi, my passionate coeditor (ex Bloomberg Businessweek), who helped me to complete this effort. Both not only served as critical sounding boards but also helped with the editing. A big thank you to Anson Bailey and Keith Wong (both at KPMG), who were kind enough to offer help with data for the various chapters. In the process, I was able to learn to appreciate KPMG's data and network power in China. I would also like to thank my copy editor Matthew Fentem for helping me turn this into a cohesive book, and the folks at Springer—Editor Prashanth Mahagaonkar and Nils Peter Thomas—for not giving up on a first-time writer.

The thoughts behind and shared in this book wouldn't be here were it not for the experience I gained while building our company in China. Therefore, a big thank you to my team for the many years of innovation and maintaining the "start-up spirit" (the secret recipe for success in China), even after 10 years. Also, a thank you to my competitors and suppliers for challenging our company and me for the last 10 years. In doing so, you have been great teachers every step of the way!

Most of all, I would like to thank my wife and children for putting up with my pursuing this at times seemingly endless project and consequently having to do without me on many weekends while we were out interviewing or writing. I hope this book serves as an inspiration to my children (and my team at the company): to learn from others every day, to embrace change every time it arises, to see the opportunity behind every challenge, and to always find unique ways to move forward. (Tip: Ideally ways that are hard to copy!)

Hong Kong   Christian Nothhaft
June 2017

Contents

About the Author

Christian Nothhaft has been living and working in Asia for the past 20 years, 12 of which were in China. He is one of the leading business minds dealing with the Asian markets, and especially when it comes to China and the Chinese consumer. A German native with a background in marketing, retail, and FMCG consulting, Mr. Nothhaft moved to Asia in 1997, raising investor capital and setting up several chain stores and food businesses in Korea, Hong Kong, and South East Asia. In 1999, he had his first experience in the Mainland China, where he set up and expanded food manufacturing businesses. After building up two high-profile online and offline consumer businesses for Hong Kong's largest conglomerate, he moved to China in 2007 to develop a consumer retail business for young female white-collar consumers. The company has since become the market leader, consisting of over 3000 stores in over 450 cities, a shopper database with over 60 million members, and a fast-growing mobile commerce platform. After 10 years, the company is still in hyper-growth, opening 500+ new stores each year. More importantly, Mr. Nothhaft has been accepted as an equal among China's leading business figures, a fact that grants him unique access to Chinese companies and consumer entrepreneurs alike.

Part I

China's Customers and How to Lead the Trend with Them

1

Understanding China's Consumers

The Background: History Won't Repeat Itself—From a Planned Economy to the World's Largest Consumer Market in One Generation

The evolution—or perhaps better said—sudden appearance of China as the world's largest consumer market happened practically overnight, or, more precisely, within a single generation. In 1970, China's GDP was a mere 8.5% of the US GDP, but by 2016 had climbed to 58%. By 2013, China had become the second-largest economy in the world. By 2020, it is forecasted that China will have almost caught up with the USA. So, China is too important for businesses to ignore in terms of consumers.

But is this evolution a miracle or coincidence? Not at all! China is merely playing catch-up with the rest of the world. China used to have a flourishing economy and consumer market. In fact, during the Tang dynasty (618–907), it was the world's largest economy. Back then, its economy was largely driven by the domestic market—trade between agriculturally and geographically diverse provinces and regions.

This phase was succeeded by one of gradual decline, right up until the late twentieth century, at which time (only about 40 years ago) the words "market" and "consumer" were practically unheard of in China. The consumer economy hit rock bottom. Following the famine of the late 1950s, the leadership recognized that they had to change their economic policies. From 1979 onwards, under Deng Xiaoping, they embarked on a series of economic experiments to test market mechanics on their home soil, initiating the main

© The Author(s) 2018
C. Nothhaft, *Made for China*, DOI 10.1007/978-3-319-61584-4_1

drivers for China's economic "miracle" through urbanization, export orientation, and establishing the country's subsequent role as "workbench of the world."

The urbanization numbers themselves are staggering. In the 1980s, three-quarters of China's population lived in rural areas. By 1998, the number had decreased to two-thirds. Another decade later, the rural population made up 45% of the total population, and by 2011, China reached the historic point of becoming a majority urban population, with nearly 52% of people living in urban areas. This process was extremely influential in the development of China's consumer market. And the urbanization process continues today.

In 2001, following 15 years of difficult negotiations, China finally became a member of the WTO. Thanks to its cheap labor, China quickly positioned itself as the workbench of the world, giving rise to manufacturing clusters that accelerated the process of people leaving the countryside to find work in or near cities where manufacturing jobs were on offer. Between 1980 and 2014, China's workforce increased by about 350 million people. A large majority of the "new additions" (83%) have now settled in the cities thanks to the government's ongoing efforts to accelerate urbanization.[1]

In parallel, between 2000 and 2010, China managed to double the average per-capita income and is currently pursuing plans to double salaries again between 2010 and 2020. What that means for the consumer market is extremely positive, of course. However, it also has its downside in terms of China's competitiveness, thus requiring a departure from the "workbench of the world" model, towards developing domestic consumption.

While urbanization, workforce development, and income growth are the key indicators of the emergence of a possible consumer economy, it is worthwhile to examine how some of the underlying market infrastructures evolved—more specifically, the development of transport systems, places to shop (i.e., malls or department stores), and means of communication or means to receive and share information.

The Table 1.1 reveals how, in an extremely short period, the fundamentals of consumers' classic shopping (malls, department stores, retail outlets, TV advertising, and PC penetration) exploded on the back of urbanization, intercity, and intra-city transport (see Table 1.1). This process is ongoing and still provides companies many opportunities. Most relevant for now and the future is the explosion of smart phone use in China, which has put millions of people directly in touch with brands, anytime and anywhere. This rapid development of the world's largest consumer market (by population) coincides with massive global advances in technology, e-commerce, and consumer big

Table 1.1 Rapid development of infrastructure in China

Source if not otherwise stated[a]	Data points (Yr)	The 1990s	The 2000s	The 2010s
Transport				
Highway ('000 km)	1994/2004/2014	1.6	34.3	111.9
High-speed trains (km)[b]	2008/2012	–	643	5180
City rail transit (km)	2006/2014	–	621	2816
Places to Shop				
Chain retail outlets no.	2004/2014	–	77,631	206,415
Department stores	2004/2014	–	2637	4689
Commercial properties for sale (million m²)	2004/2014	–	31.0	90.8
Shopping malls	2005/2015	–	1000	4300
No. of merchants on Taobao[c]	2015	–	–	9,000,000
Retrieving information				
TVs per 100 urban households	1992/2002/2012	74.9	126.4	136.1
PCs per 100 urban households	1997/2002/2012	2.6	20.6	87.0
Sharing information				
No. of mobile phones (million)	1997/2002/2012	1.7	62.9	212.6
Share of smartphones among mobile phones[d] %	2013/2015	–	–	43.0%/50.9%
Combined monthly average users of Weixin & Wechat (million)[e]	2012/2016	–	–	160.8/805.7
Web/data traffic[f] (million GB)	2010/2014	–	–	399.4/4186.8
Internet users ('000)	1997/2004/2016	620	94,000	710,000
Consumer money				
Total credit card payments (trillion RMB)	2015	–	–	7.08[g]
Online payments (trillion RMB)	2010/2015	–	–	0.06[h]/23.5 (via mobile)

[a]National Bureau of Statistics of China, http://data.stats.gov.cn/easyquery.htm?cn=C01, accessed November 20, 2016

[b]National Railway Administration, http://www.nra.gov.cn/ztzl/hyjc/gstl_/zggstL/kt/, accessed November 20, 2016

[c]Internet Retailer, https://www.Internetretailer.com/2015/04/27/alibaba-encourages-merchants-focus-mobile-shoppers, accessed November 20, 2016

[d]Statista, https://www.statista.com/statistics/257045/smartphone-user-penetration-in-china/, accessed November 20, 2016

[e]Tencent Financial Reports, http://www.tencent.com/en-us/ir/reports.shtml, accessed November 20, 2016

[f]Ministry of Industrial and Information Technology, http://www.miit.gov.cn/n1146312/n1146904/n1648372/c4620679/content.html, accessed November 20, 2016

[g]The People's Bank of China, http://www.pbc.gov.cn/goutongjiaoliu/113456/113469/3044071/2016040516445058937.pdf

[h]The People's Bank of China, http://www.pbc.gov.cn/eportal/fileDir/image_public/UserFiles/goutongjiaoliu/upload/File/中国支付体系发展报告2010.pdf

data, accelerating the way people discover and select products across a massive population.

China's consumer society has been leapfrogging the development stages seen in mature economies, and the consumer economy surpassed 50% of GDP in 2014, with rapidly changing consumer needs and technological adaptation now driving massive diversification in consumer lifestyles and needs. This has happened as the consumer economy growth rate has slowed. This slowing of growth has been quite natural and, despite a stock market crash in mid-2015 that triggered shockwaves across the consumer market, the reality is that China's economy is now shifting into what economists (and now everyone else) have dubbed China's "New Normal," characterized by economic growth rates closer to 6% going forward.

As economic growth slows and continues to shift towards domestic consumption, we can observe that the so-called middle class is being split into two parts: those who work in progressive industries with good prospects and rising incomes and those in less attractive industries, who will have difficulties improving or even maintaining their middle-class status.

China's consumer economy is still developing relatively quickly given its large size, is becoming more complex, and is leapfrogging generations of social development. Faster than some had expected, it also faces the issue of a widening income gap. The government is constantly busy managing this complex process—under the scrutiny of its people and the world at large. These issues sound familiar to other economies, but what's different here is the sheer size of the population involved and the speed at which these developments have been emerging. What is also unique about China is that, due to its aforementioned leapfrogging developmental stages, the consumer generations have also leapfrogged, creating what could be called a Six-In-One consumer generation market.

The Driver: China's Six-in-One Consumer Generations

Over the years, I have had many visitors ask me: "So what are Chinese consumers like?" And I find this question hard to answer briefly. While there are some commonalities, such as the appreciation of low prices or a good deal, this question can best be answered by discussing developments in the country's economic, societal, and consumer market side by side.

Below is a simplified model matching the period when people become consumers with an overall understanding of key events in China's social, political, and economic developmental stages. We define the time when people become consumers as when they earn their first money or—as with the younger generation, where parents supply them with money—when spending money first becomes available, and people establish their basic/first shopping habits. The decade periods are somewhat artificial, but help to explain the general evolution. The "stereotypes" are based on observation and are for general illustration purposes only; they are by no means good enough for marketers to develop a strategy. For ease of understanding, here and later during the interviews, I have assigned each group its own nickname as shown in Table 1.2.

This simplified model shows how the "early programming" of the respective consumer generations differed vastly depending on the environment they grew up in and what was available to them (including information, advertising, etc.) at the stage they became consumers. It also shows how would-be consumers get their hands on money earlier (e.g., middle-class youngsters getting good pocket money from their parents). In reality, there are more likely two generations in each decade after 1990, including consumers born from 2000 onwards, but who began consuming much earlier than the previous generations. Most relevant of all, each of these consumer groups represents roughly 200 million people. This potential alone is huge, especially for brands that focus on their core age and lifestyle group without trying to market to everyone.

As a prelude to the interviews, it's worth pointing out that for companies hoping to become successful national players in China, understanding the needs of the different consumer groups is essential—which is one reason why especially the retailers and FMCG companies discussed in this book all have big data projects in the pipeline.

The GenRed Consumer (Born 1959 or Earlier)

The consumers that this period produced (assuming they were age 20 in 1980) are today's 55+ generation. Their needs, spending behavior, and product preferences today have been fundamentally shaped by the trauma of the Cultural Revolution, famine, and rationed/assigned goods and services—also referred to as the Iron Rice Bowl. For the generation born between 1950 and 1959, the Iron Rice Bowl meant free housing and no need to learn English or pursue education or job advancement, as they were raised in a communist system with very different values and government-assigned jobs, housing, healthcare, etc.

Table 1.2 China's six-in-one consumer generation

Consumer group (nickname)	Age in 2017	Consumer and spending behavior stereotype	Matured as consumers and urbanization degree	Strongly influenced by[a]	Est. Population today
• GenZ (Born 2000–2009)	8–17	Buy quality, not brands. Trust friends, not ads	Post 2020 Est. 60%[2]	Wechat MAU 800+ million (2016) Smartphone penetration 63%+ by 2019[3]	226 million[b]
• GenMobile (Born 1990–1999)	18–27	Show (share) that you are trendy!	Post 2010 50%	656 million mobile Internet users (Jun 2016)[4] Smartphone penetration 43%+ (2013)[5] Web data/traffic: 399 million GB (2010) University graduates: 6 million (2010)	200 million
• GenNet (Internet) (Born 1980–1989)	28–37	Confident in making choices!	Post 2005 43%	Internet users: 111 million (2005) Shopping mall growth 1000 to more than 4000[6] University graduates: 3 million (2005)	220 million
• GenPC (Born 1970–1979)	38–47	More mature browser!	Post 2000 36%	Year 2010 data: PC penetration 10% Annual personal income urban: 9300 TV penetration: 117% University graduates: 950,000	220 million

Generation	Age	Attitude			Influencing factors	Market size
• GenRise (Born 1960–1969)	48–57	Feel rich and show it!	Post 1990	26%	WTO/Free Market Year 1990 data: TV penetration: 59% University graduates: 614,000	210 million
• GenRed (Born 1959/–)	58–67	Save it for the next generation!	Post 1980	24%	Experienced famine and the cultural revolution University graduates: 147,000 (1980)	160 million

Data source: National Bureau of Statistics of China unless otherwise noted

[a]Influencing factors change faster due to digitalization, smartphone usage, and international travel plus post-Olympics market consumer market acceleration

[b]Total population of age 0–14 as of 2014

For most of them, the main concern was having enough to eat. They view "savings" as a top priority and don't like to spend much on themselves. These people are now (nearly all) retired but tend to live very humble lifestyles. This is quite different from the West, especially in wealthier countries, where the baby boomer generation tends to appreciate the free time and conspicuous leisure activities, such as overseas travel, luxury cruises, sports, and hobbies like golf.

From my personal experience as a marketer, I can say that the GenRed consumers are very difficult to directly cater to. Their sense of having "missed out on" a life of abundance has instilled in them the desire to make sure the next generation is better off. Therefore, they are one of the best "indirect" consumer groups. They won't necessarily make the purchase decision but may fund the purchase, such as an apartment for their son (as the precondition for him finding a bride in China) or private education for their grandchild (with the school being chosen by their children, since they wouldn't even understand how today's school system works).

The GenRise Consumer (Born 1960–1969)

By the early 1990s, the "Iron Rice Bowl" model of state-owned enterprises relying on never-ending support from state banks was already doomed. In 1986, China began reforming the SOEs by applying "market economy" methods, most notably by introducing "shareholding structures," essentially privatizing companies.

Customers of this generation, GenRise, are now about 45–55 years old. They didn't personally experience the Cultural Revolution. They may have heard about it in detail and therefore certainly never want to go back to such a situation. Further, its historical proximity also makes them appreciate their newly earned "richness." They have been exposed to the teachings of their parents in terms of values and prudence. They have also been exposed to a "quasi-market environment," an increasing wealth divide and the acceleration of urbanization. They have witnessed reforms, the introduction of market mechanics, and WTO entry at a time when they were entering the working population.

All of these events have drastically changed the environment around them. While this generation was still privy to free housing and was partly still assigned to jobs in SOEs or the government, they were also exposed to capitalism and market prices, last but not least through immediate access to international TV programming. They, therefore, have one foot in the old world—and its values, conservatism, pragmatism, and self-protectionism—and one in today's world, characterized by modernism, a reformist drive, and the impulse to find a better future, compared to the past and its "limitations."

GenRise also witnessed the dawn of the housing boom, thanks to being in the right place at the right time, especially early urbanites had a chance to make a lucky investment in property which could reap very decent multiples, especially if bought before the property boom started (around 2002). Most likely, most of these people were first-time buyers of more sophisticated electrical appliances, mobile phones, and constantly upgraded television sets.

GenRise entered the workforce at a time when companies had to modernize and expand. Armed with a better education, this generation was able to take advantage of better-paid jobs for educated workforce members—even at the lower end, as migrant workers in cities far away from where they grew up, where salaries were several-fold higher than in their hometowns.

Consequently, as they rose up the social ladder, GenRise consumers became the prime purchasers of luxury brands. Through their life as consumers, they have tried many products and upgraded what they bought in keeping with their incomes. They have also had their experiences with fakes and poorly made products from the early consumer market and are therefore more selective when it comes to new products. Also, with many of them having risen from very humble roots, and "stepping up in the world" by working hard, they are more prone to show off their riches for the sake of status.

The GenPC Consumer (Born 1970–1979)

As previously mentioned, with its WTO entry in 2001, China became the "workbench of the world." Many fortunes were made in the manufacturing sector. Money was earned in USD and salaries paid in RMB. These salaries were in part sent to the much poorer countryside to feed a multi-generation family, thus lifting a total of 100 million people out of poverty between 2000 and 2010.

This workbench role brought a never-ending flow of product-making knowhow back into China, which was in part the intended effect. Overseas Export Manufacturers (OEMs) made good money with ever-expanding factories and product lines. Suddenly, these manufacturers had the knowhow that allowed them to generate demand in China; given this aspect, combined with an explosion of urbanization, the domestic market suddenly began heating up.

In 2007, the total length of tracks laid for high-speed trains (capable of speeds over 200 km/h) surpassed 3000 km, growing to over 10,000 km by

2014 and connecting most of the country's cities. Suddenly, a trip from Beijing to Shanghai could be made in only 5 h instead of twelve. Beijing and Tianjin alone became one giant consumer pool with a combined population of 30 million, thanks to the opening of the 300+km/h high-speed train that would reduce a 2-h car journey, or 4-h bus journey, to a mindboggling 25 min.

While, outside China, all eyes were on the 2008 Olympics, I had mine on the railroad plans with a view to growing our company. While most of my foreign branded goods colleagues were pursuing complex strategies, we focused on anticipating new booming cities by following the main new train stations, opening businesses there ahead of competitors, and establishing our brand early. In my personal view, the high-speed train was the single most important driver of consumer market growth before e-commerce finally made a breakthrough.

In 1999, China was home to roughly 800,000 college graduates, rising rapidly to 5.3 million in 2009. With a much better educated population entering the workforce, building a career during this period seemed to be relatively easy. The generation born between 1970 and 1979 grew up with TV. But, after 1999, the availability of computers exploded, greatly influencing how people spent their (free) time and how they retrieved information, including advertising or product news. Thus, I feel the name GenPC is appropriate for this consumer generation.

And, as many people knew how to access overseas websites, more and more consumers were exposed to the wider world of products and aspirations. Being able to retrieve information on their PC meant a shift in power. In the previous decade, the TV advertising value chain had greatly influenced consumers, but with the transition to PCs, that influencing power waned, as consumers decided for themselves what information they wanted to retrieve. This also accelerated the rise of social media.

GenPC customers, when I think of them in retrospect, are "apprentice consumers," comparable to a baby that is trying to learn how to walk, while their parents keep moving the furniture around to challenge them; they spend considerable time browsing the Internet looking for new things, rather than merely relying on TV/paper advertising. As a preference for brands that evolved in China, the market increasingly became a battlefield between foreign and local brands, with (not always, but very often) the foreign brand winning out. Not surprisingly, this resulted in a vast array of fake "shanzhai" products that were made locally and looked similar to the big foreign brands, but were priced more cheaply to better fit local spending power. Thanks to these developments, regional domestic brands had a chance to expand nationally.

This generation of consumers often lived in cities, away from their families, sending home money as well as products the family needed or wanted. However, this generation also started to feel the pressure of urban society, and in some respects also the pressure from families at home who needed the money, as material possessions became more dominant in their lives. This was seen as compensation for having to work hard and/or being away from their families.

The GenPC consumers continue to be good spenders, who want to make themselves feel good. A small note of caution: Overall there are some doubts about their future purchasing power, not just for the above reasons but also because their parents are aging, and they are most likely the only social security "net" that their parents have.

The GenNet Consumer (Born 1980–1989)

GenNet consumers are the "centerpiece" of a massive market transition—with the old model economy based on exports as the main engine of growth fading out, while there was a massive change in consumer connectivity as mobile-/smartphones evolved. However, this generation also witnessed the 2008 financial crises and the fallout in certain parts of China, which (in my view) was delayed due to a stimulus package. The post-2008 stimulus package to some extent propped up the old model by fueling growth and wealth development through spending on infrastructure. Eventually, this only bought 2 or 3 years of borrowed time before retail growth slowed along with spending and wealth development.

Since then, the government has embarked on a clearer path to transition the economy towards more of a consumer market bias. This ongoing transition encompasses some painful measures, such as the withdrawal of investments in sectors that have little or no future (mostly heavy industry). The government has shown clarity by even allowing (temporary) unemployment in sectors, as well as more corporate bankruptcies. Consequently, as I write these lines in late 2016, the consumer market and retail landscape shows some cities and areas in decline—regions or cities that have been overexposed to old-model industries. This process will take a few more years to complete. What China outsiders often don't see are the positive steps being taken to transition domestic industries at the local level.

Probably nowhere in the world is the contrast between the 1970s and 1980s consumers as stark as in China. People born between 1980 and 1989 are likely to be a product of a much wealthier generation. But in China this takes on an additional spin: The daughters and sons of consumers, they were raised under the one-child policy, which was introduced in 1979. That means today's younger people most likely had both sets of grandparents plus their parents looking after them, spoiling them with gifts, taking them out to Western restaurants, and often paying for privileged private early education.

In my experience, GenNet consumers—the product of a one-child policy—tend to have very high self-esteem and high expectations from their job and their life. They want to work, but consider enjoying life to be more important. Therefore, they can be fickle when it comes to their lifestyles and—to the horror of brand managers—when it comes to brands, not merely rejecting the brands favored by previous generations, but also demonstrating less brand loyalty.

GenNet consumers, aged 25–35, have finished university or have joined the workforce in recent years. In general, the incomes of those working in offices and the private sector, especially those involved in the Internet and technology, e-commerce, or marketing and sales, are rising. Young workers in other important sectors, such as teachers, doctors, medical staff, or people in entry level positions in the government may see a slower progression, and thus their incomes are being squeezed by rising living costs.

Despite all their ambiguity and a high degree of "brand disloyalty," I find that this generation offers good consumers, representing a cornerstone for building the next stage in China's consumer economy. It is a population of over 200 million people, 54% of which now live in urban areas, and this group now includes roughly 39 million college graduates. This generation combines the ability to advance their incomes with a willingness to spend—which they do in shops and increasingly online as Internet players with better products evolve.

One important phenomenon regarding this generation is the emergence of the Internet players—companies like Alibaba, which triggered a change in product distribution combined with generating global window shopping. China now has the highest number of Internet users (710 million in mid-2016) and 1.28 billion mobile phone users (practically the entire population). The market has a high concentration of successful players. Today (2016 Q3),[7] Alibaba owns a market share of 56.2%, and JD.com, the number two player, holds 25.1%, leaving everyone else to share less than 20% between them. In this regard, Mr. Zhang of Suning is leading the pack with a total market share of 4.4%. The only foreign player is Amazon, with an abysmal share of 0.8%. However, there are thousands of shopping sites in China, offering millions of products and thus constantly generating demand and sparking new micro-trends.

Consumers in this group can be easily tempted to spend on the right product, and they use online searches and friends' recommendations as the main source of information on products—often ignoring traditional advertising. What is still lacking: deep pockets, but this will change quickly as more of them climb the job ladder.

The GenMobile Consumer (Born 1990–1999)

In my view, the GenMobile generation can essentially be described as "GenNet on steroids." This is due to their adopting a lifestyle that revolves around the mobile phone as the tool they use daily to connect with peers. This is the place where they come together, and where they get their inspirations. This is where they see the lifestyle they aspire to have some day. And the lifestyle they want to have might change from day to day, depending on what their friends do.

I recently read an article that claimed the average mobile phone user spends 106 min a day using their phone, opening the phone roughly 150 times a day. The average smartphone in China has 34 apps installed, with Chinese citizens using an average of 20 a day—to read news, chat and connect, and shop. Users are very impatient, as can be seen in an app shift frequency of 100 s per usage time. What that means in terms of complexity for brands and marketers is nothing short of mindboggling.

So who are GenMobile consumers? First of all, they are usually (even) more educated and number close to 196 million people, including 68 million (35%) college graduates. Many of them were born in urban areas and have never experienced poverty, while some grew up as the children of migrant workers living in cities far from their hometown. They may have never experienced life in their official hometown and thus have no connection to a "simpler lifestyle."

If the previous generation had aspirations, they were most likely status-related—climbing the ladder or being able to afford things they didn't truly need. This generation also has aspirations, but they are significantly different, and they keep changing and evolving. Nonetheless, a common trait seems to be a high degree of digital social connectivity plus a desire to share (what they buy or experience) and to show off—not just what they own but also their "experiences."

GenMobile consumers are more likely to use social networks. Today, China has a total of 650 million social networkers (twice the number in the US), and since China is so advanced in terms of technology and consumer behavior, we can see an extremely rapid integration between social media and e-commerce.

Many e-commerce services started in China as a free service to solve daily problems, such as access to news or free-of-charge communication and sharing. The membership of China's most popular chatting app WeChat reached 160 million in December 2012, more than doubled to 355 million members by the end of 2013, and reached over 800 million by the end of 2016.

GenMobile have been raised with fewer concerns about the future. Some say they take little interest in political things or "important news." They like to be entertained, to know the latest news about stars, and see themselves at the center of their universe, cultivating a desired image of themselves through social media. Having been raised as single children, they are more likely to be attention seekers and to share on social media their best moments, what they had for dinner, who they hung out with, and what hairstyle they just got.

The GenMobile customer has a high level of education, high sense of individuality, high aspirations, high connectivity (many friends to get information and tips from), high desire to buy things that help them to express themselves, AND a low budget. This makes them probably the smartest shoppers in the world! They maximize their shopping baskets and experience on very little money, so this consumer group represents the biggest opportunity and challenge for marketers and product makers, as we shall see from the stories in this book.

Personally, I feel this consumer group can be "led" using new channels for communication and content. Most of the companies in this book primarily focus on these consumers when it comes to innovation. Most are seeking technologies to connect with them in a different way, and they currently seem to be everyone's future.

The Accelerator: e-/Digital Commerce Accelerating Consumer Desires

With about US$663 billion over gross merchandise value (GMV, e-commerce speak for "sales") in 2016, China's e-commerce market is already bigger than the US market[8] (US$322.2 billion). In addition, there were 25.6 billion Internet transactions in China in 2015, which equates to 62 per person.[9] Goldman Sachs estimates that, by 2018, China's e-commerce GMV will exceed US$1.2 trillion and be 2.5 times the size of the US market. Worldpay, a payment company, estimates that Chinese e-commerce will grow by 15% by 2020, cementing its position as the biggest e-commerce market worldwide[10].

The role e-commerce has been playing in the life of the modern consumer in China has been amazing. If you want to get a true understanding of this phenomenon, a good way is to stand in front of an office building late one morning and count the number of couriers that deliver shipments to people's workplaces (the preferred delivery option). In my office, I sometimes count more couriers than workers! The other way is to sneak up behind your employees when they're staring at their monitor screens at about 10:30 in the morning. If they look energized and excited, it's most likely not because of the work that's on the screen, but a good deal they were able to find on something they wanted to buy! Yes, 10:30 a.m. is the starting time for group buying on a few Chinese e-commerce platforms, and 10:30 p.m. (generally) is also the preferred ordering time, especially for young consumers (who also like to go e-shopping in the night)! Torn between promoting employee satisfaction (vying for younger staff) and improving productivity, employers are split in their views on whether or not to filter Internet access.

The Chinese government doesn't mind some of the portals being so big. Why not? Because they establish an industry standard and address a concern of national interest—supply and demand, creating jobs through sales and—last but not least—because Internet competition keeps prices down and makes products affordable to a wider audience, such as migrant workers and the rural population. As mentioned before, the fact that China does not intervene too much, or not at all when it comes to e-commerce, is proof of its solid commitment to the market economy.

It's no surprise that, with so much shopper traffic on these platforms, all merchants now offer attractive discounts and other offers online. The competition is so intense that it has created new shopping seasons. China's Singles Day 11/11 in 2016 raked in US$18.7 billion dollars of sales in total, with the first US$1 billion being sold within the first 5 min of trade. These are amazing numbers considering the US market in 2016 was US$32.2 billion[11] and Black Friday accounted for US$3 billion.[12] Black Friday 2016 in the USA represented 0.06% of the total annual retail sales and the sales on China 11/11 Singles Day represented a total of 0.6% of the 2016 total retail sales.

To add to the superlatives—on 2016 Singles Day, more than 70% of all sales came from mobile devices—smartphones—the preferred option for shopping anytime and anywhere in China.[13]

Since China's e-commerce traffic is so tremendous and can—unlike many physical retailers—reach all corners of China, many big brand manufacturers have decided to use e-commerce platforms as their main form of doing business online. In my business I see both the upside and the downside of this trend: the brands we sell compete directly with us on the online platforms—on the other hand, we also sell our brands online using these massive platforms. Trend-wise, this means that doing business on e-commerce platforms in China is not just unavoidable but also necessary for brand building and finding early adopter consumers.

It also means if you want to build a brand in China efficiently and, say, reach out to new consumers, e-commerce is a viable way to go. 50.1% of all transactions in 2016 came from outside Tier-1 or Tier-2 cities; in fact, 2.97% of transactions came from rural areas.[14]

Social networks (interest groups) and their APPs are a recent and accelerating phenomenon in China. At my company, we have recently started to work with social networks and their applications, including an app that allows over 100 million mothers to talk about the topics that matter most to them, or a young consumers' network with over 100 million members who are especially interested in fashion trends. Most of these companies didn't even exist just 3 years ago!

Further, a new accelerator for consumer desires has recently appeared: cross-border e-commerce—an innovative way to order products directly from overseas and have them shipped directly to China through online platforms. Originally, this started with people simply shopping during trips overseas or asking friends to bring products from overseas with them to China (I assume this allowed pilots and airline staff to make a decent buck on the side); around 2010, professional agencies began evolving, suddenly experiencing a huge boost by offering such services; then the Internet platforms got into the game around 2012. Quickly realizing that it was better to capitalize on an opportunity rather than try to forbid it, the government implemented seven free trade zones in which companies could open official "cross-border" services. At the same time, the government began reducing the duties on some of the most heavily traded cross-border items. Since 2014 this has become a more or less organized and legitimate industry, primarily shipping apparel, handbags, and cosmetic and baby-care products, to name the top three. The volume of the cross-border market was estimated at around RMB 630 million in 2016, with ongoing growth rates of 31.3%.

So this has produced an interesting situation in which overseas brands can find their way directly into China, somewhat disrupting the market of existing distribution structures—and creating more desire for consumers to explore new products.

China TRULY is an interesting case where e-commerce has been leapfrogging the consumer industries, and we see this reflected in the stories here, where especially product manufacturers are constantly challenged to rapidly evolve their brands. In traditional Western economies, e-commerce is built on the back of traditional retail, but in China, almost the opposite is true. In my opinion, E-commerce, including its young sister social commerce, is the pioneer that will pave the way for new brands in China, with offline retail following.

Evergreen Stories that Sell: Face, Family, Food, and Fun

Recently, more and more people have started asking me "what sells in China" or "what to invest in." Usually, I get asked these questions about twice a week. Though they're not easy to answer in detail, from where I'm standing the overall mega-trends are fairly clear.

For me, the mega-stories in connection with the Chinese consumer are simply the evergreens: Face—Family—Food—and Fun. To give the reader a better understanding of why these stories work, I have organized the interviews according to these topics.

Understanding the consumer in China is no easy feat, as things are extremely dynamic. So when talking to Westerners about China, I prefer to focus on illustrating the big stories that work well and which will always be worth investing time or money in. These stories are more topical and may not follow our thinking of industry patterns. Also, they are more long term if you view them from an investment perspective. For me, they are the "China consumer evergreen" stories that can be summed up as "face, family, food, and fun." For me these four Fs represent the arenas that local companies prefer to play when it comes to the Chinese consumer—this is where a tremendous amount of business expansion and value creation is happening right now, and where countless local products, concepts and business models are being created. Much of what I see here is geared to the mix of Chinese consumer groups as described above. In this evolution, Chinese companies are now changing their approach, saying goodbye to Made in China and moving on to Made FOR China.

Notes

1. http://data.stats.gov.cn/easyquery.htm?cn=C01
2. People Daily, http://politics.people.com.cn/n/2012/1112/c1026-19552279.html, accessed November 20, 2016.
3. Statista, https://www.statista.com/statistics/257045/smartphone-user-penetration-in-china/, accessed November 20, 2016.

4. CNNIC, http://www.cnnic.net.cn/hlwfzyj/hlwxzbg/hlwtjbg/201608/t201608 03_54392.htm, accessed November 20, 2016.

5. Statista, https://www.statista.com/statistics/257045/smartphone-user-penetra tion-in-china/, accessed November 20, 2016.

6. Deloitte, https://www2.deloitte.com/content/dam/Deloitte/cn/Documents/ consumer-business/deloitte-cn-cb-2014dsoppingcenterchainbrandmerchants development-zh-150129.pdf, accessed Jan, 2016.

7. iReserach, http://cj.sina.com.cn/article/detail/6044229343/142348?cre=finance pagepc&mod=f&loc=3&r=9&doct=0&rfunc=100, accessed Jan, 2017.

8. Statista, https://www.statista.com/statistics/272391/us-retail-e-commerce-sales-forecast/, accessed Jan, 2017.

9. CNNIC, http://cnnic.cn/gywm/xwzx/rdxw/2016/201606/t20160622_54247. htm, accessed Jan, 2017.

10. WorldPay, http://english.gov.cn/news/top_news/2017/01/06/content_281475 534537565.htm, accessed Feb, 2017.

11. Statista, https://www.statista.com/statistics/272391/us-retail-e-commerce-sales-forecast/, accessed Jan, 2017.

12. TechCrunch, https://techcrunch.com/2016/11/25/black-friday-online-sales-to-hit-a-record-breaking-3-billion-over-1-billion-from-mobile/, accessed Jan, 2017.

13. Alibaba, http://news.xinhuanet.com/tech/2016-11/12/c_1119898123.htm, accessed Jan, 2017.

14. Libra, http://lab.cmcm.com/sjfx/2016-10-11/119.html, accessed Jan, 2017.

2

The Leaders Behind the 21 Made-for-China Success Stories

In what follows, I present the snapshots of my interviewees for this book, China's 21 leading entrepreneurs who have developed their companies into top enterprises in their respective industries. Born during the 1950s to the 1970s, they are China's first-generation entrepreneurs. They have witnessed almost every significant Chinese market development, from the reforms towards openness, to the entry of global companies, and the rise of private enterprises.

These entrepreneurs serve as both insightful observers on the evolving Chinese market as well as the best resource as to how they surf the fast-changing business environment in China. Their companies have been growing following China's consumer megatrends—face, family, food, and fun—and are now pushed to evolve, facing even more sophisticated consumers, hyper-competition, and the increasing need to play in the international arena. The later chapters of the book present personal interviews with each of these business leaders, going deeper into how they evolved their businesses, the challenges they faced, and the future they are preparing for.

I present these portraits following the megatrends they represent and follow.

© The Author(s) 2018
C. Nothhaft, *Made for China*, DOI 10.1007/978-3-319-61584-4_2

The Face: Accelerating Customer Individuality

Inspiring Consumers' Dreams and Styles: Modern Media—Thomas Shao

A former Guangzhou city government official, Mr. Thomas Shao founded Modern Media Group in 1993. Mr. Shao is a media mogul and a highly respected art collector in China. With more than ten publications including NUMERO, IDEAT, Bloomberg Businessweek China, Modern Media is one of the largest publishing companies in China and was listed in Hong Kong stock exchange in 2009.

Getting that Dream Job: Tarena—Han Shaoyun

Mr. Han Shaoyun founded Tarena, the largest IT training institution in China, in 2002 and has been its CEO ever since. Before that, Mr. Han was the deputy chief engineer and director of the software division of Asia Info-Linkage, responsible for software research and development and corporate management.

Diversifying the Product: GreenTree Inn—Alex Xu

Mr. Alex Xu serves as Chairman and CEO of both GreenTree Hospitality Group, Inc. (USA) as well as GreenTree Inns Hotel Management Group, Inc. (China). In addition to his leadership roles with GreenTree, Mr. Xu also oversees the APH Family of Companies, a California-based real estate investment group.

Brand to Platform: Daphne—Eddie Chen

Eddie Chen is the Chairman and a non-executive director of Daphne International Holdings. Mr. Chen joined the Group in 1992 and assumed the post of GM of Daphne in 1999 and brought Daphne International Holdings to a new epoch. Today, the company has turned around from being a loss-making company to a profitable one, with a presence throughout Greater China, Asia, Europe, and North America.

Boutique Is Beautiful: Grace Vineyard—Judy Chan

Judy Chan, President of Grace Vineyard, graduated from the University of Michigan with a double degree in Psychology and Women's Studies and Organizational Studies. In 2002, Judy resigned from her work at an investment bank in Hong Kong and took over her family business, embarking on her journey of the family-owned boutique winery in China.

High Above the Rest: Toread—Wang Jing

Ms. Wang Jing is the cofounder of Toread, and it took Ms. Wang and her husband Mr. Sheng Faqiang several years of hard work to establish Toread as China's premier outdoor products brand. Ms. Wang is one of China's selected few women mountaineers. She sets down all her climbing exploits on her blog, which is staple reading among China's outdoor enthusiasts.

The Family: Enhancing Quality of Life

Reaching More Households, Offering More Products: Suning—Zhang Jindong

Mr. Zhang Jindong is the founder, and currently the largest shareholder, of China's leading electrical appliances retailing brand, Suning Commerce Group. Mr. Zhang started with a small shop and developed it into a giant business group within less than 20 years and in 2015 the Forbes's China Rich List ranked him at the 28th place.

Households Upgrading Appliances: Haier—Zhang Ruimin

Mr. Zhang Ruimin serves as CEO and Chairman of Haier Electronics Group Co., Ltd. Mr. Zhang acts as a role model for modern Chinese entrepreneurs. He took the reins of the government-controlled company in 1984, which under his leadership has since grown to become what is now the well-known global household appliance brand.

Home Style Dreams: Kuka—Gu Jiangsheng

Mr. Gu Jiangsheng is the CEO of China's leading furniture brand Kuka, a family business in Zhejiang Province he took charge of when he was 29. It only took Mr. Gu 8 years to grow the small local factory of 30 million yuan in production value to a large company with over 2 billion yuan of sales volume and products sold nationwide and globally.

FMCG Premiumization: Liby—Chen Kaixuan

Mr. Chen Kaixuan, born in 1958 in Guangdong, started his business career at 17 and founded Liby when he was 36. With its iconic products like Liby washing power, Liby detergent, and Liby soap, the company has developed its market across China and became a household retailing brand today.

Medical Care Going Private: BYBO—Li Changren

Mr. Li Changren is the founder and president of BYBO Group. In 1993, Mr. Li quit from serving at a public hospital and started his dental medical business in Shenzhen. Mr. Li has been making strenuous efforts in the field of dental healthcare for more than 20 years and is honored as the leader of private dental institutions of China.

Protecting Lifestyle and Loved Ones: NCI—Kang Dian

Mr. Kang Dian served as Chairman and CEO of New China Life Insurance (NCI) from Feb 2009 to Jan 2016. During his tenure, Mr. Kang (in his 60s) directed NCI's transformation and succeeded in bringing the company to be listed in both A-share and H-share market. Before joining NCI, Mr. Kang worked across all verticals of the financial sector in China and is considered one of the most respected leaders in China's financial community.

The Food: Aspiring to a Healthy and Fashionable Diet

Brand Trust: Yili—Pan Gang

Mr. Pan Gang has been Chairman of Inner Mongolia Yili Industrial Group Co., Ltd since June 2005 and served as its President since. Following the leadership of Mr. Pan, Yili reported sales of more than 60 billion yuan in 2016, ranking at the top 8 of world's largest dairy companies.

Supermarket Sophistication: Yonghui—Zhang Xuanning

Mr. Zhang Xuanning is the cofounder and vice chairman of Fujian Yonghui Commercial Co. Ltd, China's leading supermarket brand featuring fresh food with affordable prices. Mr. Zhang started from a small shop in 2001 and took Yonghui to the Shanghai Stock market in 2010.

Urban Fast Food Formats: Gil Wonton—Zhang Biao

Mr. Zhang Biao is the cofounder of China's most popular wonton brand, Gil Wonton. Mr. Zhang started from a humble beginning in a small street shop in Shanghai and turned it into a business of 1.5 billion yuan after 15 years of hard work. Today, Gil Wonton runs over 1000 chain shops across China.

Better Booze: Jing Brand—Wu Shaoxun

Mr. Wu Shaoxun is the founder and Chairman of Jing Brand, the most popular health liquor brand in China. Mr. Wu became the chief of Jing Brand after 7 years of work at a state-owned spinning mill from 1980. In the beginning, Mr. Wu had a modest knowledge of liquor manufacturing, but he has turned the small liquor company into China's largest health liquor brand today.

Turning TCM Classics into FMCGs: GZ Pharma—Li Chuyuan

Mr. Li Chuyuan is the Chairman of the Board in Guangzhou Baiyunshan Pharmaceutical Holdings Co. Ltd, and the Vice President of Guangzhou

Pharma Group. Under Mr. Li's leadership, GZ Pharma has succeeded in recapitalization by listing in Hong Kong and Shanghai stock markets and is today ranked as China's largest pharmaceutical group.

Fun, Entertainment, and Leisure

Curious About the World: Ctrip—Fan Min

Fan Min is one of the cofounders of Ctrip, China's largest online travel booking platform and its President since 2009. He also served as the CEO of Ctrip from 2006 to 2013. During his tenure as Ctrip's CEO, Mr. Fan was the recipient of the Top 10 Great Leaders Award of the Year on the 2010 APEC China SME Value List.

Eater-tainment: Hai Di Lao—Zhang Yong

Mr. Zhang Yong is the founder and president of Sichuan Haidilao Catering Co., the most popular Chinese spicy hotpot chain brand worldwide. The Haidilao chain started from a small singe shop in 1994 and has ever since developed across China and overseas with presence in Japan, Korea, Singapore, Canada, and the USA.

Chinese Hollywood: Wanda—Wang Jianlin

Mr. Wang Jianlin is the founder and chairman of Dalian Wanda Group, China's largest real estate developer, as well as the world's largest movie theater operator. The Economist once called him *"a man of Napoleonic ambition."*[1] According to Bloomberg, in 2015, Mr. Wang was the richest person in Asia with US$9.9 billion.

Home Entertainment: TCL—Li Dongsheng

Mr. Li Dongsheng became one of the most recognized business leaders in China by founding one of the largest home electronics appliance brands, TCL. Following Mr. Li's leadership, TCL accomplished two landmark acquisitions: Thomson's worldwide television business and Alcatel's worldwide mobile phone business both in 2004.

Note

1. Dalian Wanda—It's a Wanda-ful life, The Economist Print Edition, Feb 12th 2015, http://www.economist.com/news/business/21643123-chinas-biggest-property-tycoon-wants-become-entertainment-colossus-its-wanda-ful-life

Part II

The Face: Accelerating Customer Individuality

For me, "face" means improving customer individuality and an awareness of one's looks. Today's consumers, while keen to learn from each other, also strive to be different and want to have choices in life.

I find that Westerners tend to think that Chinese people try not to stand out and prefer to fit in. This is not true, in my opinion. Chinese people have a high sense of individuality and a desire to stand out. However, education and the concept of "self-restraint" often suppress their desire to stand out. But, with the younger generation, this is rapidly changing.

Also, "face," the feeling of individuality, is often tied to status symbols. In China, different generations have different status symbols—in fact, they are radically different. Where in GenRed a position in the government or a renowned SOE was a status symbol, a few years later (for GenNet) having a car was more important, and now among GenMobiles, the latest phone and a selfie in front of the Eiffel Tower are more significant (your father-in-law has already bought the car for you). All this social development in less than 40 years has—at least temporarily—created a society with extremely divergent status symbols.

From my observations, two of the most highly valued aspects today, especially for younger GenNet and GenMobile consumers, are to (a) express yourself and (b) go to great lengths to maximize the experience you can buy for any given budget. That is why consumer companies here often have to create a multitude of products, sometimes quite similar, but for different wallet sizes.

Among predominantly younger consumers, one of the main ways to gain "face" is to become a trendsetter. Young people thrive to become famous on social networks by creating stories—including those involving products and brands—and become a prominent blogger. In Chinese, the word for blogger—"Wang Hong"—literally means "a person who is hot/in great demand on the net." That's the Chinese concept of "face" in the twenty-first century!

In the context of preparing our recent corporate strategy, I met with more than a dozen owners of social network apps, some of whom have impressive numbers. The meetings included one team that advises 170 million mothers about motherhood concerns, a team with a running app with 100 million or so members, and a Beauty App team that boasts 130 million members and, and, and. . . .. I was amazed how Chinese people latch onto trends via social networks and then share their findings about a topic, including favorite products, so openly. The numbers taught me something about individuality. If you take even a small trend or interest in connection with a total population of 1.3 billion people, your interest groups even for small trends or interests become millions of people. And e-commerce and mobile commerce allow companies to effectively capitalize on these trends. In fact, I was so impressed that, as I write this book, we at my company are already working on creating a 200-million-member social consumer network across China, so as to reach these permanently connected and evolving consumers.

I am extremely excited about the topic of "customer individuality" as a mega-trend. In the first section, I will focus on customer individuality, aspects of how the consumer wants "the products they like"—products that maximize their experience at any given budget. I also discuss the local companies who understand the market well and are using their cultural familiarity to respond to the different consumer trends.

For foreign managed brands, understanding these trends is crucial, as the China market opportunity is too huge to ignore. Recently, I gave a speech for the heads of international FMCG companies globally about China. We talked about the scope of the opportunity, during which I tried to describe the growth of the Chinese consumer market between now and 2020 as being equivalent to the size of the entire consumer market in Germany by 2020, a snippet I picked up from a research report. Everyone was pretty much on the same page: Chinese consumers are important from a global perspective and companies must learn how to understand them!

However, understanding the consumer in connection with making or selling the right products is something many foreign companies struggle to do, with the arguable exception of companies that lead trends globally in their category, e.g., Apple in mobile phones or the German car makers, to name some examples.

In talking to those global executives (most of them you know from CNN), I did, in the end, realize that almost all of them wanted to sell their existing brands in China, but that, in principle, only a few of them had understood what the evolving China consumers want. In other words: Not that many knew how to find consumer that fit to what they'd like to sell—an approach that should be possible in the age of technology and connected consumers.

Those who had already placed their products in China had difficulties rapidly adjusting to evolving trends when it came to new product requirements, quality, pricing, and brand message. The good news—as I told some people after the meeting—is that the companies based in China face exactly the same challenge. The difference is that they are currently adapting faster.

Consumers across China, a country the size of Europe, are evolving rapidly and tend to evolve in groups, and these groups are in turn becoming more diversified. The Chinese have a famous expression—"1000 people, 1000 faces" (千人千面)— which they use to express the individuality of people and one we use a lot around the office these days.

We now have—similar to mature markets—different consumer groups that want to pursue different lifestyles. Further, in China nearly half of the population still has to evolve from daily survival to a decent income and at least an "urban-like" environment.

This diversity, the increasing trend toward individuality for those who can afford it, as well as a need for those who are at the lower end of the pyramid to improve their situation are both clearly understood by most Chinese entrepreneurs. As such, their product portfolios become more refined to tailor to different tastes and wallet sizes. Tiered pricing is applied, often with different brand messages to capture entry-level consumers as well as premium product aficionados. Also, for certain companies that follow a mainstream trend, evolving the brand message to stay in tune with the consumer has become critical. Sometimes competition has been the driver, as especially widespread brands are now running the risk of becoming obsolete, as customers want products that are more tailored and unique.

One piece of good news is that e-commerce and the tremendous popularity of messaging apps that allow commercial activities, products that are new to the market, and products that don't have a distribution system (including new entrants from overseas) finally have tools to overcome critical mass. Big e-commerce platforms, and more recently messaging services, now span the entire nation.

As we will see from the following five stories, the increasing level of sophistication and individuality currently poses challenges for marketers in China but also a tremendous opportunity.

Here, we can learn from a media company with a strong history of producing printed lifestyle magazines how the influx of trendsetting messages from around the world has been accelerating rapidly. As media companies evolve into digital content providers, trends are developing in real time and spreading across social networks like wildfire.

We will also explore a more fundamental story about individuality: the struggle in China to get a better job so you can progress in life, or at least work in the sector you want. The e-commerce revolution, as well as daily hero stories of young Internet entrepreneurs, has made the IT sector one of the hottest ones to work in. Besides, working in e-commerce has become a sort of status symbol. As such, we'll take a closer look at China's leading IT training company, which was initially intended to focus on university graduates to round out their education, but is now becoming a tertiary education company focusing on professionals who want to get ahead in their careers.

The competition in the hotel sector has heated up greatly, as the market moved from the early stage of chain hotels to customers demanding better hotel offerings to suit their available budget. With local giants and foreign entrants battling for dominance in the sector, we will see how a locally operated company has diversified its concepts to better fit the varying needs of Chinese travelers.

With fierce competition and e-commerce changing the distribution landscape, many companies in the fashion sector have been pushed toward the inevitable need to transform and evolve their business models. We'll take a look behind the scenes at China's number two shoe brand to learn how an OEM manufacturer evolved into a top shoe retailer in China, and how it is transforming its brand and operating model to address what people want today, as well as how they want to shop.

Since wine is a growing market in China, but also one cornered by large state-owned companies, we will examine a business case in which a company in China successfully positioned itself as a quality leader, allowing it to compete with much larger players.

Most Chinese enjoy being in the outdoors, and as newly defined urbanites, they like to show that preference in their fashion outlook choices, even on the way to the office. We'll explore China's number one outdoor fashion and equipment manufacturers to see how they became successful in China and what brand messages for Chinese consumers mean in their sector. Along the way, we'll meet China's most famous female mountaineer and learn about her importance for the brand.

3

Inspiring Consumers' Dreams and Styles: Modern Media

Publishing—No. 1 lifestyle publisher—Thomas Shao, Founder (photo with kind permission of Mr. Thomas Shao)

© The Author(s) 2018
C. Nothhaft, *Made for China*, DOI 10.1007/978-3-319-61584-4_3

Opportunity

In today's China, with people spending an average 4 hours a day on their smartphones, customers are getting their news and content in real time. Lifestyle publications in China are evolving, both by going digital and by offering more diversified content as consumer groups diversify. The trend is accelerating as new hobbies—such as outdoor pursuits, signature automobiles, collecting, home décor, antiques, etc.—crop up, consequently creating the potential for ongoing segmentation in the publication market. At the same time, it opens up opportunities for new entrants and for publishing houses to rejuvenate and become more efficient.

Lessons Learned

At this juncture, the industry in China is changing due to online channels, social media, as well as English-language media becoming more popular, with especially younger people now reading overseas media sites. This poses a challenge for existing publishing houses and content editors. Media companies need to internationalize their sources, to follow trends and themes professionally, and to find new revenue models, as the paid for print media business is more often than not shifting to e-content.

If you've ever walked by a newsstand in China, you might have been surprised by the variety of magazines available, including Chinese versions of Western publications. Some of the visitors I show around are surprised to see Chinese versions of magazines like Cosmopolitan, available at most street kiosks in the main cities. So, how does this work in a country with a tightly censored press? In this chapter, you'll meet the entrepreneur who makes it happen.

It's a fact that only a few companies have dared to venture into the national publication segment broadly, and those who focus on up-to-date information that is global tend to do well. Only two main segments are currently dominant in China: male-focused business and success titles and female-focused lifestyle titles. As consumers evolve, there is a desire not just to read about what celebrities are doing, but also to learn about other lifestyles AND apply them.

Social media information and lifestyle publishing are a source of evolving consumer tastes—from fashion to what to eat and to how to decorate your home. Apparently, the more sophisticated customer doesn't just want to read what his or her friends recommend, but to get information from the original lifestyle source. Therefore, global brands such as GQ, Elle, and Cosmopolitan are gaining ground.

In today's China, readers increasingly prefer to get their information from online sources. While the last and current consumer generations have little or no ability to read news from the source in English, the big elephant in the room is the next generation, which has much better English skills and will be able to read global news straight from the source.

According to the National Bureau of Statistics of China (NBS), there were 1906 newspapers in mainland China in 2015.[1] Among them, influential national newspapers account for less than 100. Some of the most important ones include Reference News, Global Times, Southern Weekly, China Daily, and Economic Observer.[2] Only 26 newspapers had a readership of over 1 million subscribers.[3]

By the end of 2014, there were 9966 magazine titles, with a total annual circulation of 3.1 billion.[4] The total revenues of the magazine industry dropped to 21.2 billion CNY, 4.5% lower than that of 2013.[5] Among the thousands of different magazines, 14 have a circulation of over 1 million, including *Readers* and *QS Theory*.[6] Generally speaking, from the commercial perspective instead of the niche interest or academic perspective, magazines fall into one of two groups: business titles and lifestyle titles.

But rather than by content, a better way to grasp the industry more deeply is by examining the format of that content, like the emergence of online magazines and newspapers, and the subsequent decline of print. According to eMarketer, 2015 was the first year in which the Chinese spent more time on online media (average 3 h 5 min per capita) than on traditional forms (average 3 h 3 min per capita). By the middle of 2015, China had 675 million online media subscribers. The online media market is estimated to be about US$160 billion. The Internet and especially mobile have been transforming the media landscape.

The first trend has been the emergence of online versions of existing publications or new online publications. As shown in Fig. 3.1, the total revenues of digital publishing in China more than quadrupled between 2010 and 2014, when they reached RMB 440.39 billion.

The second trend, which is now accelerating due to the use of smartphones and especially among the emerging younger working population in China, is the emergence of social media. Dominated by WeChat, social media apps in China not only provide a space for conversations but also offer everything from news and search functions to payment services and even cab-hailing.

So, how do traditional media operators compete in this increasingly, overwhelmingly digital environment? Part of the answer to that is in their ownership, which is predominantly on the State Owned Enterprise side—with China South Publishing and Media (market cap approx. RMB 30 billion)

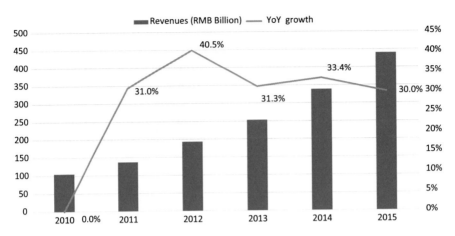

Fig. 3.1 Rapid development of digital publishing in China, 2010–2015. Source: KPMG/ State Administration of Press, Publication, Radio, Film and Television (KPMG, *2014 News and Publishing Industry Analysis Report* by State Administration of Press, Publication, Radio, Film and Television of China)

being number one, followed closely by Phoenix Publishing and Media and Zhejiang Daily. Interestingly, though, there is only one private company among the top 20: Modern Media.

Modern Media Group runs a total of 13 magazines, five of which are the mainland Chinese versions of international magazines. The company owns the rights for Bloomberg Businessweek (USA), The Art Newspaper (UK), Numéro (France), IDEAT (France), and The Good Life (France). The readership focus is predominantly on the "elite class," and the company's overall goal is to promote "taste, lifestyle, social responsibility, and globalization."

Modern Media was founded in 1993 and went public in Hong Kong in 2009 (HK:00072) with a record 120-fold oversubscription. Who could be behind such an eclectic business—magazines that focus on lifestyle, light business, art, and taste? An equally eclectic personality!

I met Thomas Shao (Shao Zhong) for the first time in 2013. We were organizing a YPO (Young Presidents' Organization) education session on China and wanted to invite someone to talk about the media world. We approached Mr. Shao, and to my delight he agreed to join us on a Sunday morning to present his company and do a Q&A session. As the audience was from overseas, I asked Thomas to share something about his life, which he did, including pictures of his workplace and some favorite works of art! In fact, he treated us to a nearly complete virtual tour of his house! It soon became clear that the company was, in fact, an expression of his personality.

Mr. Shao, who holds an EMBA from Tsinghua University in Beijing, had a head start in understanding the media industry, as well as a good grasp of how media strikes a balance between publishing and politics—his mother worked for the influential regional newspaper The Guangzhou Daily. "I was raised in and influenced by the media environment all around me," says Shao.

After first trying his entrepreneurial luck at importing printing machines from Germany and other countries, Shao set up a printing company in China, focusing on high-end color printing. Later, he became involved in Modern Magazine as a general manager. Like so many entrepreneurs, when Shao first branched out he had few resources. "I started with no money, but I was doing what I liked" is one of his favorite quotes, as well as "I started out with a passion for the business, rather than the desire to get rich."

Armed with a passion for news and style, a knowledge of how to edit the content of a good magazine and how to produce top-quality printing, Shao set out to become a market leader by buying the then-printing company in 2000.

When Shao started with *Modern Weekly* (周末画报), he focused on targeting the general public. Similar to a newspaper, Modern Weekly covers news, business, fashion, and lifestyles in a comprehensive magazine format. Along with the development of a wealthier class in China, content needs to evolve from general news to more specialized and professional information. The consumer demand led to the launch of topical magazines, such as lifestyle of health and sustainability (LOHAS) titles, young lifestyle (The Outlook Magazine), fashion (Numéro), the arts (The Art Newspaper), and business (Bloomberg Businessweek). "We adopted a T-shaped strategy, which consists of general, comprehensive information horizontally and specialized, professional fields vertically," Thomas recalls.

Modern Media's longevity as a private player in China's media industry was a positive aspect, helping Shao to cement his reputation as a style guru. A few years earlier, I asked Thomas during a discussion about how it is possible to survive in China, where the media industry is so heavily regulated. Expecting a long answer, he surprised me with a simple analogy: "Media reporting has many areas—think of news reporting as a giant traffic light (with green, yellow and red lights)—as long as you stay away from the red lights, you can successfully run a media business in China." Though simple, this is an apt analogy for Modern Media's many years of success.

On its journey from a single-magazine company to a media group with more than ten publications, Modern Media also took advantage of the growing technological developments in China's media industry. "We used flat-bed printing when our circulation was 100,000 copies and moved to cylinder printing when we reached 1 million copies, which made our product a better fit for young readers." Shao explains that cylinder printing has fewer limitations regarding colors, while also offering higher efficiency and better picture quality.

Not surprisingly, as soon as smartphones with apps became widespread in China, Modern Media launched apps-based online magazines. Shao believes there are two kinds of success factors/stories in terms of online magazines (or e-versions of traditional magazines): the success of sales/subscriptions and the success of content/creativity. "It is hard to achieve both types of success, as most e-magazine apps of this kind lack beauty in design and content. It is, therefore, much harder for the company to sell advertisements with the app alone," says Shao. He believes that Bloomberg Businessweek China (BBW as mentioned below) and iWeekly offer a better combination of content design and sales. "Both of them have impressive sales." Generally, BBW and iWeekly rank top ten in the ios App Store in the business information and lifestyle categories, respectively.

For Shao, this is an interim step. As demonstrated in Fig. 3.2, iWeekly currently allows him to reach around 10 million younger readers, and as technology evolves, he has bigger goals in mind: "The future product, based on Internet cloud technology, will help us reach the 100-million-reader mark."

The competition in the digital media arena is fierce, and this is particularly true for a major traditional media company. Shao believes that companies should try every new technology early and refine the product on the basis of users' responses. Traditional media companies may find the upsides of print media and online media, respectively, and further develop them accordingly. He has learned his own lessons: "You can never be hesitant and indecisive. In a mobile media environment like China, once you miss an opportunity, you'll never catch up." Accordingly, it's no surprise that Shao has added two more

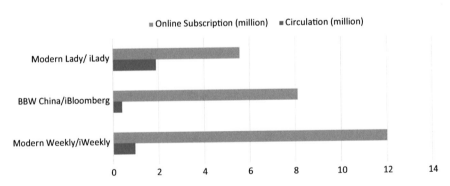

Fig. 3.2 e-Magazine is more popular than printed publications. Source: Modern Media Group

elements to the current four emphases—"taste, lifestyle, social responsibility, and globalization"—namely, high-tech and high-touch.

With regard to readers' general interests, Shao seems to believe that the core topics and themes don't actually change much. From a broader perspective, established patterns and interests seem to remain reasonably steady. "Consumer behavior and portals have changed, but regardless of age, consumers' needs for quality products have not changed," he emphasizes.

During the interview, it became clear that Modern Media's success is partly due to its consistent focus—concentrating on the content its core readers want, but at the same time managing to evolve its platforms.

> We value the high-end media market because I believe there is still a gap to fill there in terms of the system, the talent, and the market. That's why we focus on this category, instead of offering a broader range of media products.

As mentioned earlier, Modern Media's target reader is China's middle class, aged between 25 and 45, and Shao feels the future reader is the younger urban "elite class," which is more accustomed to mobile life. The company plans to cooperate with the prominent American celebrities and fashion magazine INSTYLE to cater to a younger group of quality readers, which will introduce part of INSTYLE's content in Modern Lady and iLady, especially international celebrities' resource. "Young consumers like overseas entertainment news, and we can't neglect this trend," says Shao.

He also thinks that business content, if handled in the right way, could be regarded as lifestyle reading. "With interesting and timely content, business magazines don't have to conflict with lifestyle magazines." Here, he again cites BBW as an example.

One aspect of Chinese companies are their heavy dependence on their owners—who are deeply involved in daily decisions and management. It's often portrayed as a weakness, but in a challenging operating environment such as China, or in dynamic times, e.g., today's global economy, I see it as an advantage, especially because it shortens the time between decision-making and implementation.

Thomas and I are WeChat friends, and I am always impressed by his travels, which somehow blend business and art—and often find their way into the magazines. He seems to be constantly on the road to learn about and find new things for his readers, being as much journalist as publisher. At the same time, he instructs his managers back home on how to run and transform the business. "Learning and reading are very crucial. We have to constantly work to keep up with the latest developments in technology. I believe that the integration of art and technology is always the best approach."

But, in a market where content has become freely available, and bloggers have practically taken the place of reporters and journalists, what long-term plan would a Chinese publishing magnate have? Probably flexibility. Going forward, Shao sees the need for flexibility in this dynamic market and times and, therefore, has no fixed 10-year plan. "I do have a vision, though. I always want to create the best products. We hope that Modern Media will become a global platform for Chinese and Western cultures to communicate with one another, and for the best cultures and lifestyles from all over the world to communicate."

In fact, Shao sees the company serving as a mediator for lifestyles rather than as a single-media company in the future. He hopes Modern Media can transform how people view media companies, from a customer/sales-oriented business (B2B) to a reader-oriented (B2C) community "in which products, creativity, knowledge, and services can all be exchanged."

Amongst industry leaders, Shao has a reputation for being tough and demanding on his staff, so I asked him for his leadership "recipe." At the core of Shao's philosophy is a "4S" management approach comprising: spirit—setting high standards for yourself; study—knowing the job and industry inside out and being highly professional; sharing—communicating effectively; and support—working for each other.

With regard to working and cooperating with Chinese companies, Shao believes one of the most important points is to understand their individual cultures. "For example, companies in Guangzhou, Shanghai, and Beijing are all quite different." Shao feels foreign companies' difficulties setting up in China are also related to culture. "Sometimes I see foreign companies get stuck when they don't understand Chinese culture well enough. They may have good intentions and good tools, but they'll never acclimate if they simply try to copy their success stories from abroad."

Acknowledgment This interview has been published with the kind permission of Mr. Thomas Shao.

Notes

1. KPMG, National Bureau of Statistics of China.
2. http://china.ahk.de/market-info/media-marketing/main-media-players-in-china/
3. KPMG, *2014 News and Publishing Industry Analysis Report* by State Administration of Press, Publication, Radio, Film and Television of China.

4. KPMG, National Bureau of Statistics of China.
5. KPMG, *2014 News and Publishing Industry Analysis Report* by State Administration of Press, Publication, Radio, Film and Television of China.
6. Ibid

4

Getting that Dream Job: Tarena

Private education—No. 1 IT training company—Han Shaoyun, Founder (photo with kind permission of Mr. Han Shaoyun)

© The Author(s) 2018
C. Nothhaft, *Made for China*, DOI 10.1007/978-3-319-61584-4_4

Opportunity

As the consumer economy is growing and more and more local companies are pushed to become more professional in the ever-increasing competition for customers, China is likely to become the largest vocational training market in the world.

Chinese companies could be in a unique position to thrive not just in China but also in emerging markets with experience in distance learning, low-cost operating models, and fast growth experience. Countries with a vast geographic spread, comparatively few specialists, and a workforce highly motivated for self-development would be a good choice, like India or parts of Africa.

Lessons Learned

Classroom-based distance learning provides the solution for quickly becoming a national player, ensuring consistent training quality, and keeping up-to-date with the training content that is needed to be a market leader.

As Chinese people yearn for better lives and pursue self-development, the education sector appears to be a hot topic for investment. This is especially true for Internet-based and scalable models that allow a high level of standardization to secure quality and fast growth, as well as the capacity to cover a large territory.

From 1978 (when China opened up the economy) to the late 2000s, during the 30-year economic transition, the Chinese labor market became a free market economy in its own right, with workers improving their income by moving to new cities and by constantly changing jobs in search of a better life through a better salary. The modernization of the economy required not just "workers" in urban areas but also more qualified personnel.

According to NBS, the total working population of China reached 774.51 million at the end of 2015. In the urban areas alone, the labor force is 404 million,[1] larger than the total resident population of the USA (323 million) in 2016. The most surprising number is the change in the urban workforce, which has nearly quadrupled over the past 35 years.

In the past decade, with the modernization of the economy followed by the Internet age, a huge demand for IT personnel, especially those equipped with the latest programming skills at the international level, emerged in China. With e-commerce and the use of Big Data evolving further, this trend continues. Three industries with an Internet focus, including e-commerce, software and applications, and online financial services, accounted for the greatest demand for talented people with an undergraduate or higher education.[2]

Internet-based business models have managed to overcome one of China's primary challenges (and opportunities) when it comes to creating a domestic market: its size and, in many parts of the country, its low population density. Such models also break sectoral boundaries within China and lower the thresholds for starting up new businesses. As such, it's no surprise that the Internet-related sectors and especially e-commerce-related businesses are a key target for the future workforce in China. And—as if that weren't enough—many young people see their future as entrepreneurs and view their first employer as the training ground for their future entrepreneurial ambitions. In a nutshell: today, universities and companies are full of young people who dream of going out and trying their luck in the Internet (or tech) sector.

And here we see the conflict that can't be ignored: a talent gap between university/college education or professional experience among the current workforce and a highly dynamic IT market, driven by rapidly emerging industries and an equally rapidly evolving consumer market, especially in terms of e-commerce.

The Chinese government began significantly expanding university enrollment in 1999. The reform led to a sharp increase in both the number of university graduates and the number of universities. The number of universities nearly tripled from 1080 in 1994 to 2879 in 2016. Over the same period, the number of graduates skyrocketed from 640,000 to 7.65 million—more than tenfold!

I have always been impressed by the facilities at Chinese universities and by just how many universities there are. Most universities are essentially mini-cities within their host cities, with their own roads and supply infrastructure, including supermarkets and laundry shops.

Before we delve further into the talent gap topic, let's take a look at how Chinese society handles personnel screening. The history of the "Gao Kao" system (lit. "high test"), a test held every June and taken by an average of 9.40 million students yearly (in 2016),[3] dates back to the Sui Dynasty (which began about AD 605).[4] It was intended to identify the country's brightest talents and put them in the Imperial Court-controlled education system, which would groom them for Imperial administrative roles to serve the Emperor. In principle, the basic philosophy hasn't changed, in that universities are there to prepare students for a good job in the government or at a state-run company. The system is based on ranking all students nationally, which creates tremendous competitive pressure as well as expectations from parents, family units, or even entire villages. Further pressure stems from self-expectations, as young people today are driven by aspirations for a good job, traveling, and enjoying a good lifestyle.

Today, your Gao Kao score ultimately determines which university you can attend. Once you have enrolled at a university in China, you will be taken care of (much as in the Imperial days). As an observation—one reason why university graduates are a target audience for marketers (and us as a chain store retailer) is not that their future income prospects are bright, but the fact that their disposable income is already considerable—once at a university, their food, board, and basic living expenses are covered by the university.

However, there is a discrepancy between the type of workforce China's future consumer market will need and how universities are run. Universities in China are strongly science-focused. In fact, 41% of all undergraduate students are engineers and scientists.[5] While university education in China is demanding for students, more often than not, the knowledge and practice gap for students entering the workforce—depending on the industry—can be immense. This is compounded by the fact that parents generally consider getting top grades at university to be the priority, over extracurricular activities, or following a vocation or personal passion.

As the economy kept leapfrogging during its hot stages of growth, more often than not companies had to self-train their staff and management, within their company system. This also gave rise to specialist training outsourcing companies to fill the workforce-training gap.

The Chinese government took its first steps into education reform in 1985, by allowing market-driven private schools and training institutions to open their doors in China. In the previous planned economy, workforce education had been planned according to industry needs, with people being assigned to a given industry and, in fact, to a State Owned Company to work for.

30 years have passed, and China's workforce development has now become a market of its own. Private professional education is a key enabler for people to make better choices for starting their career and, more and more, for transforming their career according to their individual needs and dreams. According to the Ministry of Education of China, there were roughly 120,000 vocational training institutes in China by the end of 2015,[6] with language training and IT institutes forming the mainstream.

Recently, China's professional training market has gradually become mature. From 2004 to 2013, the number of education and training institutions in China dropped by 48% to about 100,000 companies,[7] and few of them achieved annual revenues of more than RMB 1 billion. A report by Tencent Education published in 2014 found that the main pillars of the Chinese education market were as shown in Fig. 4.1.[8]

As already mentioned, the Internet age and e-commerce development are driving many companies in traditional industries to leapfrog and to become

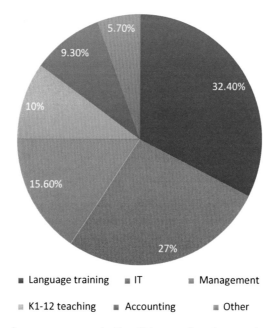

Fig. 4.1 Popular degree programs in the Chinese education market. Source: Tencent Education

more tech-oriented at an incredible speed. Consequently, new jobs requiring IT and digital-related skillsets are being created not only in the high-tech industries, but also in the traditional sectors, such as manufacturing, health, and retail. The prevailing "Internet+" concept is pushing the demand for digital professionals to new heights, as nearly every business is going digital in one way or another.

According to Essence Securities, the market size of IT training reached RMB 15.3 billion in 2015 with CAGR of 16.24% from 2009 to 2015, as shown in Fig. 4.2. Further, Essence predicts that by the end of 2020, the market size of IT training in China will be RMB 30.8, with the total professional training market worth 708.8 billion.[9]

Tarena is the only China IT education provider publicly listed in the USA and the largest of its kind in China's IT training market, with a market share of 8.3%.[10] The company was founded in 2002 and went IPO in 2014 (NASDAQ: TEDU). Its revenues in 2016 were RMB 1.58 billion (US$229 million), with net revenues growing at a CAGR of 63.1% from 2011 to 2015. According to Tarena, it produced an estimated 110,000 graduates in 2016 alone and a total of ca. 354,000 since being founded.

Mr. Han Shaoyun, Tarena's founder, chairman, and CEO is a true "model success story," On a Saturday morning, we met over coffee near his home in

Fig. 4.2 The Chinese IT training industry continues to grow. Source: Essence Securities

Beijing. It was a beautiful day, but—as so often in Beijing—the traffic was not as enjoyable as the weather.

Mr. Han is proud of having pioneered China's IT education market. Having spent over 6 years in software development in Canada, he interviewed a number of software engineers. "I found that there was always a gap between the skills the candidates learned from the Chinese universities and what employers actually need." He described the market opportunity he saw. "So I thought maybe the placement rate of young graduates would be much higher with the proper training." As such, he soon quit his job and founded Tarena.

Like so many entrepreneurs and managers I know in China, Mr. Han's main challenges when building his business involved finding the right people. In this case, the problem was trying to find the right instructors for certain courses. According to Han, Tarena found it difficult to recruit qualified instructors in tier-two or lower cities during its rapid nationwide expansion. For Han, an IT engineer, the obvious solution was distance education. Today, Tarena has over 200 qualified specialist instructors, all located in Beijing and delivering live lectures through the Internet to students in classrooms at 138 directly operated learning centers in 43 cities across China.

To ensure a comprehensive and live classroom atmosphere, a locally hired teaching assistant joins each remote classroom to answer students' questions in person and to help monitor their progress. This approach has allowed Han to overcome the bottleneck of finding specialist trainers in remote cities and thus focus his center of excellence on the best location for the resource—in this case, Beijing.

Distance learning has enabled Tarena to steadily expand into lower-tier cities, gaining two to three cities every year. According to Tarena, the instructor-to-student ratio was one to 435 at the end of 2015, and with this model the ratio will continue to rise unless new courses are launched.

Tarena also has its online course platform TMOOC, which was launched in March 2015 to help it compete with other professional education service providers like Coursera. Nearly 200,000 people have since registered, and more than 22,000 have paid for the online courses.

Although Han's main focus is on developing talent for the Internet industry through two main channels of distance learning—a live classroom learning experience and e-learning (structured programs for self-study)—he feels the live classroom learning format plays a more significant role. As Han explains, "The reality in China is that students do need an offline teaching atmosphere, as the completion rate of online courses is rather low. Further, from a corporate perspective, the number of per-customer transactions for online courses is also low."

Though Han's market opportunity may seem obvious, while building his business he soon hit another brick wall—his target customers were university graduates with no or little income. Students from junior colleges and below currently make up 55% of Tarena's total customers, and in China, the reason that families choose colleges is mostly their limited financial resources.

According to Han, at that time a Tarena course cost the equivalent of 3–5 months' living expenses for a student, and a well-rounded IT education called for attending several courses. In response, Han developed a pre-financing model whereby students pay a small down payment to enroll in the class and then pay off the balance through monthly installments once they have secured employment. By lowering the threshold, Tarena achieved critical growth momentum and successfully doubled its revenues every year from 2006 to 2008.

Inspired by Tarena's success, other players in the sector began adopting both distance learning and the down-payment model. To stay ahead, Han had to constantly innovate, which is caused by "both industries and IT requirements leapfrogging." The company launches at least one new course each year—Web Front, Big Data, kids' computer programming and digital arts in 2015 and AR/VR and kids' robot programming in 2016.

In the long run, Han is considering strategies to respond to changing needs, including expanding course subjects to non-IT areas such as digital arts, digital marketing, accounting, K-12 teaching, etc., or introducing IT subjects to a new target audience, for example, school-age youths. Tarena currently offers a total of 15 courses, including three non-IT courses. Personally, I believe that since the IT industry is constantly evolving, Han will be able to retain Tarena's market position in IT and doesn't necessarily have a pressing need to diversify, though the opportunities in distance education are vast.

Currently, Tarena still continues to evolve alongside the overall evolution in the IT sector. According to the company, its three most popular courses are Java, Digital Arts, and Web Front, with Web Front the fast-growing course.

As employees and universities are working to make themselves attractive to employers in hot industries, Han sees a shift in his customers from being almost exclusively fresh university/college graduates to past graduates who have already worked for 2–5 years and are looking for a career change.

Han also sees some changes in the client base from people with IT-related degrees and professions upgrading their skills to non-IT candidates taking Tarena courses. According to Han, non-IT candidates now account for 50% of total students. "A shift to non-IT-based candidates has been evolving." Han concludes that the rapid development of the Internet industry in China over the past 10 years "has inspired many professionals from other industries to join Internet companies and make a career in the technology sector."

Globalization is another area Han is exploring. He believes that IT technology is universal. "Successful cases of IT training in China can be adapted for other countries such as the USA, Germany, and especially the gold brick countries including India, Russia, and Brazil, as their markets are similar to that in China." Tarena now has cooperation agreements with global companies like Adobe, Oracle, and Red Hat in terms of establishing studios and developing courses.

My personal view is that, when it comes to updating the workforce with the right knowledge and skills, Chinese companies could have a strong opportunity to grow in the global workforce training market, with a global trend of private education being more dynamic than government-sponsored models.

Although very successful, Mr. Han is one of few chairmen I interviewed who doesn't have a grand goal to become the number one or two in their industry; at least he didn't say so. To my astonishment (and delight, as it matches my own thinking), he said his goal was to build "the best managed Chinese company," and the reason is to fend off competitors.

Seeing learning capability and management as a means of continuously evolving, Han believes "first class management and execution capabilities" are the core quality that allows Tarena to identify the best approaches and bring them to market quickly with good execution.

Han describes his view as follows: "In fact, the core competence of a company is its management capabilities. When your management standard rises to a higher level, other tasks will become easy."

Han hopes Tarena will become a business management model, allowing him to make contributions to improving the management of Chinese companies. According to Han, Chinese companies are very active when it comes to entrepreneurship, innovation, and the ability to seize market opportunities, but not necessarily when it comes to management. He points out that, as a unique combination of the above three elements, venture capital is very active in China, creating opportunities for entrepreneurs to expand their companies quickly. Supported by both the motivation to start up new businesses and the capital funds required, the emerging new economy can grow rapidly. As China's consumer economy continues to grow, management and operations will therefore remain a challenge for every company—and has become a part of the character of Chinese companies in many cases.

Han feels Chinese companies might be in a unique position, since most have quickly grown after starting with very little resources, and more often than not operating in an environment characterized by a lack of highly qualified staff. As companies from mature markets may be too advanced to quickly learn, digest, and apply dynamic developments, Chinese businesses could therefore prove appealing for emerging markets, and for companies in developing countries, they could also be worth learning from. As he puts it: "Alibaba is a good model for a large market like India, and the same is true for Tarena; one day we may provide professional training and develop talent for rapidly evolving, geographically large economies like India or Russia."

Acknowledgment This interview has been published with the kind permission of Mr. Han Shaoyun.

Notes

1. http://data.stats.gov.cn/easyquery.htm?cn=C01
2. http://tech.gmw.cn/newspaper/2015-05/05/content_106379729.htm
3. http://www.guancha.cn/Education/2016_06_07_363110.shtml
4. http://baike.baidu.com/link?url=kzbOfdV2K3iaa2IsgOVpOIWpDQqjnsx-rYYKpWDtcIjEULBoa4pF2hNpIIZGidOJwttBBzYhZYO9YLmH16SIvq
5. http://data.stats.gov.cn/easyquery.htm?cn=C01
6. http://www.moe.edu.cn/jyb_sjzl/s5990/201612/t20161219_292432.html
7. http://data.stats.gov.cn/easyquery.htm?cn=C01
8. http://edu.qq.com/a/20141203/077878.htm#p=1
9. http://istock.jrj.com.cn/article,yanbao,29785998.html
10. http://itpx.eol.cn/career_9921/20140829/t20140829_1169336.shtml

5

Diversifying the Product: GreenTree Inn

Hotel industry—No. 4 hotel chain—Alex Xu, Founder (photo with kind permission of Mr. Alex Xu)

© The Author(s) 2018
C. Nothhaft, *Made for China*, DOI 10.1007/978-3-319-61584-4_5

Opportunity

China's hotel industry is currently in a state of transition. Though growth of the market has slowed from the high double digits to single-digit, new generations of customers provide new opportunities for brands that are agile. The race for market share and the attention of more lifestyle- and brand-conscious consumers has provided both a challenge and an opportunity for hotel operators. We can see new boutique hotel chains evolving, while existing hotel chains with large footprints now have the chance to diversify their offer and also "premiumize" their brand. As China is an early adopter of technology and new ideas, we might see service and convenience evolving to a new level in this sector over time.

Lessons Learned

As the decision of which hotel to book or not has shifted more and more to the consumers, hotel operators are faced with a double challenge: differentiating themselves from their competitors and attracting new consumers or convincing existing customers to upgrade by offering different categories of hotels.

The goal has changed from pure expansion speed, allowing companies to outrun their competitors and build a brand, to being able to offer the right hotel product to different consumer groups. This chapter provides insights into gaining new and retaining existing customers through segmentation, exploring which services could be developed beyond the rooms, especially using technology, and what we could find in the hotel room of tomorrow according to the founder of one of China's largest foreign-invested, locally operated hotel brands.

I tried to find out which hotel chain was the first to open in China in the post-Mao era, and our research determined that roughly 50 different hotels claimed to be "the first hotel in Modern China." Yes, product claims in China are always a challenge. Giving up on that idea allowed me to pick some hotel industry milestones of interest.

In 1982, the first foreign joint venture (JV) hotel in China—the Jianguo Hotel in Beijing—opened; at the time it was a JV with the Peninsula Hotel Group. In 1983, the White Swan Hotel in Guangzhou opened its doors, being a JV with the Hong Kong-based Henry Fok Ying Dong family. That was a fairly significant milestone, as Guangzhou became the host of the famous Canton Fair as part of turning the city into the first experimental economic opening zone during the 1980s. Guangdong is, therefore, often referred to as the frontier of China's opening up and reform. Organized by the Ministry of Commerce and the Guangdong provincial government, the Canton Fair has been held twice a year since the spring of 1957. In autumn 2015, it attracted

177,544 visitors from all over the world. Therefore, those hotels became something of a symbol for the opening of China to the West.

For those interested in the history of Western hotel brands in China, it is noteworthy that Holiday Inn entered China in 1984, Marriott in 1995, Sheraton in 1985, and Accor in 1985. I still remember my previous company, Mövenpick, had a hotel in Beijing that opened in 1986—which was hugely popular with Europeans. Unfortunately, it fell on me to close it for strategic reasons as part of my then role as Managing Director for Asia (what a misreading of the market's future potential!!).

During the planned-economy era, the only target markets in China were state-owned enterprise (SOE) employees and government officials traveling between different provinces. In the Mao age, many SOEs, especially the larger ones, operated their own guesthouses. SOE employees stayed in either the guesthouse of the SOE they were visiting or a guesthouse run by another SOE in the destination city.

The same procedure applied for government officials, which explains why many cities or even district governments had their own "guesthouse." Often, the SOEs or state guesthouses had different buildings with different furnishings and room standards to accommodate different people according to their various ranks or positions. You might imagine those vast premises as being like creating a 2- or 3-star hotel, a 4-star, and a 5-star all in the same compound!

In the early stages of the opening of China, due to deregulation, many hotels sprang up. These were property projects by individuals, leading to a highly fragmented market. A major challenge for the industry, as travel in China continued to pick up, was that different hotels had vastly different standards. Star ratings were not reliable indicators of what product a consumer would actually get, and it was difficult for the consumer to pick a hotel with a good standard in the absence of any meaningful "brands" or "chains." The situation changed rapidly during the 1990s, with international chains entering China, establishing standards in customers' mindset. As shown in Fig. 5.1, sizeable hotel chains then emerged with the evolution of local brands that acted like overseas brands regarding value proposition and standards (usually based on a franchise). The growth of such chains was based on two solidly developing markets—the business traveler and the leisure traveler (see Fig. 5.1). GreenTree is one such success story to emerge from this period.

As shown in Fig. 5.2, the company GreenTree Inn is China's fourth largest hotel brand, in terms of the number of outlets (see Fig. 5.2). The company started in 2004, and it took full advantage of the rapidly growing economy and the lack of business concepts to become a market leader in the 2–3-star sector. Today GreenTree Inn has more than 2200 outlets worldwide, the majority of

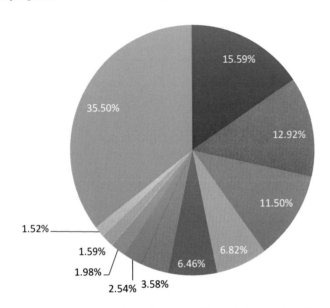

Fig. 5.1   Top ten Chinese budget chain hotel brands by market share in 2015. Source: China Qianzhan Academy

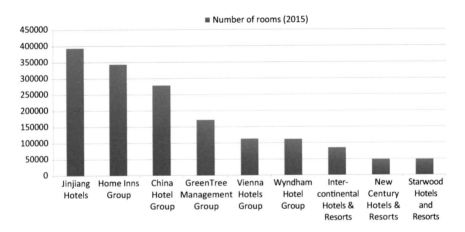

Fig. 5.2   Top ten hotel chains by room in China. Source: China Hotel Association (http://travel.sohu.com/20160720/n460194051.shtml)

which are located in China. The company primarily operates on the franchise model and is tightly managed by its open-minded and highly entrepreneurial founder, Alex Xu.

Mr. Xu was educated in the USA and holds an MA in Mathematics and MS in Computer Engineering from the University of Southern California. He started his career in retail at Broadway Stores as a finance manager and then moved to a real estate company, followed by management roles in different US listed companies. In 1997, Xu founded his own company, American Pacific Homes, helping Asian investors develop their real estate. As the housing market gradually became more difficult in the USA, Xu considered diversifying his company. At this time, a friend of his (coincidentally) invited him to invest in and form a joint venture in China, with his friend as the hospitality expert and Xu being in charge of real estate.

As the Beijing Olympics drew nearer, his friend was asked by the government to help organize the Olympics, and Xu ended up doing the hospitality by himself, facing the challenges of learning the hotel trade. Stuck with a venture in China and a company in the USA, Xu began wondering whether or not he'd made the right decision—especially when his US friends laughed at him as US real estate prices climbed rapidly between 2005 and 2006. But later, when the real estate market in the USA crashed in 2007, the decision to invest his time in China and the hotel business proved to be the right one.

"I visited many hotels in China and found there was a lack of quality products at affordable price levels. That's how I created and designed my first hotels. At that time we didn't have any networks, so we did the first 50 hotels using the lease-operating model. And then we used the directly-owned model." After 3 years, Mr. Xu had a good understanding of how the hospitality market works and then started offering franchise opportunities to others.

Mr. Xu believes it was his calling to be in hotels, yet he had a lot of doubts, as it can be a turbulent business. "My daughter was 9 years old then. She drew a picture when I first started going to China and doing hotels. In the drawing there is a busy lobby: Dad will have a great business! I still have that little pencil drawing," Xu says.

Especially for international readers, it is important to understand how huge the Chinese domestic travel market is and what Chinese consumers expect in terms of value proposition and segmentation and that means embracing the 2–4-star market.

The domestic market in China is enormous. In 2015, the value of the domestic travel market in China was RMB 4 trillion,[1] while the value of the Chinese overseas travel market was RMB 930 billion the same year.[2] The Chinese spent a total of RMB 211 billion in domestic star-rated hotels in 2015 while spending US$498 billion abroad in the same year. A study conducted by Starwood Hotels in 2012 revealed how the market had been evolving. While

Table 5.1 Forecast of a slow-down in growth on China's hotel market

Sector	2012–2015 CAGR (%)	2015–2022 CAGR (%)
High-end hotel	11	5.8
Middle-end hotel	12.5	6.6
Budget-end hotel	20.7	6.8

Source: NBS, AT Kearney

Chinese guests represented 24% in Starwood hotels in China (in part due to its portfolio focus on 5-star hotels back then) in 2010, they represented 60% in 2012.

The numbers mentioned above already represent a slowing-down trajectory after the Beijing Olympics (2008) and Shanghai World Expo (2010). As shown in Table 5.1, the industry is now growing at an average annualized rate of roughly 7%, and there could be slower growth in the next few years (see Table 5.1).

Nevertheless, there is a good future in hotels in China. Foreign enterprises still have a significant impact on the industry's development, as they have now successfully established themselves as players even in the 3–4-star market, offering a franchise or operating opportunities to local entrepreneurs looking to get into the business or to upgrade their current hotel.

According to a study released by IHG in 2014, while overall growth on the Chinese market may be slowing, spending per trip will continue to rise due to greater consumer affluence. Leisure overtook business travel as the biggest share of the market sometime around 2010, and it is now estimated that leisure travel spending will accelerate further.

IHG has been in China since 1984, and the chain expects to double its number of hotels in the next 5 years. It already has 205 hotels in the pipeline, more than half of which will be managed under the midscale brands Holiday Inn and Holiday Inn Express.

This is an example of how foreign branded budget and 2–3-star outlets appear, through smaller hotel operators upgrading and refining themselves into the branded, franchised sector. Many of the leading chains are now focusing on increasing their footprint in smaller, provincial cities and towns further into China's interior. They are not only opening new hotels but are also expanding their brand portfolios so as to appeal to an increasingly diverse range of consumer needs, from short-stay budget business to high-end, luxury boutique hotels.

The current market situation and the rapidly evolving customer offer the hotel industry an opportunity for rejuvenation and for developing more brands, targeting the lifestyle and leisure element. A good example is the brand strategy of the aforementioned company GreenTree, which has embarked on a multi-brand strategy covering different price categories, business, and leisure sectors with different intensity, even introducing highly affordable business hotels with spa services or meeting rooms, just as 5-star hotels would do.

The company ranks 5th in market share for economy hotel chains in China, with over 2200 outlets in 400 cities across the country, plus hotels in the USA, South Korea, Bangladesh, and Vietnam. The company was only founded in 2004, making it a latecomer. However, it has had an incredible growth story, growing from 30 hotels in 2006 to eightfold within 10 years. "We are the largest privately held hotel chain worldwide because most of the hotel chains (once reaching 2000 or more outlets) have to go to the public markets to raise funds," Xu says.

Mr. Xu started his business by making sure to deliver on the 3Bs—great bed, great bath, and great breakfast. "What else do you look for to make it affordable? Very simple and naïve." He chuckles during our interview.

In response to the market challenges, rising customer aspirations and the expansion of international brands at the 3–4-star level, as well as fierce local competition keeping prices down, GreenTree has pursued a multi-format segmentation strategy to tackle the future. Comparable to Holiday Inn and IBIS from overseas in terms of its positioning, Mr. Xu has designed two brands under GreenTree that cater more to business travelers. GreenTree Inn, as he puts it, is "primarily for entry level business travelers" and he adds, "I think IBM and Wal-Mart are some of our corporate accounts." The star rating is roughly 3 stars, and the pricing is somewhere between RMB 150 and RMB 250 per night.

The other brand, GreenTree Eastern, is essentially a premium version of GreenTree Inn. According to Xu, "I consider it to be a 4-star chain with limited service at a higher standard level for engineers as well as government officials, because their travel budgets are limited." GreenTree Eastern charges between RMB 400 and maximum RMB 500 per night. "With a membership discount, it will cut the price down to RMB 400," Xu adds. In his eyes, RMB 400 is probably the critical threshold.

Just as in the West, business travel for company reasons is increasingly blending into leisure travel, as customers expect more than a good bed, shower, and Wi-Fi. The hotel group has also observed a similar trend in China. CYTS GreenTree Eastern International Hotels and GreenTree Eastern Hotels are targeting both the more lifestyle-oriented business traveler and the leisure traveler. They are 4-star boutique hotels located in business districts or high-tech zones, focusing on a strong location and convenient transportation. Most of the rooms run from RMB 300 to RMB 600 per night. The hotels have a more sophisticated design and a combination of business and leisure facilities, including a business center, health food, beauty spas, etc.

Customers aged between 21 and 40 account for 70% of GreenTree's total clientele, while those above the age of 90 make up 24%. To Mr. Xu, who intends to cover a "more fashionable/trendy traveler," GenNet and GenMobile are both a challenge and an opportunity—which is also why GreenTree launched its fifth brand, Vatica Hotel, which Xu calls a "Baby-W" hotel. It is a "young fashion" hotel advocating a green, environmentally friendly, low-carbon way of life and offering a "fresh and comfortable" experience. By the end of 2016, the group had 84 Vatica hotels in China, primarily intended for young, white-collar workers and with prices for most rooms ranging from RMB 150 to RMB 300.

In total, the company is now operating five sub-brands representing the high-end, middle-end, young/fashion and localized markets. By differentiating and segmenting to best scoop up different consumer groups, GreenTree Group offers a good example that reflects the current trends in the hotel market's key economy chain sector.

What's more, competition has led most local companies in China to start offering loyalty programs with attractive perks and benefits. GreenTree also launched a membership program that offers price discounts for returning consumers. "Most Chinese post-90s are less loyal to brands compared to GenNet, and they are more practical, paying more attention to what exactly they can benefit from, like the points and rewards." The data derived from membership serves as a basis for further growth of the existing business. Examples of this data include bookings, invoice pickups, online complaints, etc.

More than 19 million members have since purchased a membership and Xu dreams of scaling up, given the huge number of potential consumers in China. "We may be able to create more than 50 million paid memberships in a 5-year period. And our goal is set at 100 million." That's fascinating; it wouldn't be possible in any other country.

In the long run, Xu wants to foster brand relationships with consumers at a deeper level. He is thinking more and more about technology and how it can enhance services to consumers. Besides offering Uber-like taxi services and meeting consumers' travel needs throughout their journey with the help of on-demand services, his main priority is the personalization of the room itself.

Xu says, "When we talk about a personalized room, that includes what is already in the plans, designs like air conditioning, the television channels, the shower temperature, the music, etc. All is going to be set to match the customer's preferences, based on his or her last visit." For him, therefore, the focus is now on providing the right product for consumers.

The Internet is already a mature tool for selling hotel rooms, and thousands of hotel booking engines and e-travel agents now dominate China. In addition, customers use social apps and location-based providers to make bookings. Every second, a consumer books a room using the Internet, mostly based on price. According to Xu, most young consumers of GreenTree hotels are price sensitive and will usually look through as many price ranges as possible before booking.

Some might deem the travel industry and hotels to be the most "disrupted industry" in the world. But another way to look at this is to call it advanced, since it delivers complete transparency of pricing and full accessibility through direct booking. With distribution so far developed, the hotel product itself becomes the paramount battleground in China.

Xu sees the Internet as an important means of establishing a deeper relationship with the customers and in part a tool for mitigating price competition. It also provides the opportunity to work with other platforms based on the superior offer. "If you have a loyal customer base and can provide excellent services at an affordable price, we can do it together. 97% of our customers come to us through our own channels. The third-party internet is only 3% or so."

Mr. Xu feels that shared resources (using your apartment as a hotel room via platforms, e.g. Airbnb) will continue to be a trend as a particular segment, especially for younger consumers and individuals traveling for leisure. For Xu, the private accommodation model will be the biggest disruptor for the hotel industry: "That means all of a sudden the supply of hotel rooms will increase manifold."

However, he also believes that budget hotels have "weapons" to combat this trend. "We can provide the customer with safety and security, thanks to a standardized product and service." GreenTree's one umbrella brand strategy also offers another advantage: segmented brand targeted for various consumers with different needs.

As "country living"—the countertrend to urbanization—represents a second mega-trend, the hotel industry may also pick up on it, taking advantage of better and faster transport systems. According to Xu: "People perhaps have less need to stay in the city, but have a keen desire to live in the countryside or at a resort. Hotels located in suburban areas, the countryside, and other environmentally friendly places are going to be more popular instead of vacation, weekend, or holiday types of visit. This could even become a business-combined-with-leisure-travel phenomenon."

"Boutique" hotels are a new segment that Xu believes will be relevant for the next 5–10 years, with an "in-home experience," such as Airbnb-type outlets with families providing one to two rooms for hotel guests in their home/apartment and "commercial boutique hotels" with only 50–60 rooms decorated with individually unique themes and highly customized services. According to Xu, many of today's "non-branded" hotels now have the opportunity to reinvent themselves and become boutique hotels.

And further automation is in store. Xu is optimistic that 10 years from now, people will see robotic technologies providing basic room services. "Even robotic companions will become available. So if you are traveling alone and feel lonely, it could be easily solved: a robotic lady (or whatever you prefer) can accompany you," Xu adds. "In fact, Japan already offers robotic companions. Just imagine: the robot will play chess with you and also help you get ready for bed."

The hotel industry in China has developed solidly for over 20 years and is now in the maturing phase of its lifecycle. Strong growth over the past 10 years has been the result of market deregulation earlier in the decade and of the expansion of chain operation businesses. Mr. Xu does not expect to see much change over the next 5 years, as the industry overall might continue to undergo an era of consolidation with branded hotels enjoying superiority over the non-brands.

He has an interesting view about integrating hotels with the surrounding community: "Hotels will become a more integral part of communities. For instance, they may share resources with the community like cafés, hotel kitchen facilities to cook for the elderly, and serving communities' other needs."

When it comes to cross-border expansion, Mr. Xu believes the coming years belong to the Chinese hotel industry, both in terms of expansion and innovation. His rationale is that the hotel industry is doing a good job of following consumer trends and, with millions of hotel nights booked annually, Chinese travelers represent the largest group worldwide. And with 120 million Chinese making trips overseas in 2015 (and growing), the future customer segment to focus on is simply the Chinese.

"In the past 50 years, America exported most of the hotel brands. That's because they had the hotel management technology. Secondly, being the world's richest country, Americans exported most of the travelers." According to Xu, things are now starting to change, with China's hotel management software already advanced and China's outbound travelers being the largest group in the world. And these trends continue to grow. "Thanks to these two elements, Chinese hotel brands will gradually expand into different parts of the globe."

Acknowledgment This interview has been published with the kind permission of Mr. Alex Xu.

Notes

1. http://news.china.com.cn/2016-01/05/content_37457113.htm
2. http://m.21jingji.com/article/20151229/herald/1202966380a1ba759569d2664c796773.html

6

Brand to Platform: Daphne

Shoe manufacturing—No. 3 footwear chain—Eddie Chen, Chairman (photo with kind permission of Mr. Eddie Chen)

© The Author(s) 2018
C. Nothhaft, *Made for China*, DOI 10.1007/978-3-319-61584-4_6

Opportunity

The underlying opportunity for overseas shoe brands is to time their market entry in line with the current transition and to potentially cooperate with transitioning companies like Daphne to get ahead in the race. Foreign companies may succeed if they can flexibly and rapidly adapt to the ever-changing tastes of Chinese shoe consumers.

Lessons Learned

The shoe market in China has always been highly competitive, as China has become the shoemaker of the world and all OEM manufacturers have created large distribution systems and brands domestically in China. E-commerce, in particular through platforms, has given customers a vast array of choices and brands, all of which they can purchase at a low price with just a mouse-click. Now, as the young generation evolves, young customers want to express their own style, either by following foreign shoe brands (and thus being trend leaders) or developing their own preference.

Shoe manufacturers have no choice but to follow this trend and become both shoe manufacturers and shoe retailers. In fact, their ultimate role might be that of "style consultants" offering trends every couple of weeks to reflect the country's numerous seasons (China is huge!). To make matters for shoe companies worse, they need to transform the way they sell, from retail outlets to creating online experiences and to potentially developing trend-leading services.

If everyone goes through an average of two pairs of shoes a year, in theory our planet "consumes" about 12 billion pairs of shoes annually. With China being the "workbench of the world," it's perhaps no surprise that 55% of all shoes produced on the planet come from China,[1] which means probably more than six billion shoes are made in China annually, a staggering number!

In preparing for this chapter, I asked around out of curiosity: What shoe brand did Deng Xiaoping wear? In fact, I could have guessed. He wore "Liberation (Jiefang) Shoes," which is the military brand of shoes that became the primary footwear of the Chinese people for many years after 1949. It is said that over 40% of peasants and 90% of urban workers wore the Liberation Shoes every day.[2]

But things have changed considerably since Deng was in power, and I have identified four key stages of development for the shoe market in China. This began with the "one-brand-fits-all Liberation Shoes" era, before moving on to the early wholesale days in the absence of proper distribution, to single-brand stores (since 1998), and lastly to the current multichannel stage, where single-brand stores, department stores, shoe supermarkets, e-stores[3], and global cross-border sales all coexist.

In connection with China's shoe industry, an interesting year to mention is 2006, when a 2-year EU anti-dumping tariff was imposed on the industry, which led more and more manufacturers to start thinking about how to grow the domestic shoe market. During this period, the EU levied additional tariff charges of between 9.7% and 16.5% on the import price of Chinese shoes and 10% on Vietnamese shoes.

Then, on February 4, 2010, China filed a complaint at the World Trade Organization (WTO) against the European Union's duties on its footwear exports, alleging the 27-nation bloc was imposing illegal duties on Chinese shoes. Eventually, the WTO ruled that the EU's anti-dumping duties were in violation of international commerce.

Since its WTO entry in 2001, and especially during the period from 2003 to 2008, the annual value growth of China's footwear exports exceeded 15% for 6 consecutive years,[4] and China duly became the shoe supplier of the world, including its domestic consumer market. Figures 6.1 and 6.2 illustrate how large the market is and what each segment of the market looks like, respectively.

When you enter a department store in China, it is highly likely that a huge shoes floor will greet you. The shoe market in China is hyper-competitive. As sales through online portals (including overseas portals) has soared since 2011, China's shoe companies have scrambled to launch their own direct distribution models online, which has forced them to evolve from manufacturers (OEM) into branded direct marketing companies. According to the data on 15 platforms (including Taobao, Tmall, JD, VIPshop, etc.), online shoe sales

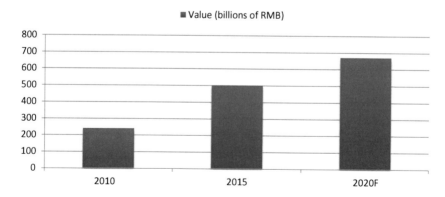

Fig. 6.1 Growth of China's shoe market. Source: Euromonitor International, KPMG (KPMG, Euromonitor)

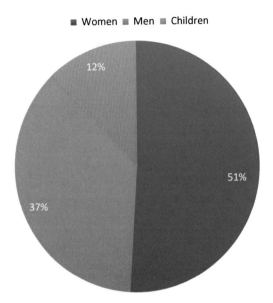

Fig. 6.2 Segments in China's shoe market. Source: Euromonitor International, 2015 (http://china-trade-research.hktdc.com/business-news/article/中国消费市场/中国鞋类市场概况/ccm/sc/1/1X000000/1X002MPH.htm)

reached 18.5 million pairs of men's and 34.2 million pairs of women's shoes in November 2015.[5]

As always we had a look at the Chinese "rich list" and realized that five of the 1000 richest people in China were shoe entrepreneurs. The days of the "Liberation Shoes" are long gone, and now the market leaders are all private companies. According to China's Shoe Association, the following brands were the top five in 2013, based on sales volume, revenue, number of employees, total assets, and number of Baidu searches: Yue Yuen, Belle, Daphne, Doublestar, and Aokang. Among them, Yue Yuen is the largest global shoe manufacturer based in Taiwan, being an OEM supplier for international sports and outdoor brands. The publicly listed Qingdao Doublestar was once a prominent shoe brand, but since 2008 it has completely repositioned itself to focus on producing tires and mechanical equipment.

I then gave some thought to what would be the most interesting things to find out about the highly competitive and transformative shoe market in China. A company that has a major focus on China's young consumers (the fastest-evolving and most individualistic consumer group, and thus responsible for the most transformation) would be an obvious choice, and a company working on a major transformation.

Daphne (the holding company's name is officially United Brands) was established in 1987 by the Chen family from Taiwan, producing for the US and European markets as an OEM manufacturer with factories mainly in Fujian. In 1990, the company launched Daphne as its "own brand" for the domestic market in China. The rest is history. The company went to IPO in Hong Kong (HK:0210) in 1995 and joined the Hang Seng Mainland Index in 2006. The company also entered into lucrative distribution agreements with Adidas Classics (2002), Aldo, Aerosoles, and Paris Hilton (2008). Having focused on the Chinese market for a quarter of a century, the company was ranked number one in sales for 16 of those 25 years.

For much of that time, United Brands expanded by more than 500 stores per year. The company currently has approximately 5000 shoe outlets across China. What we found particularly interesting was that almost 50% of the stores are in tier-4 to tier-6 cities, and two-thirds are located in tier-3 to tier-6 cities. Only 10% of the outlets were franchised. Therefore, with 90% of the stores run directly by Chairman and CEO Eddie Chen and his team, we thought he would surely be a good source to learn what's going on in China's shoe market.

Having built a business with over 3000 stores in China myself, I was keen to meet another "big store network builder." Building anything big and fast in China takes courage and relentless effort. Most of all, I was keen to get some answers about the challenges he faced and how to market to the new generation of Chinese consumers.

We met in mid-2015, during a very interesting stage in the Chinese footwear market's development. In 2014, the market had been experiencing massive disruptions through the emergence of online retailing. 2013 and 2014 were not easy years for shoe sellers in China, with many companies facing zero or negative growth, and ever-changing competition both online and offline. As such, I expected Mr. Chen to be downbeat. But nothing could have been farther from the truth.

"The Daphne brand is only 25 years old. The Chinese market is very big, and in 10 years it can create a big company (like Wanda and Alibaba). It's just the beginning of a market boom." According to Chen, there are so many rural areas yet to urbanize, that it will continue to create plenty of opportunities. That was his response. In his (and my) view, the Chinese consumer market will continue to produce opportunities from both an emerging consumer class in more rural areas and from more and more sophisticated consumers in urban areas. The question is, who will come out on top when it comes to seizing these opportunities?

Interestingly, Daphne's chairman and CEO was once a rock star. Not just a rock-star CEO, but (about 20 years ago) the keyboard player in the famous hard rock band Red Snake from Taiwan, alongside the famous singer Richie Jen. I couldn't resist asking him: "Do you miss your band? Would you rather be a rock star again?"

"All the band members are still friends, and some are trying to get the band together again," said Chen, but at the same time, he made it clear that right now his focus is on the business transition, 24/7, which he believes will be completed in 3 years.

With him making transition the key topic, I was even keener to find out how the shoe business in China works today, and what Mr. Chen's business transition plan was all about.

Daphne grew by opening regional offices around the provincial cities and continued to grow inward from there. It is a strategy most retailers and FMCG brands have applied to China. Customer acceptance had to bear pricing in mind. Mr. Chen described Daphne's pricing as "reasonable," attributing the company's popularity (then and today) to the fact that Daphne could deliver "the latest designs" at a competitive price. In addition, there was a lack of competition in this regard during the market's early stage, thus allowing Daphne to establish itself as a "fashionable top-of-mind brand."

Competition in China is fierce. It's a real example of hyper-competition, with countless OEM manufacturers calling China home. Many manufacturers see production for the local market as an incremental add-on to their business and are thus willing to run the domestic market at very small margins. Also, many wholesalers are selling their excess stock or clearance items at incredibly low prices. To me, the China shoe market already appeared to be a giant snake pit, when Mr. Chen added: "Today there are more than 330,000 shoe stores on Taobao." Wow, I thought—yes it is a snake pit, but with crocodiles, too!

Between 1987 and 1997, 90% of Daphne's business focused on overseas OEMs. Retail started with Daphne's own stores in 1997. Managing retail at that time was a nightmare, even for a company experienced in China. "A lot of problems arose, including products inexplicably disappearing from the stock, stolen cash, etc.," Mr. Chen recalls, adding that, "Cooperation with government and local authorities was cumbersome."

I made a mental note that operating in China had historically been difficult, even for locally managed companies. However, due to the lack of an overseas talent pool, Chinese companies were often forced to work with whomever and whatever was available so as to create (over time) continuity and learning. There were pros and cons to hiring local people, but apparently more pros than cons. As Mr. Chen says, "We started to feel confident in our future success, because we gained very good local staff. Together we researched cash management, people management, and stock management."

During my time in China, I have observed this process in many locally managed companies, which simply had a continuous learning curve, ultimately leading to a superior market understanding and execution. In the end, market superiority was often not achieved because they were "treated better as a local company," but because they followed a "more consistent learning curve."

Of course, OEM manufacturers have access to good designs via their clients, but how do they decide which ones would work in the Chinese market? In a world where designs are developed globally, where do good designs come from today, and what makes a good marketable design FOR CHINA?

Though European brands are also successful in China, Mr. Chen does see a difference. "Fashion originally came from Europe—Italy and France. But the tastes of the French and Italians are different from those of Asian people. Europeans' fashion concept is different from that of Chinese. 15 years ago Asian fashion came from Hong Kong and Taiwan. Now it's from Korea and Japan."

That made sense to me from an Asian perspective.

However, China's having a geographical spread the size of Europe poses specific challenges for marketers due to the different climate zones, cultural regions, and "different sizes of people."

Chen has pursued a hands-on approach to these aspects. "Every year I would have to go to shows in Tokyo six times. The style changed every 2 months. China is so big, with six seasons (spring, summer, deep summer, autumn, winter, and deep winter) and that posed an additional challenge. Winter in Guangdong is different from winter in Northern China. Shoe sizes are different because people in the North are generally taller than people in the South. Tall girls prefer short heels or flat shoes, while short girls like high-heeled shoes. The most popular colors are the same—black and white."

It all sounded like a great deal of complexity and commercial risk to me. But how do you spot designs that work in China? Without hesitation and with a little chuckle, Mr. Chen shares his secret:

> To understand what girls (really) like, I often go to nightclubs and karaoke bars to do market research. The girls in karaoke bars respond to the latest trends the fastest. If you asked the girls working in karaoke bars what was "in" now and what would be popular next year, they could tell you exactly.

We had a good laugh, and I couldn't help thinking about the millions of dollars spent on so-called market research in China, while successful companies resort to more practical methods and focus on First to Market and Speed. Most importantly, I imagined what speed to market would be possible in such a company, where the owner can spot a trend and bring it to market within, say, a month. Do Chinese companies, therefore, have a major advantage in dynamic markets or in changing times?

We started to talk about the future of the shoe market in China and the dynamics that his company will have to follow. It seems clear that the two drivers of change are "new-generation consumer behavior" and "online." According to Chen, the new-generation consumer not only wants to see new brands of shoes, but also cares about the company's image and its expression of style. As such, it may no longer be possible to have different styles under one brand.

On the Internet, Daphne is competing with a staggering number of online shoe stores on Taobao, as well as other local and international brands. "20% of the sales are migrating to the internet," Chen says.

Like many consumer companies in China, Daphne plans to launch products that are purely for online sale and to cater specifically to different price groups. Besides, as small online stores respond quickly to customer needs, Chen is working on the transformation of the supply chain to shorten the company's production cycle. "We must update our restocking system so as to respond to young consumers' needs for the most fashionable shoes," says Chen.

Also, offline retail is changing. In the past, different styles and price brackets could be combined under one umbrella brand (like Daphne). However, the new-generation customer expects a brand that is specifically tailored to her/him, which poses a challenge for consumer companies, requiring them to create a multi-brand strategy.

According to Chen, today a brand in China can survive for 10 years at most. As he elaborates, "We had one brand, then three brands and now we have ten brands, and we need 20–30 brands."

Looking back, the years when amazing growth and store expansion ensured market share are likely to be a thing of the past. When the market was young, the speed of growth was vital and typical for Chinese entrepreneurs, and high risks were taken, with those who could keep up with the speed of expansion coming out on top. Chen recalls those years, when he, aged 30, managed to grow by 500 stores per annum for ten straight years, as follows: "It was like a child playing with a big knife—he either kills the enemy, or he hurts himself."

So if the Internet is growing faster, and you have specific Internet brands, what happens to your stores? "I think the first step is to reduce the number of offline stores by closing the small ones and opening big shops. Maybe in the future, our current number of 6000 stores (in 2015) will be cut down (to 4000), but the total square meters will remain the same."

As shown in Table 6.1, that's exactly what did happen: a year and a half after we met, the number of Daphne's stores had been substantially reduced (see Table 6.1). According to Chen, the company also redecorates its stores on a regular basis, aiming to "always offer customers a fresh image."

Table 6.1 Daphne's slowed expansion in terms of store openings

Year	2014	2015	Nov. 30, 2016
Number of Daphne stores in mainland China	6757	5930	Around 5000

Chen sees the future in big mega-stores with multiple brands side by side. Today, a typical Daphne store in China has an area of about 70 m^2. Under Chen's vision, stores grow to 1000 m^2 or more. Will the fast fashion-like mega-stores soon hit the shoe world in China?

"In Europe, you may see big shops with many brands of shoes, or big apparel shops with shoes, but you seldom see shops with a single brand of shoes. That's why there are big clothing brands, but no big brands for ladies' shoes. But this will happen eventually. In fact, the mega-shops in apparel didn't emerge and develop until 10 years ago." I guess that was a yes. This would also mean we will see a consolidation of brands under mega-operators.

Mobile technology is also helping reap more sales from the Internet. Mr. Chen, like most business owners in this book, also has a big data project. "We need a platform and an app to make our products more interesting through customization and personalization."

We delved a bit deeper into the issues of "personalization," "customer power," and new enterprises using their sales force as "virtual spokespersons." In fact, the goals seemed similar to those we'd heard about in talks with other companies—a desire to use technology not just to market products, but to re-engineer the business process and relationship building with the consumer.

As Chen puts it: "Key Opinion Leaders (KOLs) are very important. Fans are very important. The platform, which is the app, is also very important. Who are the KOLs? They are our sales force and our VIPs (customers). For example, in our database, we have 30 million customers who have purchased with us before. We must interact and communicate with them. We should provide them with value and empower them in order to get their support and loyalty. In the future, maybe one million KOLs may help me sell 100 pairs of shoes each. A KOL may participate in the process of designing products for customization. She may sell the shoes to the people in her immediate vicinity, such as her husband, kids, and parents. So your wife is your KOL. Smartphone technology came out 2–3 years ago, and many business models are now run upon it. Everybody is on this platform now. In the future, the manufacturer and sales force will communicate with consumers directly through smartphones—with nothing in between."

More and more, it sounds to me like brands are turning themselves into technology-driven, multi-channel companies employing store retailing, e-commerce, and even the direct sales model, all under one roof. It would seem the convergence of hyper-rapid growth and technology in China is really cutting through the different ways we sell to consumers.

Considering what was on Mr. Chen's plate at the time—transforming his 5000-store retail empire into a multi-brand company with multiple sales channels—I wasn't sure if I should be jealous (of the interesting challenge he faced) or relieved (that I wasn't the one who had to deal with it). What infected me, though: his passion, commitment, and especially his willingness to try new things. A virtue we in the West have lost a bit over the years, perhaps.

According to Chen: "I see this as a new start-up business. I have set up a separate entity, independent from the existing company, and hired talents from outside. I will personally lead and drive the new business." And I was sitting there wondering how long such a transition, or even the willingness to take on such a huge risk, would take in a typical company from my home country.

The music in our restaurant turned nightclub and became a bit louder, so we felt it was time to either hit the dance floor or wrap things up. However, I had to ask just one last question: "Is there anything you learned from your rock band days that you apply to business—besides doing market research in karaoke bars?"

Chen's reply: "We played rock and heavy metal before. We were not so famous because our product—the songs—was too difficult for ordinary people. So when I started in the shoe business, I knew that designers might not like 'easy' products, but it works for sales and allows you to also make the price 'easy.' Everyone wants 'easy' styles." That's certainly good advice when it comes to conquering a market with 1.3 billion people in it!

Acknowledgment This interview has been published with the kind permission of Mr. Eddie Chen.

Notes

1. http://www.docin.com/p-477205551.html
2. http://baike.baidu.com/link?url=zft2TgefUBOl-wS93JbfyDDm9uY8OMHp UL_W5yL6aisd7ZhyE5vQUV268Ztohp4LJOXVwiMk4e-1oUHbUAt1oq
3. http://www.dginfo.com/xinwen-91621/
4. http://wits.worldbank.org/CountryProfile/en/Country/CHN/Year/2001/ TradeFlow/Export/Partner/all/Product/64-67_Footwear
5. http://z.zhongsou.net/info/160119_39109925456049432.html

7

Boutique Is Beautiful: Grace Vineyard

Beverages—wine—leading privately held winery in China—Judy Chan, Second Generation Founder (photo with kind permission of Ms. Judy Chan)

© The Author(s) 2018
C. Nothhaft, *Made for China*, DOI 10.1007/978-3-319-61584-4_7

Opportunity

Companies often tend to rely on China's size and population and are tempted to make "national plans" for China. Often this is costly and bound to fail, as it's hard to know how customers will respond to a product and therefore it might sometimes be better to gain a solid reputation in one part of China and then use it to "go national" later. With more product transparency and the ability to tell a product story through social- and e-commerce, especially well-made lifestyle products that customers might not have understood just a years ago, can now rise to fame. A good example is the wine market, which is now driven by young consumers.

Lessons Learned

Niche placement with a focus on quality as a means of successfully growing in a market that already seems dominated by major players. As the decision-making power has now shifted to the consumers, who use the Internet to learn about products, smaller businesses that can capitalize on their product's reputation for quality with the right position and a consistent history will be able to effectively scale up in China.

As the consumer market continues to evolve in China, customers are becoming more and more sophisticated, and with so many brands and products investing heavily in recent years, these customers are now spoiled for choices compared to a few years ago. Given the heated competition, together with younger, more educated, and connected consumers, the right brand positioning is taking on a new importance.

Most visitors who talk with me about bringing their brand to China see "the China market" as their target. Over the years, I have seen many brands do the same thing—launching in the major cities, which are the most competitive marketplace in China, and then trying to expand inland at a brisk pace and high cost. While this has worked for quite a few businesses, I have also observed many brands failing and more often than not, failing because they underestimate the investment needed for expansion.

As I operate in the FMCG sector, another strategy was to enter China with cheaper products that were more affordable for the general public. Step two, then, generally consisted in trying to make some profits by "upgrading" and introducing more expensive product lines.

Since the above strategies are very costly and thus very risky, especially for companies whose pockets aren't so deep, the business case presented here might help to show that there are other possible approaches. It is the story of a wine company that gained a global reputation while also successfully and profitably positioning itself as a "regional brand" in China.

A small business surviving among agricultural titans and growing into the leading privately owned and run wine producer makes it an interesting story. Therefore, Grace Vineyard was a prime target for me to interview. The young CEO (she insists that the Chairman title is reserved for her father, the founder CK Chan) Judy Chan gained celebrity status in 2007. This was because one of her company's wines received an honorable mention at the Decanter World Wine Awards—the first Chinese wine to ever do so. Then Cathay Pacific began serving her wine to its first class passengers in 2008.

Interestingly, Ms. Chan didn't make her start in the wine business. A graduate of the University of Michigan, she worked for Goldman Sachs before joining the family business. Her success has garnered her numerous accolades, such as the 2010 Ernst & Young Entrepreneur Award (Hong Kong/Macau), and being ranked among China's Top 25 Businesswomen of 2012 by *Fortune China*.

When I met with Ms. Chan one evening in Guangzhou, she immediately emphasized that her father had founded the company and—although she was running it—that it was a family business. Founded by Mr. Jinqiang Chan in 1997, the company was passed on to Ms. Judy Chan, Grace Vineyards Chairwoman, at the end of 2002 (when she was only 24).

Within 10 minutes, it was clear to me that having the family name involved meant never cutting corners on quality, and that this was the key to her success against much larger corporate ventures. In fact, "Chairman's Reserve" is her father's wine (= the chairman's) and not a "wine for chairmen." Her father started the vineyard in Shanxi, somewhat by accident, intending to buy a vineyard in France with a French partner. Not being able to find a good investment, they asked themselves: "Why not do so in China and start from scratch?"

> Our family principle is that we care a lot about our reputation. We always say that we are in business with friends and neighbors, meaning you should consider long-term consequences. It's a long-term business, and you don't make a huge profit from customers by ripping them off.

Today the company has a number of products, with the Chairman's Reserve priced at ca. US$100 topping the range, and very popular mid-market products such as Sonata and Deep Blue, both priced around the US$50 mark. There is also an entry-level wine called Grace, priced at around US$10, plus a

Premium version of it at twice the price. Overall, this price structure works in China by providing a lower-priced introduction to new customers who can then upgrade over time, all under a single umbrella brand, but with the premium product upholding the quality promise.

As it is extremely dynamic, the wine market in China is a good example of how the Chinese consumer market has changed fundamentally, shifting decision-making power away from distribution channels and directly to the consumer.

In the early stages, the wine market grew well thanks to government entertainment. Most wine drunk was not bought by the consumer, but by people giving gifts or sold in restaurants with expensive menus. As such, the wine did not follow customers' tastes, but rather evolved around purchasing decisions made by restaurant owners and around prestige brands bought in order to "give face" to the person who received them as a gift.

A significant disparity in tariffs, with high tariffs on already bottled wine, made the import of bulk wines an attractive business. And during this process, many locally bottled labels evolved in the country. Both trends led to wines becoming more affordable and pushed local SOEs (such as Great Wall) to raise the bar regarding winemaking quality and range. The government's promotion of wine rather than hard liquor for health reasons, and to save agricultural capacity for grain production, became a national directive in 2011.[1]

While the market was initially quite divided—cheap, low-end locally produced or bottled wines, versus high-end wines sold via mostly restaurants—wine appreciation and drinking culture have now reached China's middle class. Social media and e-commerce has done its bit in both educating consumers and showing them what's possible to aspire to within a certain budget.

Consequently, customers are increasingly buying wine on the basis of its quality rather than price. At the same time, the proliferation of wines from many countries on offer has led to confusion as to what is good to drink. Social media networks and e-commerce sites have taken a leading role in educating the consumer on what to buy, and e-commerce wine companies, as well as wine-related social networks, are relatively successful.

Wine consumption growth nearly doubled from 2007 to 2011, much of that growth came from high-end wines being sold expensively in restaurants, while at the opposite end of the spectrum, cheap retail wines were partly imported from overseas and bottled locally under bulk import tariffs.

Between 2000 and 2010, wine sales tripled at a CAGR of 15.8%. As shown in Fig. 7.1, it then grew to RMB 264 billion by 2015 at a much slower CAGR

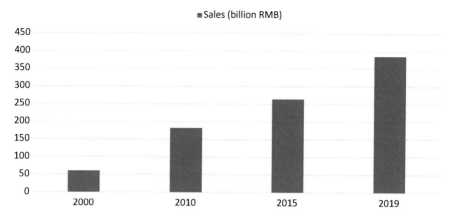

Fig. 7.1 The wine sales boom in China. Source: KPMG, Euromonitor

of around 8% (see Fig. 7.1). The market is expected to pick up and grow to 386 billion by 2019, at a CAGR of nearly 10%.

In 2013, the new government's anti-corruption campaign policies, which prohibited lavish government dinners and gift-giving, brought the wine market's growth to a grinding halt. It was also in that year that Grace Vineyard experienced its first-ever drop in sales.

The impact lasted for at least 3 years and in 2015, Grace Vineyard gained one-digit growth in spite of its double-/triple-digit growth rate in the previous 10 years. Some insiders like Ms. Chan regarded this campaign as a good opportunity, since wine sales now rely more on middle class consumers than government apparatchiks. "We reversed that adversity in 2016 and once again have a positive growth rate," Chan confirmed.

Personally, I see a rosier future for the wine market as new consumers discover wine while existing customers upgrade their drinking habits to premium products. In addition, casual dining sectors are now developing. Millennials are starting to take up champagne and wine drinking at a fast pace, partly triggered by social media sharing. The digital age of wine marketing has dramatically changed customer education, especially among younger consumers, and has made wine much more accessible, from both a knowledge and from a price standpoint.

In a 2015 interview, Ms. Chan said, "I think value for money is more important to me from the quality perspective," She elaborated how she compares their wine's performance with other wines in the same price range available in Hong Kong as part of a benchmarking exercise, and to determine the right pricing. "Also, we invite industry professionals, staff and customers to conduct blind tests."

Grace Vineyard is a classic case of an underdog that capitalized on its hard-won regional reputation as a means to compete in a market ruled by giants. In the beginning, the Chan family were the outsiders in the industry. They broke the established rules but succeeded because they understood consumers better than their significantly larger SOE competitors.

Despite being a 24-year-old CEO who knew nothing about the industry (and didn't even drink), Ms. Chan nonetheless used her personal experience and understanding of how people behave as consumers to build a market. From my personal experience, THAT is often the best place to start in China and is also why so many foreign companies fail to "grasp" China. Sometimes you need to adapt your train to run on the unusual tracks in China, but often you simply need to lay completely new tracks.

Ms. Chan believes that not understanding wine or speaking the same "language" as winemakers or wine critics were huge advantages for her.

During the interview, I came to appreciate Ms. Chan's deep knowledge of the consumers, in contrast to most wine people I know, who mostly focus on their product knowledge. It made me think that not initially being from the industry can be a competitive advantage. Ms. Chan confirmed that and was, in fact, quite critical of the wine industry: "I was able to relate to consumers much more easily than people who grew up with a wine background."

Potentially, new market entrants can read the market better than the incumbents because they can see the market from a new and unfettered perspective, since Chinese consumers are all new drinkers. Furthermore, as customers become more confident, they like to experiment with new things and consequently, more and more consumers might decide to abandon already established brands. This is a story that I keep mentioning to new market entrants who feel intimidated by the established players.

Grace Vineyard is a good business case for brand positioning from a quality perspective with a view to winning over aspiring white-collar customers. I asked Ms. Chan what some of her best business decisions had been while navigating the business after taking it over at the age of 24. The book "Blue Ocean Strategy" somewhat inspired her during what she called her three best decisions when it comes to Grace Vineyard's brand position. A boutique company size position that is reflected in a complete focus on quality and—especially important for China—a focus on using premium packaging to convey a sense of quality to consumers.

Consequently, in 2003 she asked the company to reduce its capacity from one million bottles down to 500,000. While in the West we are used to economic cycles and adjusting a company's size up or down according to what is required, in China this was difficult from a cultural perspective: in China's post-planned economy, most businesses' importance, success, and fame, especially agricultural businesses, were traditionally measured by their output capacity. Ms. Chan remembers: "(We) uprooted half of the vineyard, and compensated the farmers. But in China, shrinking is so hard. When you wanted to cut production, nobody helped you. That was a difficult time, facing farmers who protested everything."

To find a way to set her company apart in the market, Ms. Chan started to look at what other producers were *not* doing, but that she could do. She realized that producers focused on hard selling ever-growing quantities of wine. "They focused on marketing; the marketing campaigns, and all the slogans they came up with," she recalled.

Ms. Chan realized there was great potential in upgrading the packaging, both the bottles and outer boxes, and made the then-unusual decision to import bottles from overseas. "We decided to import bottles, because at the time the only one bottles you could buy in China were cheap ones." Ms. Chan started to import bottles from France at ten times the then-prevailing local cost.

As a manager in China, this is something I have also often observed with consumers—the packaging experience is part of the product appreciation. A mistake companies sometimes make is to cut corners on the packaging or to use overseas packaging without considering whether the product's position in China is the same or not. In fact, in a country where most products were new, and where customers wanted to feel "rich" and good about what they could now afford to buy (unlike in the past), the worst thing to do was to ignore or skimp on the packaging.

When it comes to product positioning, and especially to communicating price positioning, packaging designs and colors that have gained acceptance and hold certain positive connotations among consumers in the West do not necessarily work in China. In general, consumers in China have not had the same cultural history, so they have different perceptions about what the cultural signifiers of "value" are.

Examples include the fact that in the West, light packaging and pale colors signify modernity and elegance, whereas they signify a low-quality product in China. (This is now changing a bit due to the increasing appreciation among Japanese and Koreans for "clean" product designs). In the West, green suggests naturalness, but in China, it tends to be seen as medicinal. The yellowish or gold type-faced labels of some Western brands (not just in wine) combined with brown bottles could trigger an entirely different association in the consumer's mind—in China it's the classic combination used for soy sauce! (Cheers to that!). However, with younger customers' tastes now moving toward simpler, cooler, and more environmentally friendly packaging styles, this is also changing.

While being a good example of how to position a brand using quality and how to convey that quality, Grace Vineyard is also a good example of how to build a brand regionally—one might also say with less effort and a lower investment.

As said before, to build a brand in China, the standard approach that especially Western companies pursue is to launch in a leading city like Shanghai or Beijing, and then invest in a nationwide rollout. This often works, but is a highly costly undertaking. It also pitches new market entrants against many other brands doing the same thing, which in my view is less and less necessary. More often than not—at least in the past—Chinese companies choose the other way around, not focusing on the larger cities until a later stage. Western companies often blame their failure in China on local competition and pricing. In reality, the reason is usually a lack of focus or the wrong choice of positioning and strategy concerning where to start and where to go next.

It seems especially the case that Western companies' feeling the need to announce "big China plans" in their boardrooms are what triggers such choices. It is usually difficult enough to sell the idea for a massive new market expansion to an overseas board—and harder still when their geography skills are poor! Putting pins in the map over Shanghai, Chengdu, or Wuhan because they have big populations tells you nothing about how the people in those cities live their lives, or what they aspire to.

Grace Vineyard applied a regional strategy to build its brand. "We decided to focus on the Shanxi market alone. Shanxi has a population of 30 million." So Ms. Chan decided not to pursue a national brand and instead to focus all the company's energies on the Shanxi province to become the wine of choice in its true "home market." This focus doesn't seem to have changed much. According to Ms. Chan: "(Until now) our focus is really Shanxi. Seventy percent of our sales come from Shanxi, with the majority from Taiyuan, the provincial capital." The obvious advantages are having a strong brand correlation to the consumer and greater defense against competitors, but also less pressure on sales, since the costs of expansion can be reasonably managed.

We talked a little bit further about how Grace Vineyard has been able to compete against the three big wine companies Changyu (market share 9% in 2014), Great Wall (6%), and Dynasty (2%). It became apparent that, in the early stage of Grace Vineyard's development, the competition did not take it seriously because of its focus on Shanxi, until it was too late and Grace Vineyard's reputation had been firmly established. It was only then that Ms. Chan decided to expand the business to some other select cities, such as Beijing and Shanghai, and to develop an export business.

I recently interviewed the founders of the three largest wine-related social networks, which together have roughly six million users. What I found: consumers' wine consumption is now changing rapidly. Customers of all ages have become more curious and have learned quickly about different wines from different countries. The Internet, especially the mobile Internet, has become a game changer. Besides wine education and product information, it has brought about a huge change: price transparency—something particularly tricky with products of subjective value, like wines. According to Ms. Chan, most of her online buyers are between 20 and 35. "Young people are comfortable shopping online."

The Internet also helps the Chinese consumer find a fair price, which they always expect. Here's why: in a highly entrepreneurial new market like China, the customers don't understand different quality levels or what product functions are truly worth. While prices can vary greatly between brands and channels, including the fake product channel, consumers lack confidence in price and value perception paired. This has not been helped by living through a decade in which many companies tried their luck at overcharging or palming off fake products.

People are wary about the price of anything that is new to them. "I think Chinese consumers particularly hate it if they feel cheated," Ms. Chan explains, adding, "Many consumers don't have that much confidence. As a result, if they feel you might be cheating them, they get really angry, because they think 'you're treating me like an idiot.'"

As with most of the companies interviewed for this book, Ms. Chan embraces digitization and sees a great advantage in using smartphones, both from a consumer's and also from a producer's perspective. Online orders still only account for a small percentage of Grace Vineyard's overall sales, but the growth rate from 2015 to 2016 was 74%. Quoting a new sparkling wine "Angelina" that she launched in September 2015 purely via social media, Ms. Chan said, "With technology, consumers are changing even faster. I found all the things our industry people are doing are not fun: wine dinners and wine tasting, they're boring. If you want to go to a wine dinner or wine tasting for free, every day, you can do so in China. So if you do exactly the same thing, why would people choose to come to, let's say, Grace Vineyard, and not somewhere else?" She is still figuring out how to best combine the online and offline platforms.

Conquering the international wine markets is still a major challenge for Chinese wines. For now, Ms. Chan has intentionally set moderate goals for geographic expansion, instead focusing on upgrading the quality message and stretching the brand by venturing into related products, e.g., sparkling wine and potentially whiskey. "But everything will be small but prestigious, high-end and high-quality," she emphasizes. She will continue to do export business, but the main angle is to maintain an international presence for the brand, not necessarily to achieve growth. Now that her products are available in the UK, Japan, and Singapore, Ms. Chan said the global market wouldn't be her focus in the next 3 years. Wines "made in China" simply don't match people's expectations. In a nutshell, her foreign export markets will serve as a quality reference for Chinese consumers in the home market.

At the end of the interview, we talked a bit about the business leaders Ms. Chan admires most. She does admire Apple as a company for its products and Elon Musk for his long-term vision beyond business. And for strategy, she cited Zhang Ruimin's "Get in first, stay in, learn, evolve" stance as a highly admirable and very inclusive strategy for Chinese companies expanding overseas, with internationalization built on learning rather than control when entering new markets or businesses.

Acknowledgment This interview has been published with the kind permission of Ms. Judy Chan.

Notes

1. http://www.askci.com/news/201406/10/101701640181.shtml

8

High Above the Rest: Toread

Outdoor fashion/sports industry—No. 1 outdoor brand—Wang Jing, Cofounder (photo with kind permission of Ms. Wang Jing)

© The Author(s) 2018
C. Nothhaft, *Made for China*, DOI 10.1007/978-3-319-61584-4_8

Opportunity

China's outdoor market has seen rapid growth, due in part to outdoor wear becoming an expression of status and lifestyle, thus tempting urbanites to wear outdoor fashion on a daily basis. With Beijing hosting the 2022 Winter Olympics, the interest in outdoor activities like mountain climbing, skiing, and hiking is already growing, and the momentum is expected to continue. This sector still has a way to go, as customers are now beginning to appreciate the functions of outdoor products, and local brands have a good opportunity to trade up. As customers grow wealthier, the market also has good potential for foreign brands to expand.

Lessons

One of the specific challenges in the market will be correct pricing. As foreign outdoor brands are pricey and luxury items beyond the reach of the masses, pricing has to strike a good balance between product functionality and affordability. And as the Chinese customer evolves, the brand message has to evolve, too—in China, this all happens very quickly.

Local companies are more competitive here, as most of them have large retail store networks. Direct retail distribution is a major advantage when it comes to building brand awareness, as it allows customers to understand and explore first-hand functionalities of outdoor fashion and products.

Recently, I saw one of my Chinese friends Wang Jing post many pictures on her WeChat Moments (China's answer to WhatsApp) account of her climbing mountains with her daughters, and I got dizzy just looking at them! Allow me to make a slight departure here and discuss how Chinese families raise their kids and prepare them to compete in the "big, wide world." Generally speaking, Chinese families are very competitive, with two or three generations working together to raise the kids, while the middle generation is expected to increase the family's wealth. This has created a very competitive society, but today's kids are also far better off than their parents' generation, which can make it difficult for parents to convey the right messages and to keep their kids challenged and competitive. Let's see what the next generation brings.

Wang Jing and I are old friends, and we enjoy comparing notes on parenting. Sometimes it seems like we're comparing who can get their kids to do scarier things. The recipe seems to be to "push the envelope"—but we both know we're trying to prepare the next generation to live the life they want to. As she explains, "Coping with pressure is a challenge. When my kid moves on to her next task on her own, if it's not as hard as what she's already faced, she won't be worried at all. Climbing an 8000-m mountain is potentially life-threatening. When you overcome such difficulties and return to the ground in one piece, you won't find the next challenge so intimidating. It's okay to fail, since it won't cost you your life." You may be wondering why I chose to mention this, and the simple answer is: to give you a picture of how competitive the Chinese are at work, at home, and especially as entrepreneurs.

Accompanied by Wang Jing, her daughter made it to the summit of Siguniang Shan (over 5000 m) at age 11, making her the youngest female in China to conquer the peak of the mountain. "Her article on mountaineering was posted on the school's website and published in the school's brochure. Education is not easy, so my view is that we are their role models and our behavior is what influences them the most," Wang says.

Wang Jing is China's most famous female mountain climber and cofounder of China's number one outdoor brand, Toread. She started climbing mountains at the age of 32, in 2007. She's attracted a great deal of visibility by breaking records for female mountaineers, and her blog has 800,000 followers. She conquered Explorer's Grand Slam in 143 days. As an environmentalist, Wang Jing is also the fifth-term council member on the board of SEE, China's biggest environmental NGO, and was awarded the title "2014 Mountaineer of the Year" by the Nepali government. She has also released two books and films on mountaineering.

Wang's position as a spokesperson reflects a unique feature of China's consumer industry: though the concept of having a mascot and "expert" for a brand has been working well, there aren't any local heroes who—like Michael Jordan or Roger Federer—are recognized internationally and could help a brand become famous.

In China, the outdoor (and so to some extent sports fashion) market is developing rapidly. Whereas in many mature markets such as the USA and Europe, most sports brands begin as sports brands and then expand into fashion, in China it has always been the other way around. Even sportswear brand popularity there is based on coolness and fashion, with sports functionality only being of interest to those taking part in China's evolving sports scene.

The same applies to the outdoor products market. The desire for outdoor products is shaped by foreign brands that are extremely expensive, creating a good market opportunity for local companies to evolve by offering similar styles, but ones that are more tailored to the Chinese wallet size in different segments.

It seems to be a category that has grown rapidly without entering into a phase of further sophistication, where true product evolution and the brand message count. So what is currently driving the outdoor fashion market?

Consumers and especially Millennials are looking for leisurewear that allows them to express their sense of adventure, love of nature, and desire to explore. Large areas of China have a continental climate, with a substantial winter and plenty of rain. Since sports brands that focus on shoes—basketball shoes and the like—haven't responded to the demands of consumers in this climate, outdoor product brands can offer wider fashion segments.

I once took my management team to do some light mountaineering among the famous peaks and vistas of Huangshan, in Anhui province. None other than Deng Xiaoping himself praised the area for its scenery during his visit in 1979. We spent a whole weekend there and stayed overnight in one of the well-appointed hotels on the mountaintop. I decided to get up at 4 a.m. on Sunday morning, to sneak out and watch the sunrise over a small peak called "Monkey Facing the Sea."

I thought it would be a tranquil event and that the peak would provide a great view. So I got up and made my way toward the peak, which was only a few hundred meters away, only to realize that I wasn't alone! Arriving at the peak, I found that there were hundreds of people already there to catch the sunrise. I was most likely the only one expecting a tranquil sunrise in solitude. But, of course, in China you're never alone. Everywhere in China, you always have to compete, even for peace and quiet, or a few square inches of space on a rock!

According to the buzz on Baidu, modern mountaineering in China began in 1955, when a team of Chinese and Soviet mountaineers summited the Tuanjie and Shiyue Peaks, which was the first time Chinese mountaineers had conquered what could be regarded as a high-elevation mountain. Shortly thereafter, in 1958, the Chinese Mountaineering Association was founded as a government-funded professional organization. By the end of 2012, the Association had trained 6938 qualified climbers, of which 4204 had been certified as mountaineering and related sports and technology professionals. Some leading universities also have mountaineering clubs, including Peking and Tsinghua Universities.

Even if people don't even attempt to conquer peaks, they can at least wander into Starbucks looking as if they did, or at least considered it. According to China Outdoor Association (COA), by 2015, the total outdoor products market in China was worth an estimated RMB 18 billion.[1] As Fig. 8.1 shows, between 2007 and 2015, the market for outdoor products grew a staggering eightfold (see Fig. 8.1)!

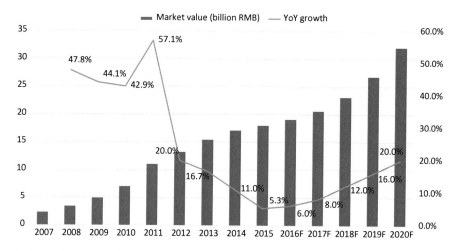

Fig. 8.1 China's accelerating outdoor market. Source: COA

In my opinion, outdoor wear has become a self-expression of the wider travel lifestyle in China, and the market has gradually evolved into a lifestyle segment. I remember a time around 2009/2010 when malls and department stores downsized their sportswear departments (which had been expanded due to the Beijing Olympics effect), and suddenly "outdoor lifestyle" sections replaced running and sports gear across entire floors. During this phase, foreign brands began pushing into the market, leading the way in terms of brand appearance, yet remaining too expensive for the average urbanite. This gave local brands the opportunity to fill the gap, offering products with comparable quality but at much more affordable prices. Some of the local companies also developed a great reputation nationally by promoting specific garment technologies.

According to KPMG, there were a total 945 brands active in the outdoor wear market in China by 2014. Between 2013 and 2014, 54 new brands entered the market. The market is so competitive that brand entrants are now trying everything they can to grab consumers' attention. In January 2016, the Italian ski equipment brand Nordica took the unusual step of opening a restaurant in China, to raise its brand profile leading up to the Beijing Winter Olympics in 2022, an event that is likely to give the industry a further boost.

Most established brands have already gained a foothold in China, including the US brands Columbia, The North Face and Marmot, Jack Wolfskin from Germany, ARC'TERYX from Canada, Ozark from Switzerland, Northland from Austria, and Black Yak from South Korea. The leading Chinese domestic brands are Toread and Mobi Garden.

Toread is a relatively young company. It was founded in 1999 and IPOed on the Shenzhen Stock Exchange in 2009 (SZ: 300005). The company consists of three business pillars: Toread branded outdoor products, the brand Discovery Expedition, and ACANU. The group has recently embarked on creating an ecosystem around outdoor products, including the travel service "easytour" and a Toread Sports Industry M&A Fund with a fundraising of RMB 110 million.

With a network of 1455 stores in 2015, it's a big company in terms of distribution spread. The company's turnover was RMB 2.91 billion in 2016, at a year-on-year sales decrease of 24%. Like most companies, Toread has an e-commerce division of Brand Toread, with sales of RMB 453 million in 2015, growing at 20% year-on-year and accounting for 28% of total sales. The company sells a number of brands exclusively on the Internet. In 2015, Toread invested RMB 230 million for a 74.6% stake in the easytour (travel service) website company, in an effort to capture the travel experience aspect of the outdoor trend.

Unlike other stories in this book, Toread's is one of a "perfect couple". I first met Wang Jing and her husband in 2013, and we have since become friends. As mentioned earlier, Wang is a legendary female mountaineer. Her role in Toread, however, is the "Chief Product Technology Advisor" and she insists her only focus is on improving the company's products. Wang's husband, Sheng Faqiang, was formerly a businessman in the textile industry, who had his first job in the railway industry, then printing, and then tent design. Together, they started Toread.

Wang Jing met with me in her office in Beijing in 2015. Her door sign did indeed say Chief Product Officer, which I found interesting since everyone treats her like the boss, but in fact, it was meant perfectly seriously, especially when she mentioned that she left the day-to-day commercial management of the company to a CEO, while she focused on brand building and product quality.

Of course, my first question was why Toread had been so successful compared to others in the market. Providing OEM for outdoor products to the USA and Europe had a long history in China, so how did Toread make it to number one?

Wang's answer was that Toread has used various channels at different stages of its development. Like many consumer brands in China, Toread has successfully changed along with its consumers—at a much faster pace than in Western economies. Essentially, during its short 16 years on the market, the Toread brand has employed three brand messages, in a sequence that reflected the desires of a newly awakening consumer in China at each stage.

In the earlier years, department stores were the major players and wanted suppliers like Toread. Soon thereafter, Toread developed relationships with distributors who were in the leading position in their regions. And here comes the most significant step. "No matter how well the distributors were doing, it was crucial that we had our own self-operated flagship stores, which represented the philosophy of the brand and communicated the brand messages to the customers directly," says Wang.

Having built a retail and consumer business, I'm often asked whether it's a good idea to have your own stores and outlets in China, or if it's better to work with third-party distributors. Brand control is a key consideration with today's more sophisticated consumers, and it's extremely difficult to achieve in China. The most successful companies I have seen so far run at least part of their store networks directly to ensure proper brand implementation and stay in touch with consumers directly. As mentioned elsewhere, one key to the Chinese market is to control the running of your stores, sales teams, and R&D.

In addition, Chinese consumers don't want "cheap products"; they want premium goods, ideally at a price they can reasonably afford. The trick is to figure out exactly what they can afford. Most seasoned China marketers would recommend focusing on segments in which customers appreciate quality and function, instead of considering the masses. Within these segments, companies can gradually develop a focus on product evolution, from a mid-price point to higher price points.

Wang Jing's products and strategy are a good example. She cites an anecdote of how an award-winning down coat from overseas became successful in China, but only after introducing a "value engineered model" that sold at a third of the original US$1300 price tag.

The company invests approximately 4% of its profits into research and development of new products, with Polar Bionic Technology being a signature R&D project. Over the past 4 years, 12 of Toread's patented products were awarded the China Red Star Design Award.

How does one build a sustainable brand in China? Why don't certain products succeed? Why do some foreign products fail, while others don't? These are typical questions visitors ask me. Actually, it's not that hard to explain. First and foremost, the Chinese consumer in general is, in fact, a very conscious consumer—with a tendency to seek information and weigh the pros and cons before making a purchase. People want to make sure they understand the functions and quality of a product objectively, which is due in part to their budget constraints.

Building brand reputation is a central aspect of establishing a sustainable brand and often requires a premium segment to develop the message and cultivate expertise, while the bulk of sales may come from slightly lower-priced products under the same umbrella brand. We should also bear in mind that many consumers are now buying lifestyle products for the first time, and there is no user experience or commonly accepted standard for different categories, or "commonly accepted quality." Therefore, customers might tend to buy a mid-priced item from a brand that is famous for its premium range.

Since China is still in an early stage of market and consumer sophistication, you will find many brands here that encompass different price levels or subbrands under one brand, which is quite different from the West, whereby more often than not, each brand is linked to a specific image and price bandwidth.

According to Mrs. Wang, high-end products are used to communicate the brand message, while the focus of Toread's business is on the mainstream market. She reaffirms: "High-end products are like the spiritual leader of the brand, and build up the brand reputation."

Toread's first slogan was 'Follow Your Heart,' intended to connote freedom. As Wang Jing explains, "I think freedom is the ultimate goal of life that everybody wants to achieve, even though people may have different understandings of freedom."

In China, it is important to have an inspiring brand message that is relevant for the current and upcoming key consumer groups and is something they can relate to. Here Toread's slogan portrays a picture of a good future, which strikes a chord with consumer across age groups.

As customers became more mature, individualism and a desire to stand out from the crowd have become more prominent. Customers have begun dreaming of being different than their neighbor. As the Toread brand evolved, so did its core message—the second slogan was 'Brave Heart,' representing the courage to do and create more.

"The transition needs to be more tangible and to stay closer to customers' reality versus ambitious dreams. The new slogan was a shift towards the efforts and risks people have to take in order to achieve their dreams. It also constituted a good connection to mountaineering, which requires courage and tenacity," Wang explains.

More and more consumers in China expect a deeper story behind a brand. With China's environmental struggle, many consumers are becoming interested in the concept of sustainability. Over the last few decades, many Chinese locations including mountains have been negatively impacted by tourists, resulting in anything from ugly property developments in the most beautiful areas to the garbage left behind wherever tourists go. However, the government is increasingly putting a stop to this, and society is also changing. Among my younger teammates, for example, it's self-explanatory that you don't leave behind any garbage; you might even pick up others' garbage.

While we talked, Wang Jing kept stressing the brand's sustainability message. When I met her for the first time at a YPO close-up session, she immediately impressed me with her speech about how business in China was quickly turning into an environmental discussion. I was surprised back then, but studying her blog, which includes reports from her campaigns to remove the garbage in Nepal's mountains (left behind by expeditions), her actions speak for themselves.

As a passionate conservationist, one of Wang Jing's priorities is that innovations are not only made for the market's sake, but should also serve a purpose. Further, she feels one of Toread's main goals is to conserve resources. "It's true that individuals and companies need to innovate, but we need to think more about whether or not our innovations can make a change in the lives of human beings." Though such comments are rarely heard, her stance is perfectly reasonable, since the digestion period for new products is very short in China. In my company, I am constantly amazed by how short innovation cycles have become in China—roughly half as long as those in overseas markets.

With regard to further expansion, Toread's ambitions are currently focused on the domestic market (I'm not surprised, given the tremendous boost the Winter Olympics are likely to provide). Wang Jing explains that the goal now is to maintain the company's number one position in China. "I tell my team we should maintain our leading position in China, and in the future, we may become number one in the world. It's possible that we'll eventually become number one globally, but we're not there yet."

In China, setting targets for staff and teams is not as negative as in many Western countries—in fact, it's a good thing. Chinese managers and staff love pursuing a big dream together as a team, while also individually competing against each other. However, there is an art to doing this right.

As Wang Jing relates: "When we started the business, we grew the team all the way up to thousands of people. When the targets you set are achieved or over-achieved, it's easier for people to keep following you. They were willing to embrace the vision we put forward and work hard to achieve it."

Keeping a workforce united while highly competitive does put a lot of pressure on leaders in terms of balancing short-term and long-term efforts. On the other hand, since China is a more cohesive society where "achieving goals together" is more important than "outperforming your colleague," at least on the surface, big companies can sometimes be run more flexibly.

Wang Jing sums it up nicely: "I do believe, though, that the key to success is collaborative willingness. They (the staff) must believe that the dream can be achieved. If they are not convinced or hesitant, it will be very difficult to succeed."

In order to portray a brand, having the right talent at all levels of the company is an important step. When it comes to management talent, opinions are divided in China as to whether technical experts are more important or generalists with high EQ. I've seen both types succeed, but I've never seen technical experts without high EQ excel in China. I would always pick a person with high integrity (someone who practices what they preach) and high EQ, and who puts technical expertise second. Technical expertise can always be brought in using project groups, expert roundtables, or projects on a temporary basis, while retaining good EQ means keeping leaders in charge of the teams. This is less threatening and less culturally evasive.

In my view, in China working for a low-EQ boss is not only a daily problem at work but also means a loss of face among your peers. Chinese workers and especially managers want to have a boss they can be proud of, and leadership with courage is essentially the pinnacle. Leaders' integrity and behavior are of central importance for delegation in China, because that behavior will literally be copied without a filter—both the good and the bad.

Wang Jing believes that a good manager doesn't have to be a top expert in their field, and that there is in fact no Chinese leadership style or European style. "It's the leader's individual style. His charisma works if he can make his team believe in him. As a leader, he should know the direction and have the courage to lead his team in that direction. These qualities can't be measured in numbers."

After the interview, I thought to myself what a productive day it had been—with lessons on distribution building, brand building, and parenting, all in one chapter!

Acknowledgment This interview has been published with the kind permission of Ms. Wang Jing.

Note

1. http://sports.sina.com.cn/outdoor/2016-07-01/doc-ifxtsatm1135172.shtml

Part III

The Family: Enhancing Quality of Life

Given the nature of the Chinese culture, family value always ranks highly and translates to the goal of providing the entire family (consisting of three generations) a better life. This is quite distinct from the situation in many Western cultures, where the idea of well-being is more focused on the individual, and where, in extreme cases, the welfare of the older generations is perceived as being the responsibility of the government.

During my career, I have been blessed with the opportunity to build companies in different countries and cultures, from Europe to the USA, the Middle East, and Asia. In comparison with other countries, Chinese culture truly revolves around the family. In my view, the country is held together by the glue of families sticking together, working together, and pushing and supporting each other through whatever hardships they may face. In this book, you will find many examples of the desire to improve a family's well-being. Many of the most successful consumer marketing campaigns focus on connection with the family, starting from the house people purchase to live in, the appliances they use, and daily necessity products. Chinese families, especially when they are young, want the latest in terms of technology, sophistication, or brands that they can buy depending on their budget. Once couples have children, their concern shifts to giving their children the very best.

As lifestyles evolve, especially for slightly older consumers, questions about securing their wealth arise, or about health and well-being. Consumer products and service opportunities related to "family" are abundant.

China has a population of 1.3 billion people: 603.46 million in rural areas and 771.16 million in cities,[1] with about 558.6 million registered households.[2] The well-known one-child policy was introduced in 1979 to control population growth. It was established as a direct outcome of the conflict between the rapidly growing population and underdeveloped economies in the 1970s. The average number of children per household thus sank from 1.85 in the 1990s to 1.05 in 2015,[3] which is even lower than that of Japan.[4]

As the society is aging, an incredible burden lies ahead, predominantly for those who have grown up under the one-child policy. As the social network in China is still under development, this generation would have to feed two generations. 2016 marked the fourth consecutive annual decrease of China's labor force population,[5] and it has been predicted that China will essentially "run out" of labor by 2030.[6]

Therefore, a typical modern Chinese family in tier-1 or tier-2 cities consists of two adults born after 1975, sometimes with one child. Occasionally, the child's grandparents, who come from lower-tier cities, will visit the family and spend some time together. In their early 30s or 40s with growing purchasing power and increasing knowledge—and dubbed the emerging middle class by the local media—young husbands and wives are the decision-makers when it comes to family purchasing.

More and more Chinese women participate in the decision-making process, no matter whether it concerns fast-moving consumer goods, clothes, or durable consumer goods like a car, and sometimes even insurance and housing. In most cases, for more strategic/expensive purchases, the wife might first go to the Internet and have a look, providing several choices to discuss with her husband, and then they might come back to make the purchase together. The two make decisions together, while the elder generation might offer a few suggestions (with the young generation listening politely but in the end sticking with their original decision). Younger consumer generation families, however, make purchasing decisions more independently, i.e., in the interest of saving time, husband and wife divide the purchase-making responsibilities.

The dynamics of how households, their purchasing habits, their concerns, and their lifestyle will evolve hold many opportunities for the growth of the Chinese consumer market. This section illustrates some of those dynamics. These are stories of how to reach more households and win over more consumers, as well as how to innovate and improve products to keep abreast or even ahead of customers' trends and level of sophistication. As families become more modern, households are developing new needs and new industries are possible, e.g., insurance and medical services.

The first chapter introduces China's no. 1 electrical retailer (and no. 3 - E-tailer) and how it has created a huge ecosystem to capture more consumers, to better cater to their evolving needs, and to help find more products domestically and from overseas. The chapter also describes the advantages that e-commerce provides for existing consumer businesses as well as the interesting reasons why Chinese companies like to build their brand overseas, even if it means buying soccer clubs.

Directly related to this topic, we then introduce one of the most internationally well-known Chinese companies, Qingdao HAIER, the global no. 1 in white goods manufacturing. The company is huge, with global sales of US$ 27.15 billion.[7] As Haier has evolved from a single workshop to a global leader, it now has to focus on staying consumer centric in every market, especially in its home market. In a world-renowned business case, the chairman has been pushing forward a radical agenda to turn the company into a platform for incubating small and micro-start-ups, rather than a giant manufacturer.

As the Chinese urbanized, many people became first-time homeowners or—better said—first-time urban apartment owners. In the early stage, having a fashionable home was not important, but now with consumer tastes evolving, plus urbanization and work pressure promoting a cocooning effect, more and more people are thinking about what furniture to buy—or how to create their own "home style." Kuka is the number one sofa and bed company in China in terms of sales volume. We talked with the CEO about how to position products, how important pricing is, and what innovations are in the works when it comes to furniture.

Having a modern household also means you need the products that you use to take care of your house and family, including washing powder, detergents, and personal care products. The company that best understands that need in China is Guangzhou-based Liby, the no. 1 brand in several categories in the Chinese FMCG market. With its elaborate dealer system, the brand can reach every inch of China. Besides insights into FMCG trends, the story demonstrates how a simple dealership chain without complex arrangements can outsmart and outrun "Western-type" giants in China, and how companies equipped with excellent distribution channels can start focusing on building premium brands.

As households become more sophisticated, the concern for good looks, good health, and well-being is also becoming more prevalent, and people are increasingly willing to pay for it out of pocket. In fact, more and more Chinese people don't mind paying more for higher quality medical service. We visited the owner of China's leading dental chain and looked into how he has succeeded in opening nearly 100 clinics a year[8] and why people would prefer private dental services.

Life insurance has little history in today's China and has become a "one-client agent" business, as Chinese people are not overly concerned about the future and their lives. And since there hasn't been a generation of life insurance payouts, the benefit doesn't seem tangible to consumers. As such, insurers are forced to find different distribution channels and new angles. Now, with customers becoming richer, wealth protection, health, and private education concerns for the family provide potential opportunities. We met with Mr. Kang, the (now retired) chairman of China's no. 3 life insurance provider.

Notes

1. http://www.ce.cn/xwzx/gnsz/gdxw/201601/19/t20160119_8371558.shtml
2. http://www.ce.cn/xwzx/gnsz/gdxw/201604/26/t20160426_10870058.shtml
3. https://botanwang.com/articles/201610/中国生育水平已是全球最低.html
4. http://www.thepaper.cn/newsDetail_forward_1375303_1
5. http://m.21jingji.com/article/20160227/herald/99d3951e3823d7a6bca252c34225230b_baidunews.html
6. http://news.takungpao.com/mainland/focus/2014-07/2576811.html
7. http://www.haier.net/cn/about_haier/
8. http://med.sina.com/article_detail_100_1_11722.html

9

Reaching More Households, Offering More Products: Suning

Electrical retailer—No. 1 electrical retailer, No. 3 e-tailer—Zhang Jindong, Founder (photo with kind permission of Mr. Zhang Jindong)

© The Author(s) 2018
C. Nothhaft, *Made for China*, DOI 10.1007/978-3-319-61584-4_9

Opportunity

As large retail companies have been penetrating the Chinese market for 30 years, they are now in an advanced stage whereby they need to cultivate existing consumers, find new ones, and adapt their business model to cope with the onslaught of e-commerce. Electrical retailers have broad networks and extensive consumer data—resources that can help them innovate their business models. Given China's vast size, the best companies manage to use e-commerce to extend their reach into households. This allows them to transcend the boundaries of their current business and the products they are associated with.

Lessons Learned

While the e-commerce transition might make headlines, the underlying aspect of building ecosystems around online and offline stores including logistics to reach more consumers, consumer finance, and services for merchants to sell on their products is just as important. As companies seek to source from abroad, they need to overcome reputational issues and investing in sports is one means of doing so.

I came across Suning for the first time in 2006, when I was running Hong Kong's number one electrical retailer. At that time we were trying to get a good entry into the China market and were looking into acquiring a regional brand called "5Star" in Jiangsu—which was quickly snatched up by Suning.

In fact, the race to be the biggest home-appliance seller in China during the early days of development was between a company called Gome and Suning, with Suning emerging as the clear winner.

Originally, a pure offline retailer selling air conditioners in 1990, Suning now has branches throughout China, with 1600 outlets in 600 cities, including some rural areas. It also owns stores in Hong Kong and Japan. According to Suning's information, the company manages over 30 million SKUs (retailer jargon for products) including traditional appliances, consumer electronics products, supermarket, mother-and-baby care, general merchandise, financial and recreational products. Its annual sales in 2015[1] were RMB 163.4 billion, and Zhang Jindong and his persons in acting concert in Suning Holdings Group holds ca. 24.29% of the company Suning Commerce Group.

Over the past 6 years, the company has been transitioning towards an online/offline model, i.e., building the business in stores and through e-commerce alike. It launched its e-commerce platform in 2010, after opening an R&D office in Silicon Valley in 2013. Since then, the company has been working strategically to optimize its retail offerings and services across China using both channels.

The latest news: Suning struck a strategic partnership with Alibaba Group in 2015. With Alibaba investing RMB 28 billion into Suning and Suning investing RMB 14 billion into Alibaba, they have created a gargantuan "online to offline" alliance. As shown in Fig. 9.1, currently, it's the number three online retailer, with an online GMV (Gross Merchandise Volume) of RMB 50.2 billion in 2015, following Alibaba's Tmall and Jing Dong (see Fig. 9.1).

I met Zhang Jindong, Suning's Founder and CEO/Chairman, for the first time around 2009, when our retail network was expanding. We became partners when it came to real estate and at the same time, competitors of sorts in the area of female customers, namely, beauty and baby-related products.

However, I always felt he was a very detail-oriented retailer, treating his competitors with respect, and learning from them at any given opportunity. Our first lunch—with both companies in heavy expansion mode—turned out to be a long one, with countless questions on both sides of the table. We have

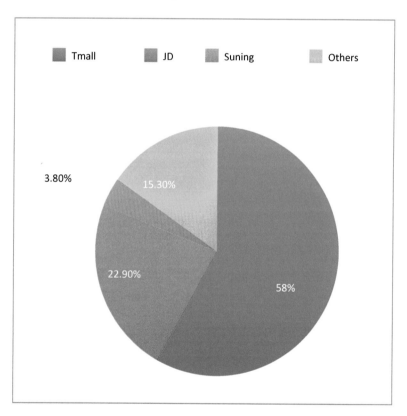

Fig. 9.1   China's Top 3 B2C e-commerce platforms by market share. Source: iResearch (http://report.iresearch.cn/content/2016/05/260788.shtml)

maintained a practice of regular exchange over the years and gotten to know each other a little better. At some point, I remember how we toured his new headquarters (literally an entire city) and were shown the data centers, while the CEO was talking about employing data usage to better serve consumers. It wasn't long after that Alibaba and Suning pooled their resources.

I personally found Suning to be more consumer-centric than other companies. A few years back, when Chinese consumers rushed to electrical stores to buy appliances, the demand was so great that companies didn't really put much effort into serving their customers. Instead, more often than not their business model consisted in renting a big mall space and then subletting it to the manufacturers of individual brands, focusing their core skills on gathering rent from suppliers and more sales from customers. Therefore, not all electrical retailers were retailers at heart. Over time, as the market became more saturated, retailers had to fight for customers by offering better service, better consulting, and online sales. For me Suning, which we'll examine next, was a company that had demonstrated good consumer service and professional retailer behavior from the outset, focusing on improving customer service rather than simply collecting rent from suppliers.

As Fig. 9.2 shows, Chinese enthusiasm for online shopping could be partly reflected by the tremendous growth of Alibaba's Taobao, the first-ever platform that enables person-to-person deals online.

Zhang and Suning are a good example of how quickly Chinese companies, especially those in the retail sector, need to evolve or reinvent themselves so as to learn and embrace new ways of working. In his remarks to commemorate the company's 25th anniversary, Zhang spoke of "corporate culture reshaping" to break the boundaries between old concepts and new concepts, e.g., the Internet and the age of mobile commerce.

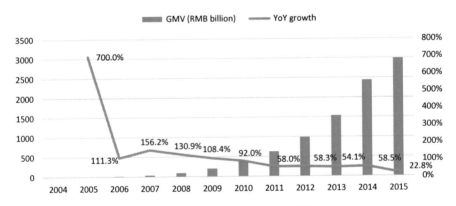

Fig. 9.2   Taobao's transaction value 2003–2015. Source: Zhihu

We met to do this interview over lunch together with his team, most of whom I had known for a few years, which reflected Zhang's style of having "everyone in the same boat" and everyone working on the same dream. Of course, the most obvious question was whether Suning, after the share swap with Alibaba Group, had shifted gears towards a whole new business model and if he believed that offline retailers are doomed.

Zhang replied that he felt the Internet was only a tool: "I don't believe Alibaba and JD can transform retail. Ultimately, retail will return to its basics—products and service."

Zhang went on to describe how the Internet is a new channel and therefore presents an opportunity, especially in China, where many consumers have no access to good products yet (in part due to the location, and in part also due to existing distribution structures). But in the end, the decisive factor is to provide the right products for consumers.

Zhang sees his company's journey as an individual path, allowing Suning to source strength from online as well as offline. He points out that, due to the fast growth and the still-evolving market, this is possible in China. For Zhang, neither traditional retailers such as Wal-Mart and Carrefour, nor Internet retailers like Amazon and Alibaba are his role models. As he explains, "We are a retail business and are now becoming an Internet retailer. We will go our own way as an integrated O2O retailer."

Zhang and his team see Internet integration not as a change of business model but as an add-on, an evolution to the business model, unlocking the potential of store locations (again). According to Zhang: "Once the traditional retail is associated with the Internet, the offline resources, previously seen as huge burdens, will suddenly become treasure troves, and the balance will also tip toward the retailers who have both online and offline channels."

I am often asked why large retailers (or E-tailers) create such huge ecosystems of companies around them? Is the goal to create a monopoly? While indeed those are business opportunities in and of themselves, as the country has only recently begun evolving, many service industries in China that enable large retailers to do business well are underdeveloped or, better said, under construction. Therefore, large and cash-rich companies fill or have to fill in voids to grow. More often than not, this creates vast ecosystems from logistics companies, to marketing service companies, to even consumer financing. Companies like Suning, which seek to create entire value chains for the manufacturer, are just one example.

Even though China is such a huge market and has been the manufacturing bench of the world for decades, the country still has a shortage of good products and brands that appeal to today's consumers. One reason is that foreign brands have had a hard time surviving here. Although there are countless consumers, many have failed to "find them," to successfully market to them, or to understand how to win out against local competitors.

Another reason is that local manufacturers have not had enough time to evolve, i.e., learning over at least two generations to move from, say, a craft/trade to a brand (see the example of Kuka in this book).

Also, as small companies have almost no chance of getting funded by banks in China and intercompany loans are illegal, many smaller companies are heavily restricted in their evolution due to lack of money. This also holds true for distributors who need cash to buy stocks to expand their merchandise.

Therefore, big companies like Suning offline and Alibaba online have an interest in working together with merchants and manufacturers so as to have broader offerings and to make new products. At least, these two make the products available in most parts of China. They also form large ecosystems, either themselves or by partnering with "service providers" to make good logistics available and provide other services such as professional marketing and funding. They somewhat fill the gap that, in mature markets, are fully covered by logistics providers or marketing agencies and even banks, all of which are lacking in China. According to Zhang, Suning's core strengths are in logistics, customer data, and finance, which are all applied to improving the product.

For example, Suning now offers its logistics services to 1200 other enterprises. At present, the company has huge logistics capacities, comprising 12 automatic picking centers, eight national logistics centers, 47 regional logistics centers, 465 urban distribution centers, and 19,359 endmost express points.

As with many international and domestic retail companies, Suning is engaged in financial services from consumer and business loans to crowd funding and selected wealth management.

Traditionally, Chinese consumers from past generations tended to save and stayed away from credit. When I started in my business, credit card-related sales accounted for less than 5 of my total sales, and by now credit card and other online payment systems together represent over 40%.

With customer habits and needs evolving—more and more faster than their means, especially for younger consumers—credit financing is becoming an important topic. Again, here, the non-regulated sector such as retailers and online platforms are jumping in to fill the gap. According to Suning's consumer credit division "Credit Pay," a total of nearly 20 million people and over 8 million consumption loans were offered both online and offline.

To acquire new consumers and penetrate rural areas, Suning has implemented a five-stage strategy for rural areas, putting its newly found e-commerce strength to use. Focusing on e-commerce outlets, cultivating local e-commerce talent, and establishing the brand by sponsoring e-commerce education, Suning has promoted locally manufactured/agricultural products through its e-commerce network and crowd funding. Though some of the initiatives are not directly revenue generators, they lay the foundation for demand and nurture both the market and new talent.

As many readers are likely aware, loans for SMEs barely exist in China, which has led to a shadow banking system. Major companies like Suning have been working to provide an alternative solution. According to Zhang, the company provided loan services worth RMB 30 billion for enterprises in 2015. "We've helped many SMEs overcome their difficulties in fund shortage." Says Zhang.

Providing suppliers and users with quick service through technological development is a trend I have observed in China (and which is also reflected in some interviews in this book). So, funding suppliers/vendors/merchants, providing logistics and a stream of consumers via big data, is the future business model. In my view, it will not be much different than today, except for the tools used.

As the company transitions into an offline and online comprehensive retailer, Zhang and his team see the cooperation with Alibaba as a matter of simply executing customer-centricity. They describe the current "Suning-Alibaba operating mode" as a "common commitment-oriented approach to consumers." Zhang sees the cooperation as a natural next step to targeting more consumers and to bringing more merchants to China.

While working on its cloud service to help its merchants business pursue a more scientific approach, Mr. Zhang sees a bright future with the Chinese consumer and intends to expand the company's merchandise base globally. Suning has already made steps in Europe, the USA, and Korea, based on Zhang's rationale of meeting the evolving Chinese consumer's rising expectations for quality.

Chinese companies are now seeking to grow their ecosystems overseas. Similar to other companies in the book (discussed in later chapters), like Wang Jianling's Wanda looking for attractive brands for his shopping malls, Zhang Xuanning's Yonghui looking for great food products overseas, or Yili securing overseas milk stocks, Suning is working to establish its name overseas in search for opportunities to source products and find consumer-related services.

And that's where Suning's then-headline-making soccer club acquisition comes into play. In asking Zhang—who was, as mentioned, someone I had known for years—about his business rationale, I was trying to find out the true story behind the Inter-Milan acquisition.

In fact, the official answer was fairly simple and in keeping with the above-mentioned "ecosystem building" approach. "Investments are there to make money, but instead of making money from football, Suning's investment in football was intended to help the Italian and European enterprises to get acquainted with Suning. By leveraging football, Suning may foster new collaborations with Italian enterprises," explains Zhang.

I remember well the advertising I spent with my company in China in an effort to build the brand, so this step suddenly made sense to me.

But as always, every deal has a personal story, and Zhang was happy to share the back-story. International Milan was partially acquired by an Indonesian company, whose owner was having difficulty in making continuous investments in the club. Zhang met him, they got along quite well, and the businessman ultimately decided to sell his shares to Suning. Next, Zhang flew to Italy to meet with the founder of the club, who held another 30% of the shares. "He liked me right away and agreed to sell his shares to me so that I could be the majority shareholder," says Zhang. He further adds, "I think this is like the old Chinese saying—we had the right timing, geographical convenience and good human relations (tianshi, dili, renhe天时地利人和). So it was serendipity (yuanfen缘分)."

Zhang went on to illustrate that Suning had invested over RMB 2.7 billion (ca. EUR 360 million) for 70% of the club's shares, including the cost of acquisition, players and so on. Since Suning's takeover, the company had recruited some good players, getting IM fans excited. Zhang thought it was well received by the Italians. "The Italian people are happy to see the club is being taken care of by a creditable enterprise like Suning."

Zhang had two more reasons to support this deal. First of all sports, especially soccer, is a critical component of, content. With PPTV (the previous PPLive, a peer-to-peer streaming video freeware popular in China, acquired by Suning in 2013), Suning has established a cross-media broadcasting platform, focusing on new media development and targeting cross-industry integration and content management. Considering soccer to be a long-term source of content, Suning had previously invested millions of dollars in the broadcasting rights for the Spanish League, the German League, the Italian League and the Premier League (three seasons between 2019 and 2020). The Inter Milan deal is a follow-up investment aiming to enrich the content in conjunction with its PPTV users.

The other reason might be new to the reader. Suning's hometown is Nanjing, the capital of Jiangsu province, and the company is its pride and joy. The company took over the leading local soccer team, which was founded in 1958, and renamed it the Jiangsu Suning soccer team. Now the team ranks no. 2 in the Chinese Super League. In addition, Nanjing has a population of 8.22 million people and Jiangsu alone has 79.8 million, which is another aspect of the soccer excitement (with Milan having 1.3 million inhabitants and Italy 60.1 million in comparison).

Zhang believes that Chinese soccer clubs have a lot to learn from experienced international ones, and this cooperation will help bring the Jiangsu team resources from Europe. "For example, IM has created a comprehensive system for youth player development. It can be an excellent model for the Jiangsu Suning team to learn from," Zhang relates.

Simply put, Suning is now a huge and sprawling company, consisting of two public listed vehicles, one in China (SZ: 002024) and one in Japan (a source location for appliances), with its six groups. In addition to what we have mentioned above—e.g. the financial services group, commerce group, media and entertainment group, sports group, and investment group—interestingly (though hardly a surprise) the company also has some residential and tourism-related real estate like hotels in its portfolio. The real estate group now predominantly involves commercial properties, including logistics centers and shopping malls in roughly 80 Chinese cities.

Running the number two of China's Top 500 private enterprises in 2016 and number one electrical retailer as well as number one retailer overall, Mr. Zhang now has over 180,000 employees in his daily operations. So, how can such an enormous company manage evolution and change effectively in such short periods of time?

It occurred to me that the tightly controlled large private enterprises, though benefitting from a rising consumer economy, also have to stay extremely agile. The tight top-down management has some disadvantages, but in China where things evolve and can change surprisingly quickly, this approach may help giants adapt quickly, or even to leapfrog over stages.

Despite being a high-profile company, there is less scrutiny or adversity in Suning regarding its embarking on a new or difficult course. This is unlike in the west, where the media and commentators don't just report the facts but in fact also form judgments. In a tightly managed, owner-driven company, technical innovations can be implemented more quickly, even at a stage when concepts might not be fully proven.

In addition to all these factors, the hyper-competition in China constantly puts pressure on companies to evolve and try to fend off competitors, which usually means that at every level, staff are willing to drive evolution and changes as long as the leaders believe in these policies. This is contrary to the common belief that Chinese companies are slow and cumbersome.

The advantages of strong leader management at the current stage of the market seem to be overwhelming. The downside—too much decision-making power in the hands of the chairman—is somewhat mitigated by what I observed at Suning, as well as other companies in this book. The chairmen pay close attention to details, especially when it comes to competitors' activities and technological developments.

In fact, my personal view is that Chinese entrepreneurs follow technological advances much more closely than many Western CEOs I know—some of whom delegate the task to a CIO or simply the IT department in general. Second, although companies seem to be managed top-down, chairmen spend a great deal of time listening to their close-by managers, most often informally, before making decisions. They also receive extensive input regarding their competitors' moves and—for the better—their competitors' future plans.

Of course, as all this is complex and requires a 7-day work week. Most bosses in China work non-stop, even at odd hours. Suning had a practice that the end of the workday (around 9:00/10:00 p.m.) was "sign-off time," when managers would go to their bosses to receive approval for their work and projects, raising everyone's awareness for the importance of details.

As the world of consumer products is now changing around the world, Chinese companies might take on a better role in it, since—though they may look slow from the outside—once decisions have been made, these companies can implement them quickly and take a long-term view on ventures. This is an important aspect that Western companies should be aware of as competitors.

Mr. Zhang has two dreams, the first of which is derived in my opinion from China's dream, namely that Suning can create a better and more widely affordable life to consumers through its ecosystem and multi businesses. As for the international arena, Zhang hopes that more enterprises and customers will come to know Suning and its business culture, as well as its social responsibilities. After 30 years of rapid development in China, he feels that "a small group of outstanding enterprises have stood out by participating in global competition, and their characteristics are worth exploring."

Acknowledgment This interview has been published with the kind permission of Mr. Zhang Jindong.

Note

1. http://www.srssn.com/TongZhiGongGao/516018.html

10

Households Upgrading Appliances: Haier

Household Appliances—No. 1 in household appliances—Zhang Ruimin, Chairman (photo with kind permission of Mr. Zhang Ruimin)

© The Author(s) 2018
C. Nothhaft, *Made for China*, DOI 10.1007/978-3-319-61584-4_10

Opportunity

The Chinese white goods market is huge—nearly the same size as the US market, and urbanization is still intensifying. With only half of the country's 1.3 billion citizens urbanized, the population's median income is lower than the USA, and in the past, consumers didn't give much thought to upgrading or changing appliances. The opportunity, therefore, comes from the volume as well as upgrading. Foreign brands (potentially owned by Chinese companies) also now have a great opportunity to capitalize on this stage of the market. Further, as Haier—which is in an advanced learning stage overseas—demonstrates, manufacturers in China can venture abroad both by acquisition and organically.

Lessons Learned

In fact, customers in China don't want to take shortcuts in terms of quality. They need products that fit their wallet, which gives local manufacturers who offer good quality an edge over foreign brands. For those with higher incomes, foreign brands are still attractive. Companies like Haier have good chances if they continue to pursue a multi-brand strategy and add overseas brands to their portfolios. This makes them more flexible and means that they have more opportunities than others when it comes to generating business by entering new markets with different strategies and even with specifically developed products, as opposed to big branded players that have to stick to their established brands and product lines. When companies grow extremely large, they struggle with customer-centricity and execution speed, and the best companies constantly reassess their business model and corporate setup so as to remain agile.

When my family and I first came to China in 2007, I remember very well how boring electrical retailers' sales floors were. Most products were lower-priced to mid-priced, with very few added features. Today, hi-tech features and a modern, designer look and feel are all being stressed, and high-end products take up the front row in showrooms.

The China Electronic Chamber of Commerce Office conducted a survey in 2014 and found that the top three brand selection criteria for high-tech consumer appliances were: (a) use of high-end technology, (b) internationally popular brands, and (c) user-friendliness.[1] In a nutshell, the consumer now wants a high-tech, internationally branded product that is easy to use.

Electric home appliances didn't enter Chinese households until the 1980s, accompanying the economic reforms. In fact, the development of China's home appliance market took place long after the rest of the world, mostly due to its isolation during the Cultural Revolution. "Officially," the country's first home refrigerator was introduced in 1956, the first television in 1958, the first household washing machine in 1962, and the first air conditioner in 1965. All that changed with the gradual opening-up of the market economy after 1979.

Since then, China's home appliance market has developed rapidly. As most couples both worked during the day, the most basic expectations from home appliances were that they reduce household chores and provide entertainment for relaxation after a long day of work. Although in the 1980s a TV set cost as much as a car, it didn't stop consumers' needs from driving growth in the market. People were willing to pay 2 years' wages for a television. Interestingly, China has always had more TV sets in its households than refrigerators—it seems that two or even three generations living under one roof can equitably share a fridge, but may have difficulty agreeing on what TV shows to watch.

Especially our GenPC witnessed that in the 1990s, the economic status of Chinese families continued to improve. The home appliance industry also entered into a golden era of rapid expansion. Consumer demand began to truly blossom, and refrigerators, TV sets, and washing machines began to be commonly found in Chinese households.

Thanks to rising incomes, large home appliances were no longer luxuries by the early twenty-first century. The bar had been raised again, and today prospective grooms need to have an apartment, a car, and liquid assets before they can even consider a conjugal future. Home appliance manufacturers are happy to see this trend—for every apartment sold, there will be a new family in need of various home appliances.

The growth of China's home appliance market has been closely following urbanization and lifestyle changes. Anecdotally, there have been other drivers that were more culturally related: wedding prerequisites. As seen above, the evolution of this market is perfectly reflected by the changing prerequisites to marriage. There is also an informal rule known as "three large appliances that lead to marriage" and set by Chinese mothers-in-law, who are also evolving. Applied to the consumer groups discussed in this book, it would look roughly like this table (Table 10.1).

Table 10.1 Chinese preferred bethroal gifts are changing

Consumer generation	Preferred bethoral gifts
GenRed	Bicycle, wristwatch, and sewing machine
GenRed/GenRise	Refrigerator, television, and washing machine
GenPC	Personal computer, air conditioner, and motorcycle or DVD player
GenMobile	Apartment ownership, car, and cash (mobile phones are too cheap)

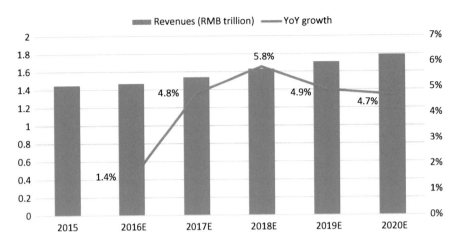

Fig. 10.1 Forecast for China's home appliance market. Source: CIC Consulting

The market for consumer appliances grew from RMB 119 billion in 2001 to RMB 1.45 trillion by 2015. Although market growth has slowed from the double-digit years up to 2013, and slower rates of growth will persist in the future, thanks to the ongoing urbanization and upgrading for existing households, the market nonetheless still has plenty of room to grow.

According to Euromonitor, in 2015 the Chinese large appliance market was nearly as large as its US counterpart at roughly US$61.2 billion, but the Chinese population is four times larger than that of the US—yes, as also shown in Fig. 10.1, through penetration as well as upgrading products for families with evolving lifestyles, it still has massive room for growth!

Product upgrading, especially for a "more modern home," has become one of the major battlefields for home appliance brands. Fortunately, ongoing urbanization and rising levels of disposable income remain key driving forces behind consumers' pursuit of better living standards and increasing replacement demand for home appliances among Chinese households.[2]

Domestic brands dominate the home appliance market in China, as represented by Haier Group (2015 market share: 31%) at the top of the ranking list, followed by Midea (market share: 13%) and Rongsheng (market share: 11%).

The leading players have broad product portfolios in both large and small appliances, extensive nationwide distribution networks, and enjoy high penetration rates all the way down to lower-tier cities and rural areas. They enjoy a positive brand reputation among local consumers and a large consumer base.[3]

Haier emerged as the dominant player in China's refrigerator industry in 1988, when it won the first gold medal in China's refrigerator history at the

National Refrigerators Appraisal. It is ranked as the number one global major appliance brand, with a worldwide market share of 10.3% in 2016, according to Euromonitor.

It is an amazing story, starting with a small state-run factory, and is still only 30 years old. The company's chairman Zhang Ruimin has been at the helm of the company ever since it began evolving from a single workshop. In the span of three decades, Haier has gone through five distinct development stages under Zhang's leadership, to become what it is today.

Market demand for household appliances exploded in the early 1980s, and everything could be sold quickly regardless of its quality. Back then, the price of a refrigerator was about the equivalent of 2 years' salary.[4] Manufacturers were focused on expanding their production capacity to make quick money.

Zhang Ruimin chose a different path. Bearing the market economy in mind, where customers have a choice, he focused on quality from day one. In 1984, Zhang had his workers publicly destroy all the faulty output from the factory with sledgehammers, making his stance on quality management loud and clear. Haier's reputation for quality refrigerators, therefore, began to be established, laying a solid foundation for its future development.

The centerpiece of stage two for Haier was diversification during the 1990s. Encouraged by government policies, Haier managed to create the framework for a home appliance empire through mergers and acquisitions with some 18 businesses. While the rest of the industry was engaged in price wars, Haier was able to position itself as a value-added service provider by introducing a "Star Service" system.

Then, after China joined the WTO in December 2001, the Chinese government encouraged Chinese companies to expand overseas. Unlike most companies, which aimed at product sales in developing countries or becoming OEMs for maturing markets, Haier implemented a three-stage strategy, for which it became famous: (1) enter a new market on the basis of price, (2) stay in the market at a cost and learn, and (3) advance by using your newly acquired market expertise to develop better products catering to the market's specific needs. These three steps are still in use as part of the company's strategy today.

Haier is now focusing on using global resources to produce even better products. As a global brand, Haier operates 10 R&D centers around the world: in China, Japan, Australia, Germany, and the USA. Interestingly, Haier's globalization strategy was built upon localization—products are designed locally, manufactured locally, and sold locally to cater to local customers' needs. The company decentralized its 1150 R&D personnel into different countries, so they can bring back shared knowhow. Haier calls this the "three in one" model, which combines design, manufacture, and sales to provide ongoing support for global brand development.

Products manufactured overseas account for approximately 50% of Haier's total overseas sales, and the number rises to 70% in the refrigerator category. Step by step, Haier has accumulated valuable brand equity in the mainstream sectors of the global market, instead of being a no-name OEM supplier behind the scenes, or just another cheap but low-quality brand from China.

Along the way, Zhang continued his quest to gain access to specialist know-how by entering into joint venture agreements with foreign companies, first with the German company Liebherr in 1984, then with Panasonic Sanyo of Japan[5] in 2012. The list of subsequent acquisitions and collaborations is long, including Fisher & Paykel, New Zealand in 2012 (US$766 million[6]), and a US$5.4 billion[7] deal with GE closed on June 6, 2016.

According to the market data provider Dealogic, the GE deal is the third largest acquisition a Chinese enterprise has ever made in the USA. With nine manufacturing facilities, 12,000 US workers and a world-class brand, the deal will significantly expand Haier's US and global presence and help move the company forward as a premium brand on the US market.[8] Euromonitor predicts that Haier will rank no. 5 globally, accumulating GE's related sales with a market share of 3.4% and surpassing Panasonic and P&G.

Therefore, I was keen to find out how an underdog grown out of Cultural Revolution-era China has been able to quietly chip away to become a global leader, overtaking the likes of GE, Panasonic, and Hitachi.[9] Due to his never-ending quest for quality and innovation, Zhang Ruimin, one of the best-known Chinese global business leaders, is a symbolic figure for the future of "Made For China." I was thrilled when, after reviewing the planned questions, he accepted the invitation for an interview.

Arriving at Haier's headquarter, a huge campus covering 10,000 m^2 and home to more than 10,000 employees, I knew I had entered something of an empire. Container trucks, shipping parts, and products were everywhere. Tour groups were wandering around the campus, as the Haier Park is a popular industrial tourism site in Qingdao.

The challenge such a vast company that has grown so quickly faces is how to stay agile, so as to follow customer trends and market complexities: e.g., the different consumer generations in China today, and various customer clusters in markets where the company competes with brands that have a longer history there. So how does Haier stay close to the consumer in so many product categories and places?

Zhang struck me with his opening words, in which he stressed how opportunistic Haier is. "One of the most important factors is that we never considered ourselves to be successful. We just seized the opportunity. When we did well, we always kept looking for the next opportunity." He then put the (in)famous refrigerator smashing into context:

When Haier started up, it imported a production line from Liebherr of Germany. The staff believed that with advanced technology and with great demand on the market, whatever was produced would be well received by the market. This was the typical thinking at the time, in the absence of choice. However, with regard to advanced products and manufacturing overseas, Zhang had a point about the staff and management mentality, and about where the technology to make the product was heading. He insisted that if the quality of staff couldn't keep up with the quality of the equipment, the latter was not going to work.

It was in 1985 when Zhang received a letter from a customer complaining about Haier's product quality. Zhang went to the warehouse and ordered a quality inspection. 76 out of over 400 refrigerators in stock failed the test. His managers suggested selling these problematic refrigerators to Haier staff at a low price, which was the most common way to deal with quality issues back then. Zhang decided to smash these refrigerators in front of his staff because he believed that defective products were a waste and that they didn't belong in any consumer household—even at a discount.

Many employees were in tears when they witnessed the smashing, since the price of a refrigerator was (as previously mentioned) roughly equal to 2 years' salary for them! The event attracted a great deal of publicity and ultimately became the hallmark of what Haier wanted to stand for in terms of quality.

According to Zhang, he had no choice but to smash the defective products. "I didn't expect the smashing would improve staff quality, but it did change their mindset," says Zhang. In fact, the event sparked a new quality awareness among Haier. Three years later, Haier became the number one refrigerator brand in China. "I believed that in an enterprise, changing the staff's mindset is the most important thing. Otherwise, there will be no effective implementation," he adds.

Further, Zhang believes execution capacity was the main reason that Haier developed so well and so quickly in the past. "Many companies may come up with a good idea, but lack good implementation. At Haier, our rule is that once we decide to do something, we must implement it one hundred percent."

However, Zhang also understands that this does not necessarily work in the Internet age: "Customers choose all companies and products today, and decision-making is in the hands of the consumers." Every entrepreneur I interviewed claimed the Internet is changing how businesses interact with their consumers. Companies are empowered to communicate directly with their end users, which helps them to satisfy individualized consumer needs. In response to the disruptions brought by such technological advances, Zhang is convinced that Haier needs to change further.

In this vein, he decided to change the role of Haier from providing jobs to providing employees entrepreneurial opportunities. People form their teams and start up their projects or businesses. The change in direction was radical when at one point Zhang offered roughly 20,000 managers two options: either start their projects or leave Haier. It caused considerable repercussions at the time, but most managers chose to stay and participate in the transformation.

Ever since this model was launched in 2005, though inspiring, it has also been viewed by some as controversial, which has put Zhang and his management team under tremendous pressure. Mr. Zhang also mentioned some of the challenges: "We transformed our structure from the previous hierarchy to entrepreneurial teams. The next step is to have the entrepreneurial teams actively "live out" their new roles, which has been very difficult for us."

Zhang firmly believes that each holds great potential and what's important is to bring the best out of every one. His further aim is to give front-line employees maximum autonomy and decision-making power so that they can respond to user requirements as quickly as possible. According to Zhang, this user/customer-centric approach empowers staff to take a leadership role in independent innovations. Their income level is subject to how much value they can create for users. The challenges, therefore, include a major change to the employee mindset, from "being managed" to managing themselves.

Take an employee named Zhong Hui and two of his colleagues from the after-sales service department, for example. In the very beginning, Haier paid them each a monthly salary of RMB 1800, and each would have to leave if they failed to propose a practical startup project after the first 3 months.

The result: Zhong's team managed to provide a "delivery locker" service in communities to solve the "last mile" problem in the express industry. With Haier's more than 17,000 service stops across the country, Zhong's service reached nearly 10,000 communities, and the project completed its second round financing in December 2015.

As an innovation, teams are also in charge of getting the best players to join them. "In other words, if you want to reach a first-class goal, it takes first-class people to make it happen. This is a difficult task because you need a good incentive to convince world-class professionals to join your team," says Zhang.

In a nutshell, instead of a hierarchical system, Haier aims to make the company more and more of a platform to incubate teams and independent entrepreneurs, where every employee is seen as an entrepreneur responding directly to specific consumer needs. The company increasingly sees itself as being an incubator and facilitator of new ideas for products and businesses and invites external resources to join in with and contribute to the Haier business.

With China having so many entrepreneurs—in fact, millions of them—in company jobs and just waiting for their opportunity to start something on their own, this approach certainly matches the country's current opportunistic culture. I was amazed, though, to see how systematically Zhang attempted to capitalize on this on a grand scale. Of course, we can see that this transition in his company—albeit a few years in—is still in an early stage, and my personal hunch is that it works much better in some sectors of the business than in others. However, as more and more industries become platforms (e.g., the taxi industry), maybe this approach will gradually provide new avenues for major companies to transition over time. At the moment, I would imagine there are many limits and challenges, but I guess if someone had told me 10 years ago what Uber would do to the taxi industry (namely, revolutionize it) or what Google's self-driving cars would do to the transport industry, I would have had my doubts, too. So, at this point, I certainly admire Mr. Zhang for taking on the challenging task of transforming such a huge company in such a fundamental way.

Haier's current "networking strategy" is now a frequently discussed topic at Harvard and other business institutions—and scholars are divided as to whether it's a stroke of genius, or simply too complex to manage. The verdict is still out, but according to Zhang, it is a 20-year plan.

In the blueprint Zhang has designed for the company, Haier no longer plans to be a controlling body. Instead, it will be a platform for entrepreneurial projects, which provides both Haier staff and individuals currently outside Haier an opportunity to start up their own businesses. Haier will play the role of investor, while its employees and external stakeholders become entrepreneurs. According to Zhang, Haier's goals are "enterprising collectively and winning together. Together, people can achieve their common goals and realize individuals' value."

In a way, Zhang is trying to build one of the largest incubators in the world. And it has been working. Haier's revenues reached RMB 100 billion in 2004, and RMB 188.7 billion in 2015, which means average annual growth of nearly RMB 10 billion over the course of a decade.[10] According to Zhang, there are now 200 entrepreneurial teams at Haier, more than 100 of which have annual revenues of over RMB 100 million each.[11] Besides, 41 of those teams are already having VCs (Venture Capital).

As for products, Zhang is confident that Haier will go beyond home appliances in the future. In the Internet age, consumers may have diverse demands in their daily lives. Therefore, what Haier provides is no longer products, but solutions to the various problems consumers encounter.

According to Haier, the open platform HOPE (Haier Open Partnership Ecosystem) has now provided more than 22,000 solutions.

Zhong Hui's delivery locker is one example, and Zhang illustrates the point further with gaming laptops. Haier is now the second largest supplier of these laptops in China. "However, considering that the market potential for hardware is limited, we have shifted our focus from gaming notebooks to the gaming industry. Users are engaged in the whole process," says Zhang.

The entrepreneurial team LEISHEN, which focused on the gaming laptop, was incubated on Haier's platform and is now focusing on gaming software and other products. Haier holds 49% of the startup's shares now and helps it to coordinate with OEM factories. Mr. Zhang believes that in this way Haier will expand to a broad range of industries, starting from home appliances.

I'm confident Zhang will continue to make headlines with innovative management solutions and more global acquisitions! And I can personally attest: he is an iconic character.

Acknowledgment This interview has been published with the kind permission of Mr. Zhang Ruimin.

Notes

1. http://www.fool.com/investing/general/2014/01/28/the-winners-and-losers-in-chinas-home-appliance-ma.aspx
2. http://www.euromonitor.com/consumer-appliances-in-china/report
3. http://www.euromonitor.com/consumer-appliances-in-china/report
4. http://news.ittime.com.cn/news/news_1272.shtml
5. http://www.reuters.com/article/us-panasonic-haier-idUSTRE76R1VS20110728
6. http://www.reuters.com/article/us-haier-fisherpaykel-takeover-idUSBRE8A505J20121106
7. http://www.forbes.com/sites/russellflannery/2016/01/15/haier-to-buy-ge-appliances-for-5-4b-in-chinas-2nd-big-u-s-acquisition-this-week/#326d16a64c41
8. http://www.reuters.com/article/us-ge-divestiture-haier-elec-idUSKCN0UT0AG
9. https://technology.ihs.com/499925/top-3-home-appliance-makers-see-growth-in-the-first-quarter-of-2014
10. http://news.xinhuanet.com/tech/2015-09/16/c_128234368.htm
11. http://news.sohu.com/20160125/n435721629.shtml

11

Home-Style Dreams: Kuka

Furniture—No. 1 sofa manufacturer—Gu Jiangsheng—Second Generation Founder
(photo with kind permission of Mr. Gu Jiangsheng)

© The Author(s) 2018
C. Nothhaft, *Made for China*, DOI 10.1007/978-3-319-61584-4_11

Opportunity

In the early stages of China's consumer economy, owning an apartment/house was considered important. More often than not the decoration of the home was secondary, as Chinese placed more emphasis on things they used outside the house, and that could be shown to others. Entertainment usually happened in restaurants. Cocooning and a shift in priorities especially with younger consumers, as well as an influx of "style advice" through social media and further enhanced by the success of IKEA and Internet home decoration companies, Chinese's dreams of home interiors have now become more ambitious—and present a good business opportunity.

Lessons Learned

As this trend applies to consumers of all budget levels, smart companies provide their offerings in different segments catering to entry-level customers as well as well-heeled ones, while the core of sales and profits are made in the mid-market. Thanks to the "young consumer effect," companies that are establishing a consistent and solid brand, and which lead the way in design and service (which involves explaining to consumers what looks good and is IN) will tend to grow much faster. Again, the Internet is a critical opportunity to stimulate demand.

Companies have also begun going to great lengths to introduce more contemporary designs, either by developing international design teams or by considering M&A or cooperation. Profitability in this sector appears to be good, so we assume the leading companies will be in a good cash position, and they will start consolidating the market.

My family had been living in China for more than 10 years and we'd been inside numerous homes in China. My wife and I always enjoyed looking at new properties, partially to be amused by the glitz and bling that would often overwhelm us, not only in luxury apartments but also in small apartments on the 25th floor in faceless towers. In most apartments owned by "my generation," you could find anything from Versailles-style chandeliers to faux Mondrian tables to Chippendale-esque sofas and would-be classic Chinese furniture. Best of all, a hodgepodge of everything combined in one room!

Things have changed a great deal over the last 5 years, and homes in China have become more tasteful. Most of all, style directions have begun to settle in. This development seems to be a bit late in coming, but in fact it represents part of a natural evolution considering the "Chinese characteristics" of consumer priorities, which in my view looks as follows:

1. Investment in self-education and progress to achieve a better life and make more money
2. Investment in status and conveying "I am up to date"—cars and houses for big wallets and the latest mobile phones for mid-market wallets (which explains Apple's phenomenal success in China); this includes investment in beauty (skin care, branded makeup, aesthetic surgery)
3. Investment in self-indulgence; e.g., nicely decorated apartment, bedding, spa trips, ethnic food, etc.

This pyramid is now in flux, while the Millennials might turn it upside down. And "cocooning" as a consequence of urban lifestyle might accelerate this trend!

Although China is huge, due to the desire to live in urban areas, Chinese apartments on average are small. Therefore, in general, entertaining and meeting friends (contrary to many Western countries) have traditionally happened almost exclusively outside the home. The choice of restaurant/venue was intended to demonstrate the wealth and status of whoever did the inviting and whoever was invited. With the arrival of the wider consumer economy in China, other "status symbols" became important, such as clothes, jewelry, and anything you can put on a table during lunch or dinner for everyone else to see (including handbags, the latest mobile phone or gadget, etc.). Very often these items were short lived, because part of the game of being recognized was not necessarily having something expensive, but always having the latest and most exotic things! Such is "social status," especially in the consumer era of the Millennials.

With higher job and social pressures, we are now observing a trend of "cocooning" and simplicity. More and more people are beginning to show concern for their direct "sphere" and personal space, and in my view, this refers to the content of the home and mobile phone in particular. For a few exceptions, it might also mean the car interior (which is the opposite of my fellow countrymen).

This is where we see the concept of "home sophistication," which revolves around personal happiness within the home, expression of your personality through how you decorate your home, and how you arrange that home to impress your peers. This has recently manifested itself in more and more people attempting to impress friends that come to visit by providing a cooking demonstration, arranged and rehearsed to impress of course. Not only is this driving growth in cookery and wine-tasting classes but also the wider development of home interior-related industries like furniture making, soft furnishings, decorations, kitchen items, etc.

According to the findings of a consumer survey on furniture conducted by the Hong Kong Trade Development Council in 2014 which is shown in Fig. 11.1, mainland middle-class consumers are placing an increasing emphasis on home decoration, with 73% of survey respondents saying that they are more willing than before to spend money on purchasing or replacing home decorative items. Also, trends have a strong influence on their buying decisions (see Fig. 11.1). Regarding the interval of replacing furniture, the average period mentioned by all respondents was 7.6 years.

Given this trend, we decided to dive into the home furniture industry. Clearly, this should be an interesting one: an industry that in China has been very traditional, with very few lasting success stories of foreign companies coming in to teach consumers how to pursue "home improvements." But now, suddenly, it is being hit by a new generation of consumers, and further accelerated by social media ("Hey everyone, see my new kitchen!") and by online retailing ("Hey everyone, I found something cooler AND CHEAPER!").

I tried to find a good representative company for this trend. The association of furniture producers names 96 brands/companies as the leading representatives of the industry in China. After analyzing the competitive field, we found Kuka (China's premier modern sofa brand) to be a good fit. In fact, I asked

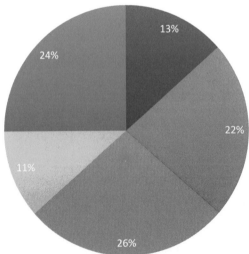

Fig. 11.1 An overview of Replacement Interval of furniture with Chinese people. Source: Hong Kong Trade Development Council, 2014

many people about the company, and most of them knew Kuka and exactly what it stood for (branding at work!!), which was a good indication that I had found the right candidate to interview.

The company, in fact, goes back 70 years as a family carpentry business. In 1982, Mr. Gu Yuhua then "formally" founded Kuka by consolidating several workshops, eventually building the company to one with US$6 million in sales. In 2000, Old Mr. Gu passed the business on to Mr. Gu junior, who has since expanded the company's size 100 times over (yes one hundred times!).

This was no mean feat, especially considering the fact that China's furniture industry is very fragmented and looks like an ants' nest from above. There were an estimated 4467 or 4942 (depending on how you define them) furniture companies of significance in China, as of 2013/2014. There are probably many more that slip under the statistical radar! Traditionally, these companies grew from family carpenter businesses just like Kuka, and most of them started by making traditional Chinese-style furniture.

The first furniture boom was the direct outcome of housing privatization. Following the great sell-off of state-owned housing in the late 1990s, from 2001 to 2012, the Chinese government rolled out a range of favorable policies to open up the real estate industry so that it might function as a pillar of China's consumer economy. As shown in Fig. 11.2, with owning an apartment at that time became the dream for hundreds of millions of urban dwellers, the real estate market exploded, and with it came the need to furnish all those newly acquired apartments (see Fig. 11.2). In 2001, investment in real estate totaled RMB 624.5 billion or 17% of aggregate fixed asset investment.[1] This amount and percentage rose to RMB 71.8 trillion and 25.3%,

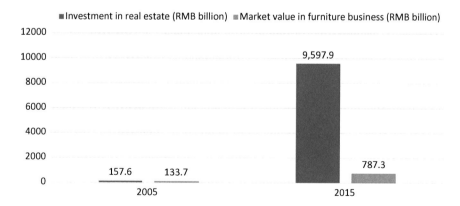

Fig. 11.2 China's furniture business grows with real estate development. Source: NBS, CINIC

respectively, by 2012.[2] To put those figures into perspective, between 1997 and 2014, real estate investment grew from about 4% to 15% of GDP.

Back to the carpenter and furniture businesses and Kuka's story: Of course, in China labor costs were especially attractive in the early stage of the economy, leading to it becoming the "workbench of the world." Some companies also evolved into OEM manufacturers, mainly for foreign furniture retailers in the USA and Canada.

Similar to other industries, OEM allowed a few skilled companies with the right mindset to assimilate design knowledge and to develop their design capabilities and apply them to the domestic market. The hotbeds of OEM furniture in China are the provinces close to the coast, and ports of export, including Guangdong, Zhejiang, and Liaoning.

Being one of the most experienced OEM manufacturers, Kuka initially built its reputation on designer sofas and acted as an OEM manufacturer in several countries. Kuka had RMB 3.68 billion in sales in 2015. As with many Chinese companies, sometimes the sales volume is not the most important KPI to define it as a well-managed company. In Kuka, net profit is 13.3%, or RMB 490 million—profits that most companies would be envious of. By June 2016, 65% of sales came from sofas, but the company is now positioning itself more towards providing comprehensive solutions for the living room and bedroom.

The way people shop for furniture today in China has been changing dramatically, especially since the Olympics: With urbanization entering into a second stage before the Beijing Olympics, from about 2006, most large cities became important domestic markets for the furniture industry. Developers began opening "home improvement centers," which were initially nothing more than large buildings showcasing different furniture suppliers who needed a platform to get access to urban consumers. Poorly managed, usually half empty, they were initially the place to go for local consumers to find out "what could look good" in their house or apartment. Customers had to hop from store to store to compare (and bargain on) tiles, floors, kitchen furniture, and all other things homely. Then each company independently delivered and installed its products, resulting in the previously mentioned mix and match styles of Chinese home interiors.

Some of the furniture/building malls evolved into better-managed establishments (some of them huge, more than 100,000 m^2). However, customers still had to find their own way between stores and styles. With the arrival of IKEA and the development of print and online lifestyle media, a desire for a more "harmonious design" and "style" evolved. And with access to overseas media came the desire to "own the original."

Kuka seems to have strengths that match this consumer trend. The company has roughly 3000 branded stores worldwide, with the majority on the Chinese mainland, as well as several brand cooperation agreements with top international brands such as LA-Z-BOY from the USA. It has hired over 50 international designers from Italy, Germany, France, and Japan to introduce different new designs every year. Its products are now sold internationally including in the Netherlands, Bulgaria, Central America, South America, Singapore, North Africa, India, Korea, France, Indonesia, Australia, and the Middle East.

We arranged to meet with Mr. Gu Jiangsheng, born in 1973 and the son of the company's founder, on a Saturday morning. We expected a lesson in management, but what we got was a lesson in (corporate) fitness, staff welfare, health, and succession planning!

Mr. Gu, a passionate runner, started talking about fitness right at the start of the interview, claiming, "I think a company's real competitiveness lies in the health of its staff. That's why I promote sports and exercise across the country."

Gu then told me with pride how he makes weight control mandatory for his staff to be able to get into the main venue of the company's annual meeting. In fact, the company has maintained a practice of ensuring that 5% of staff salary was based on people keeping a healthy weight/BMI!

Mr. Gu's ambitious dream for Kuka came out in the opening round of questions. Many Chinese private companies and/or family businesses have a generation-spanning vision of being a global market leader. In China, according to Mr. Gu, the change in consumer habits between Generation X and Y is the primary opportunity.

"Chinese consumers are changing. A few years ago they were satisfied with basic furniture for simple living. Now they have gradually made a significant improvement in aesthetic quality by pursuing taste, keeping up with design, and purchasing matching sets of furniture."

According to Mr. Gu, 10 years ago Chinese customers generally didn't believe that furniture could be categorized by different styles. Furniture was one single category of product; there might be subcategories, but they were not distinct. "Now the categories are becoming clearer and clearer, which proves that customers from various segments each know what they need," Gu points out.

To effectively cater to this segmentation, Gu explains Kuka's tiered product strategy using one of his favorite personal topics: "In general, we have three categories based on age group and spending power," he emphasizes, drawing a parallel to BMW's car segments. "Kuka has the 7-series and the 5-series, as well as the 3-series for online business," he elaborates, adding that online customers are very sensitive to price.

Knowing the trickiness of segmentation from my own business (it's easy to get lost and to dilute a brand), I had to ask about the company's core focus, which Gu claimed to be the mid-market. It reflects the trend that the furniture market now deals with reasonably affluent masses rather than the elite or first-time homeowner. "We will focus on the mid-range category, like the 5-series. We will be rooted in the mid-range market. We won't invest too much in the high-end series. Instead, the 5-series and the 3-series will be enhanced. We call this the 'Close to the General Public' strategy." While Gu summed up his strategy, I was happy to have cars as an analogy, which made it a bit easier for me to translate.

It made sense to me that companies would focus on the mid-market white-collar customer, as it's the fastest-growing market segment. Many feel the competition in the mid-market is now particularly fierce. To our surprise, Mr. Gu does not consider it that fierce at the moment and believes Kuka can use its superior capabilities to engage in and even take a lead in market consolidation. According to Gu: "There are 60,000 furniture companies in China. This number is not reasonable in the development stage of any industry. Eventually, it will drop to 6,000 or even 600. From that point onward, the real competition will begin."

I feel the same way. At this stage, the market game is not a game of equals. Many small companies may have grown rapidly in the past few years, but more recently, customer demand and aspirations have begun forcing the better players to emerge, succeeding over others. Design and product development capabilities are at the forefront of the race. The furniture market will soon enter an age of consolidation, and larger companies with design and marketing capabilities will have better odds of surviving. Given the current economic challenges, my subjective assessment is that this will probably happen sooner rather than later.

Chinese companies are very technology-oriented and extremely forward looking, even if sometimes the reason is not entirely clear. I find more often than not, rather than discussing innovations the owners simply decide to experiment and "buy technology" ahead of the market—in part as a status symbol but also with a future use in mind. I was surprised to learn that Kuka is now experimenting with 3D printing technology, which Mr. Gu seemed serious about that and considered an early "get-in" investment: "At the moment we are at the pilot stage, printing only a few models. The advancement of science doesn't guarantee the success of the corresponding products. 3D printing's situation is the same as that of solar energy in China—the cost of solar is 10 times that of hydro-electricity. Once the cost sinks to a level comparable to that of other products available on the market, 3D printing will lead the trend. Currently, the cost of 3D printing is too high to launch products. We have been conducting research to bring the cost down." In the company's plan, 3D printing will be used to explore new production technologies and customization potential.

The company is also innovative with regard to customer service and marketing. It launched a service campaign from March to May 2015, sending 2500 store managers to clean old Kuka sofas for customers' onsite. According to Mr. Gu, as people in major cities and small cities have fundamentally different types of apartments especially in terms of the available space, Kuka thus employs various marketing strategies in their stores in these cities. To drive innovation and service culture, Kuka has launched a Kuka University to develop its sales teams and workforce. The company is also at the forefront in cyberspace, including promoting O2O via a Virtual Home experience QR code, which helps to drive website sales.

Online plays a significant role in this industry and—as in other industries increasingly—so does social networking. First of all, social networking creates styles and peer pressure to upgrade your home. Second, customers in China compare prices online, just as they compared them long before online existed. They expect a brilliant design for a good price—and the manufacturers are best positioned in the value chain to fulfill this customer desire. Therefore, we expect integrated manufacturers will take the market in the long run. With this market shaping up for consolidation, it's hardly surprising that the online-and-offline combination represents an opportunity rather than a threat.

Mr. Gu agrees with this and cites some examples of how Kuka has used customer data to presale test products and boost success rates during launches, e.g., selling 100,000 sofa units (online alone) in just 2 months. Given that younger customers are more mobile-friendly, 80% of Kuka's online sales currently come from mobile orders, and the percentage keeps growing.

As Mr. Gu is a second-generation entrepreneur, the intriguing question was to see if he preferred a "following in the footsteps" approach, or if he was keen to diversify or even turn the company into something very different. My curiosity came from the stereotype of Chinese business people tending to do many things at once, without ever getting particularly good at any one thing (a false assumption for successful businesses in China). Therefore, some argue, Chinese companies might not be able to develop superior products or services.

Gu had a clear stance on this: "Many people have tried diversification and found out that the success rate is very low. Among 100 individuals who tell you they would like to be focused, 90 people suffered from diversification. Few people were born to be focused. They are brought back to their core business by the failure in diversification." It is very encouraging to hear this from a second-generation entrepreneur, not to mention good news for quality consumer goods aficionados!

Kuka went IPO (SH: 603816) in October 2016, so I asked Mr. Gu about his 10-year plan and vision. As with many Chinese entrepreneurs, he is leaving ample room for flexibility and to develop step by step—or as Deng Xiaoping is often quoted as saying, "crossing the river by feeling the stones under your feet."

Gu doesn't think that IPO will lead the company astray; instead, it will be even more focused. Though I tried to nudge him into talking about a 10-year pan, he had his own view: "I have never seriously thought about a 10-year plan. I only have plans for the next three to five years. And I also think about what the next 20–30 years will bring, which is that I will be more and more interested in and passionate about furniture and will devote myself to the furniture industry as a lifetime business." He then elaborated by saying: "20–30 years from now, Kuka will become a big brand like IKEA. We may not have as many products as IKEA, but we will provide a full-house furniture solution." According to Gu, the company has already made some rough long-term plans on how to evolve into a Chinese version of IKEA with furniture as its core business.

Good idea, Mr. Gu; that's exactly what the market is looking for!

Acknowledgment This interview has been published with the kind permission of Mr. Gu Jiangsheng.

Notes

1. http://www.stats.gov.cn/tjsj/tjgb/ndtjgb/qgndtjgb/200203/t20020331_30015.html
2. http://www.stats.gov.cn/tjsj/tjgb/ndtjgb/qgndtjgb/201302/t20130221_30027.html

12

FMCG Premiumization: Liby

FMCG—No. 1 in laundry care and dishwashing—Chen Kaixuan, Co-founder (photo with kind permission of Mr. Chen Kaixuan)

Opportunity

International FMCG brands have had mixed success in China, with local companies often dominating entire segments. As a general principle, local companies have formed powerful, multilayered and far-reaching distribution networks, while initially they sold more "me too"-type products. However, local companies are now evolving, partly triggered by an increasingly sophisticated consumer and by stiffer competition, including from direct sellers overseas. Domestic FMCG manufacturers are enhancing their skills in terms of both brand building and product evolution. Also, M&As of foreign and domestic brands alike have become a regular means for Chinese FMCG companies to strengthen their brand portfolios.

Lessons Learned

This chapter describes how a Chinese FMCG company has focused on a CapEx light model that gives good income to distributors, using this approach to grow a national sales network quickly and become the market leader in several FMCG sectors before venturing into manufacturing.

Privately held brands of the local giant Liby Group dominate the household detergent category, beating out international giants by means of a highly refined distribution system. Thanks to the widespread network across China, the company is now venturing into more premium brands and catching up to the global players in terms of its skills.

In building our company over the last 10 years, I have traveled to over 250 cities across China. Most trips were to decide whether we should start a business in those cities and, if so, to assess how many stores we could put in each one. I have seen the huge progress in real estate and living standards, bringing with it nicer apartments and better clothes, both of which need cleaning.

One of the things I was always amazed at was the competition between household detergents in the FMCG sectors, clearly seen in China's supermarkets and hypermarkets. Adding to the mix in a competitive market, online retailing has taken a sizeable share of many FMCG categories, with massive discounts heating up price wars amongst the leading brands. Sometimes, it truly looks like a war of attrition.

Chinese consumers buy a large variety of detergents and soaps—the country has moved on from bar soaps to hand-wash, disinfectant hand gels, various shower gels, face washes, facial cleansers, and different types of washing powders (including antiallergenic washing powders for kids). And don't even get me started on all the various shampoos that have now penetrated China.

For example, given how finicky Chinese consumers are about their hair, the country has more than 3000 different types of shampoos and over 2000 shampoo manufacturers[1] on the market.

The Chinese homecare market was worth approximately RMB 44 billion in 2001 and grew at a steady 3.5% CAGR until 2005. As Fig. 12.1 shows, then it accelerated, driven by the previously described urbanization process, to a CAGR of 6.2% from 2005 to 2010, and even to 7.2% from 2011 to 2015. As a result, the already sizeable market more than doubled to RMB 96 billion between 2001 and 2015 (see Fig. 12.1). Going forward, the Chinese homecare market is expected to grow by 5.4% to reach RMB 125 billion in 2020. That modest growth of 5.4% represents an increment of RMB 29 billion, which is about the same incremental market growth as 2010–2015.

Instead of being dominated by a single player, China's homecare market is dominated by a mix of domestic and foreign players. In the top 10 companies shown in Fig. 12.2, we can find a combination of three international and seven local players, with GZ Liby holding the biggest market share, followed by Nice, Unilever, P&G, Blue Moon, and SC Johnson, respectively (see Fig. 12.2).

During my years here since 2007, I have seen local players become more professional, proving the point that stiff competition drives everyone forward. From 2011 onwards, I began to hear complaints that more and more managers were deserting the big international brands, and that those companies' best

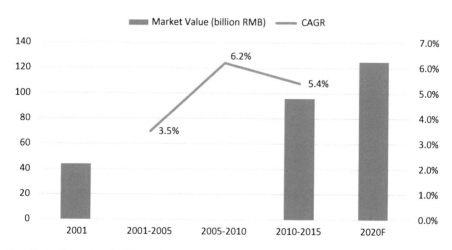

Fig. 12.1 Growth of China's homecare market. Source: KPMG/Euromonitor International; 2001–2010 data of market value are missing

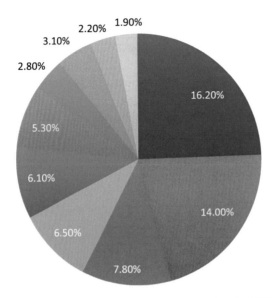

Fig. 12.2 Top 10 players on the Chinese homecare market in 2015 (http://www.hzpgc.com/article/content/7756.html). Source: Euromonitor International

sales people (initially attracted by working for a foreign company with good training) were now starting to work for local companies to improve their career prospects and payment. Originally, local players had always been reasonably aggressive when it came to sales tactics and to out-discounting foreign competitors. However, over the years, I have seen a major change: local companies are adopting better marketing strategies, better packaging, and—most of all—better innovations.

In looking for a good example of a top local company in the personal and homecare sector, Liby was a very obvious choice. It stands out both for its reputation and its high sales ranked brands. Its story also appealed to me: a family business that grew from a P&G distributor to a P&G competitor, and then to a market leader in its own right.

In 2015, Liby Group had annual revenues of over RMB 18.5 billion. Its products are household names that everyone in China is familiar with. The company has built a diversified personal and homecare portfolio similar to that of Unilever or P&G. It comprises products in nine categories—laundry care; dishwashing; disinfectants; sterilization and bleach; surface and toilet care; air care; oral care; body wash; hair care—and, most recently, skin care and cosmetics.

The business was initially based purely on distribution strength and built on an OEM model using local contract manufacturers. It now also comprises 13 directly owned manufacturing facilities. Today Liby employs over 150,000 staff. This is quite different from how other FMCG companies built their businesses in China. While many personal care companies started as manufacturers, this company started "CapEx light" and focused on marketing and distribution. The company began as a distributor (initially for P&G) and entered different business segments through acquisition. For example, it entered into oral care in November 2005, by acquiring Tianjin BlueSky Liubizhi (a local toothpaste brand); into hair care in April 2006, buying Chongqing Aoni (a local shampoo brand); and into skincare/cosmetics in July 2006, by acquiring Shanghai New Cogi (a local cosmetics brand).

I began my visit to Liby with a visit to a showroom for the companies' brands and factory expansion, which was rounded out with a view of the new office building planned. What came next was a surprise: a visit to the companies' staff gym and recreation rooms. I thought we'd arrived in a combination of Olympic Gym, Theme Park, and Club Med in the middle of a Guangzhou factory! A huge space of prime real estate made available for running tracks, gym rooms, ping-pong tables, and a swimming pool, and all indoors to make it available 24/7—even during Guangzhou's notorious rainy days!

The FMCG business in China has been very competitive, with big foreign players like P&G and Unilever directly investing in China, and with these foreign employers being attractive to job seekers. This is a delicate situation: while the frontlines are the fight for market share, the underlying war is a war for talent. While foreign invested companies often have the upper hand in terms of employer brand and better training systems in general, local companies are good at creating loyalty through staff community. So, offering better staff facilities is something local companies are particularly good at. What Liby has done in this area beats pretty much everything I have seen so far. As Chen elaborates during the interview, "We have a culture of treating our staff and business partners as family members. The culture of family creates an atmosphere of win-win."

Then, Mr. Chen Kaixuan—a cheerful and feisty man at 58—joined us. He made it clear that he is truly a fan of P&G: "P&G is the company I admire the most and also the role model I keep learning from. It's a great company worldwide."

As a successful entrepreneur, similar to others in this book, Mr. Chen felt a sense of gratitude to Deng Xiaoping for bringing about the changes to the country. "I greatly appreciate the Chinese government and Mr. Deng for reforming and opening up, which changed China and created an environment that allows us to do what we want to do," Chen said.

In the initial stage of the reform and opening up period, Mr. Chen was still in his 20s. He remembers: "I was energetic and had no burdens, which allowed me to embark on a journey of adventure. We felt much more free compared to the past, when we had to travel with all kinds of permit documents. We were not dependent on our parents or the government." According to Chen, the business environment then was so good that he had the opportunity to succeed based on his own abilities. Along the way, the company evolved from a small business to wholesale trading, and eventually to the brand Liby.

I wrote earlier in the book that during the early years of the Chinese consumer economy, entrepreneurs had to determine how to build a business with no money. The concept of banks did not exist as we know it today, and the role of banks was to support infrastructure, national construction, and SOEs with money, not necessarily private entrepreneurs. Like in the case of the Chen family and entrepreneurs in other chapters, personal wealth or collateral was nonexistent. Therefore, with no other options, networks of friends (remember Alibaba made more than 10,000 millionaires[2]) and learning from others HAD to work.

Regarding the Chen family, breaking the market rules was the edge that made them successful. In the early days, most manufacturing companies in the consumer sector were SOEs. They would sell on credit to distributors, who would in turn sell (also on credit) to consumers. In this way, sales were boosted by extending more and more credit, thus filling shelves with products that might never end up finding a paying consumer in the end.

In 1988, as a P&G distributor and with dreams of marketing his brand nationally, Chen realized he had to change the credit-based industry practice for his products; he was determined to get distributors to pay first. You can probably guess the initial (non)result!—Chen negotiated with the distributors in person, but none of them accepted his terms. Determined to get started, they turned to their network of friends, assigning a region to each of them with a promise that they would make a profit of RMB 4.00 for each carton of detergent sold—which at that time was about eight times what a regular distributor could earn per carton. Attracted by a new and more profitable model, distributors would desert other brands to work with Liby over time.

The early 1990s were also the era of privatization of SOEs, a time when foreign companies started to buy out local businesses, most of which were the manufacturing parts. Whether intentionally or simply due to a lack of money, Chen and his family had somehow found the right focus: to build distribution first rather than focusing on being a manufacturer. "Since we had no money, we had to insist on cash on delivery," Chen remembers.

The only thing Chen had was the Liby trademark, six people, and a modest amount of capital—about RMB 1 million in today's currency. While others were building factories or trying to find the money to do so, Chen was one of the first to use OEM for locally distributed products. Having devised a model that would bring in cash, Chen was keen to build national distribution (and a brand) quickly.

Many of the successful company founders we interviewed were early movers and could also ride the wave of inflation during the 1990s. Chen remembers well: "Everything sold well. The price was not determined by the market, but by the seller." The truth was, whatever price the seller set, the products quickly sold out. That was how people like Chen quickly made a fortune in those years.

In Mr. Chen's view, the cash-on-delivery model is the reason for Liby's success today. "The distributors paid the OEM factory directly. The OEM factory shipped the products out upon receipt of payment. We managed to roll out the business and became number 1 in detergent sales in Guangdong in three years using this model," says Chen.

Backed by the sales volume and money made in these 3 years, Chen bought a property in Panyu (Guangzhou) district to build the company's first factory in 1997. From that point on, Liby products went national, and it then took the company another 11 years to become the no. 1 in detergent sales in China.

The company's success was also built in less competitive areas, the countryside first. Mr. Chen drew a parallel to Mao Zedong's strategy "from villages to cities." "We also developed the company from the countryside to the cities. This was the same strategy Mao Zedong used," he explains.

Mr. Chen then raised another aspect with regard to his strategy of working from villages to cities, which was the use of a profit model (cash on delivery) that was very easy for distributors to understand. It is a model that works especially well in emerging markets, and he thinks this could also work for Liby overseas at some stage.

"It has been over 30 years since China opened up and reformed. Other countries may be just now starting that process. Some people may just be starting their business, and now face the same situation that we did 20 years ago," Mr. Chen says.

The simplicity of the business model is perfectly suited for transferring overseas. As we talked, I began wondering if:

(a) Chinese companies are perhaps well placed to take advantage of the last remaining developing economies in the world?
(b) As China has lifted so many people out of poverty through its "planned market economy approach and entrepreneurism,", this model could apply equally well to other emerging countries?

However, Mr. Chen emphasized a rather cautious approach with regard to going overseas. In contrast, he seemed rather bullish on using the existing distribution system and venturing into other categories within China: "Since we have been the best in the detergent business, we are now expanding to the household and personal care sector including cosmetics, dental cream, pesticides, disinfectants, air fresheners, furniture care, and shampoo. For the future, a broader category of household care and personal care products is our direction."

Chen also stressed that the key is service improvement, and getting used to a "new normal" under which "Competition will be harder and harder, the margins will be lower and lower, and business will be more and more difficult to secure." Through innovation as well as M&A in search of new brands and upgrading existing portfolios to premium, Liby is striving to cement its unique selling points against other players in the market.

Developing with the evolving Chinese consumers, Liby is now focusing on the innovation of environmentally friendly products, concentrated products, and food-standard level products. Fiercer competition also means more mergers and acquisitions. "If we find appropriate targets, we will consider an acquisition," Chen mentions. As previously mentioned, Liby has already had a few domestic acquisitions.

Overseas expansion may or may not be in the cards, as part of the government's One Belt One Road initiative. Liby signed a partnership agreement with CP Thailand in September 2015. Chen says, "Chairman Xi is pushing for the strategic concept of the Belt and Road Initiatives. We are following his initiative to enhance cooperation with neighboring countries such as those in SE Asia. There will be more and more such partnerships."

This made me think about how easy it is in China to align political targets with the development direction of major companies to give China Inc. a major advantage in a globally connected world.

E-commerce is another aspect we shouldn't neglect. Every week my sales figures tell me about growth rates of 50 to over 100% online for some FMCG brands. As e-commerce has been disrupting FMCG markets, manufacturers have started to circumnavigate distributors and retailers to sell to consumers directly through Internet platforms. Platforms in China are reasonably large, so the entry barrier for brands to launch online is minimal.

I asked Mr. Chen for his thoughts on the online phenomenon, suspecting that as both a maker and distributor of brands he would not be overly affected by the Internet. I assumed he walked the thin line between using the Internet as an advantage to directly reach consumers, while keeping existing distribution chains and agents happy. He seemed to agree, saying that in the long term, the market is played out by manufacturers and that the Internet is currently "in a bubble."

The company saw a year-on-year growth of 90% in online revenues in 2016 and more than 200% growth with its Cheerwin products. Further, according to Chen, the majority (80%) of online sales come from mobile orders and the percentage is still increasing.

However, Chen believes that the Internet cannot work solely without products and the economy should rely on the product industries. "We should return to the products," says Chen. That explains the cooperation between Liby and online laundry platform Edaixi, through which Liby will provide both detergent products and services to Chinese families.

If you ask me, I don't think the Internet alone can be the driving force of an economy.

During a break, I managed to sneak in a very personal question to Ms. Chen Danxia, the founder's niece and Director of Liby. Obviously, this was a particularly interesting interview, with a first and a second-generation interviewee in the room at the same time. I wondered: where is the border between business and "family"? I asked Danxia, "How is it working with your uncle?" "Terrible," was her joking answer. Ms. Chen first launched her business in cosmetics and later joined Liby. "My dad and my uncle always hold the meetings on the weekend. It's a family gathering," she added.

Somehow it made me think about the question of sustainability of Chinese companies. If you built something for your family, why wouldn't you build it sustainably? In this and other interviews that reflected Chinese entrepreneurial philosophies, I realized how there is a guidance or "stability" that is passed down from generation to generation. The business focus, business environment, and technologies might change, but the approach to doing things and values remains the same. And this thought always pops up when I am sitting in meetings with international brands where "temporary hires" make up the bulk of decision makers, often made worse by the fact that board compositions may include more lawyers and macroeconomists who have never run the day-to-day of a business or faced consumers.

All the corporate success stories we've seen in recent decades in the West were never seen among Chinese family-run companies. While Danxia was "complaining" about working with the family, in reality she stuck to a very disciplined approach to doing business. Besides the purpose of growing a family empire, Chinese companies often pursue a value-driven philosophy that Western people don't know about. It often comes from the owners' state of learning and the region they come from.

In my mind, it raised the question whether such "family principles" are a valid, yet informal alternative to the "corporate values" often produced in boardrooms or by PR agents. As for longevity, I observed that they also provide frameworks for succession planning, as well as evolving corporate culture over time.

Our time was up, and as with other interviews, I wanted to conclude by asking if there was a message the entrepreneurs wanted to share with the world. As expected, Chen replied with the philosopher's touch, incorporating temporary Chinese values born between communism and the market economy: "Chinese entrepreneurs, including me, love our country very much. We don't run the business simply for money and our own interests. When we grow the company, we want to do more charity work and do something good for the public. A large business belongs to the society and the country. We don't think the company belongs to us. Many entrepreneurs share the same thoughts."

Here is my observation: Foreign companies rely on their systems to create employee "belonging"—local companies go to great lengths to create a sense of community, even building sports facilities, or organizing staff activities, including charity events involving large donations, etc.

We had set out to explore a company that has successfully beaten out the number one in the world across some important FMCG categories in China and to learn from it. I returned from the interview with a deeper understanding of how to create a successful distribution business, as well as a philosophy lesson on and important clues to leadership transition in China. What a day!

Acknowledgment This interview has been published with the kind permission of Mr. Chen Kaixuan.

Notes

1. http://www.chyxx.com/industry/201606/422847.html
2. http://media.people.com.cn/n/2014/0921/c40606-25701216.html
   bar chart http://china.mintel.com/baogao-jiajiyongpin-yiwuxihuchanpin-2015

13

Medical Care Going Private: BYBO

Medical Care—leading dental chain—Li Changren, Founder (photo with kind permission of Mr. Li Changren)

© The Author(s) 2018
C. Nothhaft, *Made for China*, DOI 10.1007/978-3-319-61584-4_13

Opportunity

Traditionally, hospitals were the only points of dental service delivery in China, as single-focus private dentists as we know them in Western countries were practically unheard of. Since the service experience in the hospitals was subpar, this created opportunities for specialist private clinics. The vertical integration of other industries can and must happen in keeping with the evolution of technologies, laboratories, and consumer services.

Lessons Learned

As the service in large hospitals is price competitive, developing and maintaining a reputation for quality is crucial to the rapid development of successful private dentistry chains. As is typical for chain-store development, the training, recruitment, and development of dentists with the experience and quality of care needed for private clinics is the critical aspect. Branded chains of dental practices need to build penetration in the main cities to establish a brand reputation and effectively manage fixed costs.

In China, private ownership in the healthcare industry wasn't allowed until 1980, when the State Council of China approved the application submitted by the Ministry of Health. Between 1949 and 1980, there were only two types of clinics and hospitals in China—state-owned and collectively owned. Most of the practitioners and administrators in the healthcare industry were employed by the government. The family doctor system did not exist in China. When people got sick at that time, no matter whether it was a cold, toothache, or cancer, the first place they went to was a public hospital.

Unlike in the West, where outpatient service is only available from emergency rooms or specialist clinics, public hospitals in China still provide both outpatient and inpatient care. As the public healthcare system was the only source of help for patients, working at a public hospital was regarded as one of the most respected professions. Due to a dearth of medical resources and allocation imbalances between urban and rural areas, doctors were also considered among the most powerful groups of people in Chinese society.

When the central government decided to open up and reform in the early 1980s, healthcare was one of the most important areas to consider. Reforms began loosening the leash on private ownership. Private clinics and hospitals emerged and by now have been developing for over 35 years. As shown in Fig. 13.1, the number of private hospitals grew to more than 14,500 by the end of 2015, accounting for more than half of total hospitals across the nation[1]

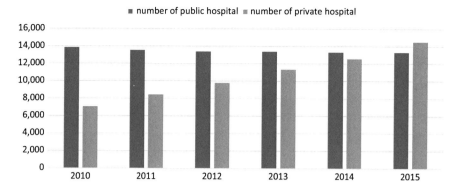

Fig. 13.1   Private clinics continue to grow in China. Source: ZhiYan Report (http://www.chyxx.com/industry/201701/490158.html)

(see Fig. 13.1). The major focus areas of private clinics and hospitals include dentistry, gynecology, and obstetrics, infertility, and plastic surgery. The number of patient visits to private hospitals accounts for only 11% of total visits.[2]

However, while between 2005 and 2015 the number of visits to public hospitals doubled to 2.7 billion (two per capita per annum), visits to private hospitals increased fivefold to 370 million visits, reflecting a growing middle class and wealthy citizens' preference for treatment at private hospitals.[3]

The development of private dental clinics and hospitals is a good example of the growth of private healthcare over the past three decades. Before 1980, only two types of facilities were licensed to provide dental care—the dentistry departments of general hospitals, and stomatology hospitals. Small, private dental clinics began emerging when private ownership was allowed after 1980. However, many of them weren't licensed.

By the early 1990s, private capital was allowed to contract and operate in the stomatology departments of public hospitals. During this period, government policies on private investment in public healthcare facilities went back and forth. The regulatory environment for private dental care was unstable and varied according to regional and local authorities' interpretations and enforcement of policies.

Then, the market entered into a new era when the central government reaffirmed its stance on supporting a "completely market-driven" hospital reform, starting with local-level hospitals, in 2000.[4] Independent, private dental care providers have since enjoyed rapid development. Currently, there are 65,000 private dental clinics and 187 private stomatology hospitals across China. Operating more than 200 clinics (10–15 dental chairs each) and

Table 13.1 Number of dentists vs. population

Country	No. of dentists per one million people	As of year
China	89	2013
UK	530	2012
Canada	580	2008
Japan	800	2010

hospitals (over 30 dental chairs each) in close to 50 cities in China, the BYBO Dental Group is one of the most successful players on the market.

Mr. Li, the founder and Chairman of the BYBO Dental Group, believes China offers tremendous market opportunities and "can hold thousands more clinics." His reasoning: the UK is a country with a population of only 63 million, but it has over 10,000 dental clinics. Taiwan, with a population of 23 million, has 6300 clinics. "The demand is there. Clinics are often surrounded by competitors, but they all manage to survive," says Li.

Another indicator of market potential is the ratio between the number of dentists to the total population. In developed countries, there is one dentist for every 500–1000 residents. As shown in Table 13.1, in China, there is less than one dentist for every 10,000 residents. People usually use the one million population to one dentist ratio to show the market potential, and as you can see from the table below, there is massive room for growth in this industry (see Table 13.1).

According to Euromonitor, the revenues of oral health hospitals reached RMB 11.3 billion in 2014, growing at a CAGR of 21.4% from 2010 to 2014.[5] Private service providers now contribute a significant percentage of the business. In terms of the number of treatments per patient in 2014, general hospitals (with their dental departments) still made up 51% of the market, mostly due to penetration and being able to offer lower prices. However, by 2014 specialist oral health hospitals already took a 24% share of all patients, while private health service providers, including dental chains, already had a 25% share of patients.

While BYBO with its 200 clinics is one of the biggest dental chains in China, the market is still fragmented, with most dental chains enjoying only regional relevance. There are thousands of individually run small clinics, as well as a few other dental chains.

Mr. Li observes that as a result of the reforms, the dental care business has been growing rapidly in China. During our interview in the city of Shenzhen, he joked with me that dental health is referred to as a malady of the rich. "In the past, Chinese people could only afford treatment when a tooth problem came up. As their quality of life has improved since the opening-up and reform, a consumer mentality has been evolving. People pay more attention to oral health and are willing to take preventive steps such as brushing their teeth more frequently."

According to Li, the dental care market in China has been gradually evolving from treatment-centric towards prevention-centric, adding: "This is a trend every dentist loves to see!"

In China, the cost of most dental care treatments is not covered by government-funded medical insurance. Given the poor experience many customers previously had in hospitals, with overtaxed doctors and nurses, and endless queuing, customers are now both more willing and able to pay for a nicely decorated clinic, better client service, and the zero waiting time offered by private clinics.

BYBO provides more specific services, like one particular catering to children, or offering affluent people more choices beyond tooth treatment. The prices remain slightly higher than those at public hospitals and vary depending on the specific products and services (unlike the uniform prices at public clinics). Customers no longer have to choose public hospitals because they're all they can afford. This is the opportunity for private dental clinics that Mr. Li is currently chasing. To build reputation quickly, he has applied a concept often quoted by Chinese entrepreneurs: "the 100-year-heritage business." His goal is to make his chain a household name, and one that has established a new standard.

Li dreams of creating a "100-year business" in the industry, as he sees dental care as an industry where "every individual has different needs at different stages of life," offering the opportunity to establish long-term relationships with clients. "If a family signs up to be our clients, I hope they will remain our clients in future generations, too."

Mr. Li was already a passionate dentist before he left the public hospital he worked at and went to Shenzhen to join a small private clinic. He believed there would be great opportunities when Deng Xiaoping visited southern China and made his famous speech in 1992. "I was sure that the future government policies would encourage individuals to establish private businesses. So I took unpaid leave from work," Li recalls with a chuckle.

With the simple goals of building a better life and realizing his personal potential, Li started his own business. Then came a setback, which again shows how complex it was to build a business in China back then, amidst constantly shifting regulations. Li contracted the stomatology department of a public hospital in Zhuhai, which was making losses at the time. He signed a 10-year contract with the hospital, renovated the facility completely, and turned it into a 30-chair, state-of-the-art dental clinic. Half a year later, the business was on the right track and began making profits. However, 2 years later, the Ministry of Health issued a new policy that prohibited public hospitals from contracting out any business. The hospital thus ended the deal, and Li had to spend another RMB 4 million to acquire a new clinic and continue operations.

Despite this blow, Li didn't lose his passion or confidence and endured his difficulties. In the early years of building his dental empire, he lacked the capital required for rapid expansion and instead relied on his profits to open new clinics. He remembers that even before he secured capital funding, none of his shareholders or the management team supported his plans to invest in the site. "At the beginning of operating this site (where we were sitting), we had only one clinic, and the profitability was poor. Many people eventually withdrew, and I was the only one who insisted on this site." Thanks to the brand power of BYBO and Li's persistence, the turnover of that Shenzhen clinic has since grown from RMB 200,000 per month to RMB 8 million.

By the end of 2010, Li operated seven clinics and one hospital, spread across four cities. Based on his understanding of the government's messages and new policies, Li expanded his dental chain by accurately anticipating changes. In October 2010, he heard that five ministries of the central government had made a joint announcement encouraging the development of private healthcare. "I believed the market potential would be stimulated by the government policies. The level of government support would be higher and the restrictions would be loosened," says Li. So as not to miss out on this opportunity, Li arranged an internal share reconstruction to prepare the business for embracing the capital market. Since then, on average more than 30 BYBO clinics have opened every year, and 100 new clinics opened in 2016 alone.

Mr. Li has a strategy for building network penetration, working down from provincial capital cities to regional cities and eventually to county-level cities. This is quite a common approach for chain stores. In each capital city, Li and his team strive to provide the most convenience for customers. Taking Shenzhen as an example, he explains, "There are eight administrative districts in Shenzhen. I hope we cover all districts, so consumers don't have to cross the district border for our dental care service. I want to have a few clinics in each district covering the most convenient locations, so as to provide consumers with high accessibility."

One factor that also applies to dental chains is economies of scale; therefore, chains tend to pursue funding to foster expansion early on—achieving deep penetration in each city also brings down overhead costs, especially those for supervisory talent, marketing costs, and management costs.

BYBO received a RMB 1 billion investment from Legend Holdings (the parent company of Lenovo Group) in mid-2014. The reasoning was that, since Legend Holdings has always been good at dealing with the government, it would help BYBO expand in the market.[6] Li feels that, since the government recognizes the BYBO brand and the management, it enjoys a competitive edge in terms of getting licenses. In China, it usually takes a clinic 6–8 months to get licenses from both the health bureau and industrial and commercial bureau. "The governments give us a great deal of support in the license application process, which gives us a great advantage in terms of opening new outlets," Li explains.

As the Chinese government encourages private healthcare, many investors coming from other industries have recently entered into the market. During this process, Li still sees a role for the government. "The government assumes supervision responsibility for the private healthcare industry. If outsiders come for profits only and go after achieving their short-term targets, their management may not be able to stay up to standard. When a problem occurs and consumers complain, the government will have to look into it and bear responsibility."

In Li's eyes, "attention to detail is the key to success." For him, "detail" refers to every aspect that ensures the quality of service that clients can enjoy at his clinics, including a spacious and comfortable clinic environment, advanced medical techniques, and state-of-the-art equipment.

Many of the clinics in Shenzhen, Zhuhai, and elsewhere that Li invested in were upgraded from the previous facility. For example, the previous owner of one of BYBO's sites in Zhuhai reported revenues of RMB 20,000 per month. Li managed to grow the revenue to over RMB 1 million per month at the same street location, on the same floor, and with the same signboard location by expanding the clinic from 4 chairs to 30 chairs. At the time, there were no large dental clinics in Zhuhai, and existing clinics used outdated equipment—so Li's new clinic stood out.

The greatest challenge Li encountered in growing a dental chain in China was getting the right talent, especially senior dentists to lead the clinics. Like other entrepreneurs, Mr. Li had to get creative in order to convince good people to join him—and, like many entrepreneurs in China, the first thing he did was to purchase apartments for those dentists who were willing to get on board. "By offering attractive packages for leading professionals, I managed to raise the quality of my team to a higher professional level," he says, adding, "That's how we managed to boost our revenues so quickly, and to enhance our brand image."

Most of the entrepreneurs I have interviewed for this book see the Internet as both a threat and an opportunity. Li primarily sees it as offering valuable opportunities, the first of which has to do with property: as retailers reduce their number of outlets, that real estate becomes available for BYBO to take over. Second, he sees technology as an enabler, helping him to reduce the time needed for dental treatments and to improve service. "The Internet is very helpful in terms of marketing and client service. Therefore its impact on us is not as disruptive as on traditional industries."

In Li's plans, BYBO will eventually become the largest dental care service provider in China and even in the world. Li sees quality at the center of his strategy. "The dental care market in China is vast. To stand out, we need to build our reputation upon quality and service. Along with BYBO's network expansion, quality has become the key to ensuring brand equity."

Further, Li aims to create a complete chain of upstream and downstream industries, such as medicine, materials, equipment, R&D, and manufacturing. For example, BYBO now provides a denture implant service, and Li wants to expand into denture design and manufacturing. He explains, "Building an upstream and downstream chain will empower me to operate in a positive cycle, with no dependence on any third-party suppliers."

In Li's view, introducing international standards is an indispensable step, because it gives private operators like BYBO a competitive edge over public hospitals. "We take talent development and the benefits of new technologies and new materials very seriously, especially knowledge transfer from abroad and the import of new materials." At BYBO, Li has established communication channels to overseas peers, including universities and colleges, to further enhance his clinics' management and technologies.

In China, private companies currently have an edge when it comes to learning from abroad, because they have the freedom to quickly implement changes on the ground, avoiding long, complicated approval processes unlike, say, SOEs or public facilities. This especially holds true for Medicare and especially for customer orientation. Li also sees how private companies can move quickly to improve entire industries. "When anything new comes up, we can watch and learn immediately. Fast decision-making is one of the reasons private businesses prosper."

I asked Li what kept him up at night. Not to my surprise, he said, "It's people"—in other words, the competition for talent. "The market lacks enough qualified practitioners." Also, though the Chinese government encourages the development of private clinics and hospitals, not many qualified professionals have pursued this path (yet). Lastly, many branded chain stores are now also growing, which has increased the competition for dental talent.

At the moment, the speed of training new dental care professionals can't keep up with the speed of BYBO's growth. To fill the gap, Li has taken a very aggressive move—he is currently in the process of creating his own dental college. Partnering with selected universities in the USA and Spain, Li will soon begin recruiting prominent dentistry professors to teach at BYBO's college.

As we neared the end of our interview, Li concluded that China's dental market is still in its infancy compared to the markets in developed countries. There is a huge gap in development, as well as substantial room for growth. "Through my efforts in the next ten years, I want to lay a solid foundation for a 100-year chain and build a Chinese brand that goes global. Few Chinese brands are well known globally. Many products carry an international brand name without any brand building of their own. I have the confidence, and I am ready to build a global brand made in China."

Impressed by the (shiny!) smile of confidence on his face, I can't wait to see it happen!

Acknowledgment This interview has been published with the kind permission of Mr. Li Changren.

Notes

1. http://finance.people.com.cn/n1/2016/0611/c1004-28425208.html
2. http://news.hxyjw.com/news/show-168873
3. http://www.nhfpc.gov.cn/guihuaxxs/s10748/201607/da7575d64fa04670b5f375c87b6229b0.shtml
4. http://www.askci.com/news/chanye/2015/06/16/171729mo15.shtml
5. Ibid.
6. http://china.caixin.com/2014-06-18/100691980.html

14

Protecting Lifestyle and Loved Ones: New China Life Insurance (NCI)

Insurance—No. 3 life insurance company—Kang Dian, Former Chairman (retired in 2016) (photo with kind permission of Mr. Kang Dian)

© The Author(s) 2018
C. Nothhaft, *Made for China*, DOI 10.1007/978-3-319-61584-4_14

Opportunity

On the basis of creating large agency networks and promoting customers' basic understanding that life insurance is something valuable, the industry has grown with a push to market approach. As consumers evolve, they might critically question the need for life insurance and might reject the agency selling model that has worked for selling life insurance so far. Life insurers are now reinventing themselves, offering a broader and more customized range of insurance products aimed at different concerns (e.g., family and kids concerns now), as well as products that provide security or a benefit now rather than in the distant future, e.g., life insurance.

Lessons Learned

Besides creating new insurance products, innovation in terms of sales channels is at the top of insurers' minds. As the distribution chain is crude, insurance companies are now repositioning themselves as life partners; covering different concerns, including health care; using big data to segment consumers according to various life stages and needs; and taking a softer and more customized approach to building distribution.

At my company—a large retail network of over 3000 stores—every year we have dozens of insurance cases: everything from customers slipping and getting injured in stores, to recently one of our contractors losing an entire truck, for which the insurance company had to pick up the entire bill. I had always been baffled how the math of insurance works, so writing this book offered me an opportunity to delve into the inner workings of insurance. And, when it comes to individual consumers, nothing is more consumer-related and personal than life insurance.

As an insurance customer in a mature market like Germany, I personally use several insurance products. I was wondering what the insurance market was like in a country like China. What I found: China's insurance industry, though not small, is still in its infancy. Key indicators such as penetration rate and density are among the lowest in the world, which means the potential for growth is huge.

As shown in Fig. 14.1, in 2015, the insurance business in China had reached RMB 2.4 trillion[1] (about US$353.4 billion) in size (by net premiums written), less than a third the value of the US insurance business, which reached US$1.2 trillion in the same year[2] (see Fig. 14.1). According to the National Bureau of Statistics (NBS), insurance represents a 6.4% share of the

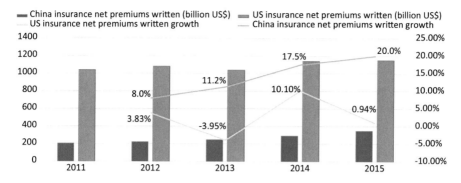

Fig. 14.1 Insurance premiums written in China vs. the USA. Source: NBS, Insurance Information Institute

Chinese consumer market. The life insurance industry in China is worth RMB 1.6 trillion (based on 2015 original premium revenues, according to the China Insurance Regulatory Commission[3]), which represents a 5% share of total consumer spending.

Operating an insurance business in China is no mean feat. The major players are fighting in the lower end segments of various consumer groups. A key revenue stream is the one-off insurances sold by low earning agents to one or just a few friends. Agent behavior and the fact that customers have not seen a benefit of insurance (the insurance industry is so young that we are still in the generation that is paying rather than receiving) have given the industry a bad reputation. The agent channel only remains stable by maintaining a huge workforce, and staff poaching is rampant. The bank sales channel as we know it in the West is expensive, but it only drives volume, not profits. Despite all these challenges, the insurance business is a profitable one, thanks to the overall market size of 1.3 billion people. These are the ingredients for the Chinese insurance market story.

The top 10 life insurance companies in China had a premium volume of about RMB 1.2 trillion in 2015. As Fig. 14.2 shows, the top insurer, China Life, has a market share of 30% of the combined Top 10 and 24.8% of the total market, making it the dominant player in that market. The number two, Ping An, has a share of 13% and the number 3, New China Life, a share of 7% (see Fig. 14.2). With the top three companies holding a combined market share of 43%, I suspected they would be huge behemoths, and no one would agree to an interview, especially not the chairman.

I was extremely pleased to get a positive reply to my invitation from NCI's legendary chairman Kang Dian after I explained the intentions of my book. Kang Dian was born in 1948, and he is extremely well connected in China's upper echelons.

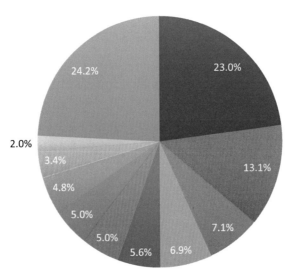

Fig. 14.2 Top 10 life insurance companies ranked by share of premium revenues, 2015. Source: China Insurance Regulatory Commission

Kang took over NCI in 2009 after a scandal, and it was no surprise that the government sent him to reorganize NCI (the ex-chairman was sent to prison then), as he had previously dealt with reorganizing Guangdong Enterprise Holdings (GDE) between 1998 and 2000. When the 1997 Asian Financial Crisis hit Hong Kong, GDE, a provincial-level state-owned enterprise, found itself insolvent of HK$9 billion at the end of 1998. As GDE was a so-called window company of the local government, government creditability was seriously jeopardized. Then-Premier Zhu Rongji assigned Mr. Wang Qishan to be the executive deputy governor of Guangdong and deal with the financial crisis. Kang Dian was the director and vice president of GDE and was also referred to as the soul of the debt-restructuring project. He demonstrated outstanding PR capabilities during a crisis. Through joint efforts made by the Guangdong government, GDE, and the debtors, the company's restructuring was completed in 2000 and has earned Kang Dian a good reputation, as have subsequent cases.

Since then, Kang has become very well known in the industry as a "cleanup chairman," and he certainly managed to turn NCI around—in fact, in

December, 2011 he took the company public in both Shanghai (SH: 601336) and Hong Kong (HK: 1336).

NCI is currently the number four in the overall insurance market and number three in life insurance and since 2014 has been listed as a Fortune 500 as well as a Fortune Global 500 company. In 2015, NCI had revenues of RMB 112 billion, and assets of RMB 660 billion, with profits of RMB 8.6 billion and a year-on-year growth of almost 35%. Unlike some of the other insurers, NCI is specialized in life insurance, and, according to the company, it served more than 27 million individual and 71,000 institutional customers by the end of 2016.

According to its annual report, the company has formulated a specific customer-centric strategy to capture the demographic trends driven by China's urbanization and aging population. This piqued my interest in understanding how this can be done with life insurance—one reason being that I was rewriting our customer strategy and I was wondering how to sell life insurance (a substantial investment in the future) to people who are more worried about their daily survival and their latest consumer dreams.

Since Mr. Kang couldn't make our first planned interview, the first step was meeting his secretary to the Executive Committee, Mr. Yang, with whom I shared a meal in the humble yet very clean NCI management staff canteen, which served as a conversation starter for us, discussing how to establish an open, Western-style corporate culture in a Chinese company.

On the way to their offices, I was still wondering about how to sell life insurance best—especially to young consumers who are more concerned about buying things or having a good night out with friends than life insurance. How can a company build trust with its consumers in a "new" market like this? How can people even afford life insurance here?

As it turns out—no matter how impressive NCI's numbers are—it all boils down to hard work. As Mr. Yang emphasized, "It's a new industry; penetration is only 4%—below India," making the point that it's both a great sector for potential growth and a hard sell.

Mr. Yang explained that the industry experienced a period of runaway growth until 2010, then slowed down dramatically after new regulations were imposed, and subsequently went through a trough from which the industry is only now emerging. Yang emphasized that the previous years had been good for NCI as consumers became more open-minded towards life insurance. This has been primarily driven by low interest rates offering little returns for the consumers' savings, which makes life insurance an alternative long-term savings option. However, growth from here onwards will be harder unless insurance companies find new products that address consumers' different concerns at this stage of development and unless they create a more effective—and less people-intensive—distribution system.

In my home country of Germany, the situation is just the opposite, where the insurance industry can penetrate all sorts of sectors, creating a culture whereby the middle class and well off see life insurance as a kind of wealth protection tool for their family or as a long-term investment tool for—say—retirement. But what is the situation in a country like China, where retirement seems far away for many young people, and the time between now and then is full of challenges and a "sense of uncertainty"?

According to Mr. Yang, around 60% of NCI's premium income comes from the lower end sector. In fact, its agents sell to friends based on personal trust, and many of the sales are one-offs (i.e., one agent, one customer—and that's it). As Yang puts it, "NCI now has 200,000 agents." However, since working as an agent doesn't pay well and is often viewed as being "pianzi" (meaning "cheater") in China, it's hard to recruit well-trained agents or agents who have access to a more extensive network of clients, as he elaborates.

Almost all staff that work for NCI are "one-person agents." The share of (more sophisticated) agencies with a larger or more extensive customer pool is very low.

According to Mr. Yang, in North America as well as the UK, 90% of the business comes from agencies; and in France, Spain, and Italy, 60–70% is from banks as the distribution channel. In Germany, the business is divided roughly 50/50 between agents and banks, with very little of the business coming from direct sales. "In China, the rule of thumb is half sales from agents and half from banks, but 90% of profits come from agents," says Yang, stressing that the bank channel is not so profitable and thus "ready for disruption."

Despite having a substantial cash flow, the life insurance industry has low penetration, a somewhat lower end positioning and an unsophisticated sales force—yet it is profitable. While Mr. Yang was elaborating, further challenges occurred to me, leading me off in another direction: what would it take to change all that, especially in the digital age, and what advantages would doing so create? Visions of dollar signs and happy, smiling customers kept filling my head. I also wondered if we retailers can play a role in distribution (with an agenda to check if my company could sell insurance, as we have some 10 million consumers walking into our stores every week).

I was trying to find out why the industry has not been disrupted in the way that retail has been impacted by online retailing. One apparent reason was regulation—it's more complicated to offer insurance in China and get the necessary approvals. Another reason is the fact that chairmen of the government-linked companies change every 3–5 years. Therefore, it is hard to find a pioneer who will take the risk of disrupting the industry—apparently, it would take more than one tenure to achieve the goal. Ping An is an exception, where the chairman is the major shareholder and can, therefore, push innovation harder than anyone else.

Given all of the above, it's no surprise that NCI is working on consumer-centricity and planning a more direct approach to customer sales. In fact, Mr. Yang stated that a quarter of the sales agents they have today alone now produce more sales than ever before. Technology is partly key to this, as well as CRM (customer relationship management).

Mr. Yang explains how the company serves existing customers. NCI has established a separate team to serve "orphan customers," whose agents have now gone (as agents in China are highly mobile). "We see a lot of opportunities among them, like cross-selling and upselling," says Yang.

NCI calls its strategy "one center—three pillars—two opportunities." What that means: customer-centricity (one center); improving the existing business, maintaining investment in innovation, and focusing on the core product of insurance (the three pillars). The two opportunities to pursue are taking advantage of urbanization and the aging population.

I felt my thoughts drift away a bit, from the issue of building more and more distribution towards starting with consumers' needs. According to NCI, the focus has to be on creating more suitable insurance products that address the concerns of different consumers and then finding the right channels to reach them—directly or potentially more indirectly. We shared further thoughts about how social networks can help to establish direct consumer relationships, and how CRM data can help understand consumers' current and future needs.

Leading the conversation towards what advantages the direct consumer relationship has to offer, we touched upon the agents once again. Loyalty is a significant challenge when it comes to agents in China.

Interestingly, in the "one agent, one client" insurance business, a key form of competition involves poaching staff. Yang shared that once NCI almost had to close their offices in a tier-two city, when a competitor simply hired their GM, and nearly all of the employees resigned and theirs agents switched to the competitor.

Of course, that led to the question of how to retain people, and to my surprise, Mr. Yang singled out "having better products than the competitor" as the key. This reminded me that, of course, Mr. Yang had worked for P&G before and was aware that the product is the key differentiator.

Once product development has been innovated more, NCI's plan would be to have a strong push in different consumer sectors, especially in the urban population, but with a clear focus on the younger generation. Equipped with more segmented products, the aim is to reach both affluent consumers with individualized premium products and to reach the mass consumer with a better value offer. All this is financed via efficiencies in distribution, such as a more efficient agency system or direct Internet sales.

NCI appears to be working on the respective IT platforms and social media networks to deliver this within the next few years. At the same time, it is developing a more varied agent network that will bring in more people from different walks of life. The banking sector will still play a role in distribution, but as yet, better ways to improve profitability have yet to be defined.

To better illustrate what this all means, Mr. Yang quotes an example of using "indirect customers" to build new product sales, quoting children's accident insurance, which allows the company to leverage parents' data with a view to selling them other products step-by-step, including life insurance for the "next generation's prosperity."

NCI has cooperated with the local government of Tianjin (a city of 15 million within a 1-hour drive from Beijing) to provide free accident insurance as a gift to all children going to school there. The children need to activate the product after they are granted the gift. NCI then calls the families after 1 or 2 months to ask them if they can take part in a survey once their child activates the product. "Then we build the connection," says Yang, adding, "We acquire the kids' data, parents' data, and a lot of other things. We carefully screen and filter to find out some people we can approach using a very gentle approach."

In effect, this involves filtering customers from a huge pool to a smaller one, but with stronger connections. Children (and their families) suitable for other NIC products will be assigned to high-performing agents. According to Yang, the conversion rate is very high and obviously higher than that of a cold call.

"We are trying to lead the new generation in acquiring new customers." The number of new customers aged 25–34 reported the fastest growth last year. Currently, customers aged 25–44 account for 52% of total customers. "'To be a life adviser first' might be the new slogan for NCI's future customer relationship agents," Yang says. This approach is comparable to what is happening at other companies we interviewed for this book.

As mentioned before, Mr. Kang was unable to attend the first interview, but we managed to find a new opportunity a few weeks later. I felt so lucky when I arrived at his Beijing office (for tea, of course) just in time for his retirement 3 days later. And it turned out to be a very interesting hour with a chairman who has now reached mandatory retirement age, but whose mind and health are still in their prime.

Mr. Kang was well informed as to who I was and made perceptive remarks about my company's leading position in the market. He mentioned that the market is imbalanced now, as e-commerce platforms allow so many merchants to trade—many of which enjoy cost advantages by simply not paying taxes or employee benefits. Great! A good start and it set the tone for talking about disruption and how established companies respond to it.

Mr. Kang, though nearing retirement, appeared to be well informed about the digital world, which is at the top of his agenda. He seems to be the pioneer when it comes to digital at NCI. "I once held a nearly three-hour internal speech about the Internet. I have been pushing forward digitalization within our company." He proudly stated his openness for the modern age and was quite specific about NCI becoming a big data company and changing its distribution system.

Kang: "One direction that is highly likely to work is the integration of online and offline with the support of Internet technology, Cloud, and mobile technology." For this purpose, NCI had several projects in the pipeline—small scale for now—and it sounded like some of them would be rolled out sooner rather than later.

According to Kang, this is in keeping with the global trend for insurance companies. "We have done extensive research on insurance companies around the world. Many companies are thinking the same way and doing trials at a small scale. I haven't seen anybody else who has thought this through more systematically and completely than I have."

Mr. Kang immediately followed up by clarifying that he was thinking about a revolution rather than an evolution, and this might even take the regulators by surprise. He also pointed out that the market is consumer driven and change is necessary, since large companies based on existing models have been successful for too long.

"The regulators have even less time to think about this. It's about rebuilding a new model." He indicated that disruption is already happening in the insurance industry and that—likely by default—regulators will potentially have to adapt, to follow what the consumer wants.

The fact that even a rather traditional peer like NCI is working on a customer evolution took me by surprise and yet made good sense, since understanding consumer needs and the rapid evolution of consumer spending in new sectors is crucial to any business. Entire industries, such as insurance, are in competition for both more consumers and more wallet share.

As part of their strategy of becoming a "life partner," NCI is building health centers focused on health checkups. The company currently has 16 centers up and running, and the core centers are offering blood testing. Mr. Kang seems to have a broader vision, highlighting that services like blood testing are too rudimentary in many areas of China, and could be improved. "For example, a blood test conducted in a Chinese hospital now tells you the results for 200 indicators. We have learned that in Germany new technologies can cover 2,000 indicators in just one blood test."

This sounded very strange to me! We have so many crossover business formats these days. Could there be a new healthcare company in the making? I don't want to start any rumors here, but simply to show how a new market provides the opportunity for sectors to evolve faster if driven by nontraditional players—a phenomenon we're now seeing around the world. Let's see how this pans out!

At the time we met, some major overseas investments by Chinese companies were in the works, so I was eager to ask Mr. Kang about his views, and he seemed to be in favor of the right overseas investments but somewhat appalled by insurance companies' apparent lack of strategy when it comes to investing clients' money. His most important point was the need for a self-restrained and strategic approach when investing overseas. His view was some of the deals are done for the wrong reasons and are therefore overpriced. The government is also now reacting to some of the "show-off" investments made by some insurance companies overseas. "Starting from last year we have been increasing the size of overseas investments. We had planned a further increase, but the government has been enforcing tighter controls on outbound capital."

Mr. Kang seemed particularly open-minded that morning, so I couldn't resist asking him what he would do if he didn't go into retirement, and where he could see NCI being in the next 5 years.

"If I could stay with this company for another term, I would be able to bring more new things to NCI."

It seems Mr. Kang would like to see his vision of innovation and a new insurance model fulfilled—hardly surprising for a chairman who never stops thinking and innovating.

Acknowledgment This interview has been published with the kind permission of Mr. Kang Dian.

Notes

1. http://data.stats.gov.cn/easyquery.htm?cn=C01
2. http://www.iii.org/fact-statistic/industry-overview
3. http://www.circ.gov.cn/web/site0/tab5179/info4014824.htm

Part IV

The Food: Aspiring to a Healthy and Fashionable Diet

As a nation, China has a dark past, with the great famine still remembered by many of today's society. Feeding over a billion people in a country that is not universally blessed with water and good soil has been at the center of politics for thousands of years. In today's consumer world, supply may not be at the top of consumers' priorities but rather the healthiness and safety of food. Food safety is most likely consumers' primary concern, as even reliable brands have made headlines over the years due to food scandals arising from supply chain issues.

China has a hugely diverse set of local cuisines. As such, food is deeply engrained into Chinese culture. This can be seen in the fact that traditionally one asks: "Have you eaten?" as a form of greeting, meaning: "How are you?."

The Chinese have a preventative attitude toward health, and food plays a key medicinal role. Depending on the season, your age, and state of well-being, if you have Chinese friends they will keep reminding you what you should and should not eat. In fact, they will bring you the goodies to eat and drink that will ensure you will get well or simply protect you from catching a winter bug. The same applies to ordering in a restaurant, which might include scorpion soup in winter (an extreme example) or ginger tea when you are sneezing. Besides the daily food order, Traditional Chinese Medicine often replaces the function of Western supplements like Vitamin C. As society continues to evolve and people grow more used to Western products, I see more and more blends of traditional products or flavors presented in a modern form, which means there are plenty of opportunities to blend "food beliefs" with the capabilities of Western consumer brands to create future Chines megabrands.

Dietary habits have also changed and keep changing in China. One example is that traditionally Chinese people like to drink soymilk, yet more consumers now drink cow's milk and all its sweet derivatives. Some of these trends are creating real problems regarding future supply, which explains why China (via its private or state-owned companies) is now buying up more and more land overseas or making direct investments in the food industry. Chinese people have also quickly latched on to Western shopping formats, and supermarkets or convenience stores have become ubiquitous. Likewise, fast-food chains have largely replaced street vendors or individual restaurants.

What has not developed well is the Chinese consumer's overall confidence in the food supply chain—from farming to the supermarket shelf. There have been many big scandals over the decades in the food sector, so that consumers have a general concern about food safety, often resulting in mistrust of local brands and local manufacturing. Ten or so years ago, I built and managed a food manufacturing business that brought me close to the primary production sector, as well as to the food supply chain, and has given me some insights into this issue. What a huge area of opportunity!

And then—in my view—the biggest area of potential is the fact that China is due to run out of protein. According to a report prepared by RABOBANK in February 2016, China (and Hong Kong) ranks no. 1 among consistent importers of animal protein. So the food sector, from farming to production to any form of the supply chain from restaurants to supermarkets is a great area for current or future business growth.

So, with the memory of the Great Famine (1959–1961)—which killed 36 million people, or 5.4% of the population at the time—still in mind, feeding a population of 1.3 billion people is the core task at hand for the Chinese government.

Back to food safety: When we look at the food value chain the interesting thing is that the gap in values, mind-set, and even basic education between people in the primary sectors (farmers, most of them around the poverty line with little or no education and a value system that halted evolution for half a century) and the urbanite consumers is very extreme.

Customers have high expectations regarding product quality and food safety, while farmers want to increase their incomes, as they are on the slow track of wealth development. This creates all sorts of challenges and opportunities from increasing basic production yields in the primary sector and securing healthy livestock to building efficient, traceable supply chains, improving food production facilities, and developing products that are safe and suitable for different types of consumers.

The challenges, like a lack of awareness regarding food safety in the primary sector and ruthless businesses selling unsafe products to consumers, were the source of many headlines in the news over the past several years: the 2008 melamine scandal that killed six infants; pigs that washed up in Shanghai's Huangpu River in 2013, dumped by farmers in outlying provinces to reduce production; and five crises involving fast-food chain stores like KFC within 8 years, starting from 2005.

Helping to improve the food chain in terms of productivity and safety is one of the greatest tasks and thus provides one of the largest opportunities for business and investment in China—in the short and medium term, perhaps even THE largest!

Demand, especially among young urbanites, is evolving and here it's not just about the food they buy or the drinks they like to consume. Younger consumers have grown up with a very different lifestyle. They like traditional food but maybe not served in the form their parents were used to and prefer more urban and Westernized formats, e.g., air-conditioned fast-food stores over street corners or tea type drinks that are marketed like a Coca-Cola type of FMCG over brands that focus on emphasizing their long heritage.

The following section describes various aspects of the Chinese food consumer market.

The dairy industry is highly concentrated in the hands of only a few companies. When I came to China, most people I knew loved to drink soymilk, and by now, especially the younger generation appreciates milk, and especially latches on to functional drinks related to dairy and yogurt. Yili is China's number one dairy company and a good example of how companies can build sourcing (globally), increase product know-how, and establish professional consumer brands.

We will meet the owner of the number one supermarket company and hear his thoughts on food safety and what supermarkets need to do to stay close to the convenience-seeking urban residents. We will learn what kind of shopping formats are in the pipeline and why overseas sourcing is becoming more and more important for local supermarket players.

The largest dumpling chain in China is a reflection of what has been happening in the area of daily staples—a quick lunch or convenience foods—which has been changing dramatically as cities "clean up the streets" by removing street vendors, while urbanites are more and more turning to branded chain-store types of outlets for their daily lunch.

"Old China hands" are still familiar with the heavy (binge) drinking culture that the country used to be famous for, including perhaps painful memories of hangovers from Chinese Baijiu (pronunciation of liquor in Chinese) and

Moutai (the most famous Chinese distilled liquor brand). The consumer conscience, which is now moving toward healthier drinking, has opened up an opportunity for traditional health wines combined with marketing for younger people.

Staying with the "health" trend, some large-scale pharmaceutical companies heavily engaged in regulated areas are not seeking to go beyond those sectors, venturing not just into OTC (over-the-counter) drugs but also making real consumer goods, competing with the likes of Coke and Pepsi (and winning).

15

Brand Trust: Yili

Dairy—No. 1 dairy company—Pan Gang, Chairman (photo with kind permission of Mr. Pan Gang)

© The Author(s) 2018
C. Nothhaft, *Made for China*, DOI 10.1007/978-3-319-61584-4_15

Opportunity

Chinese dairy companies evolved from large state-controlled monopolies, some of which were later privatized. As Chinese consumers change habits, including drinking more and more milk (think of all the lattes that Starbucks sells, and you can see the trend), keeping up with dairy supply is a challenge for China and a huge opportunity for dairy companies to expand.

Following the global consumer trend, dairy companies now offer more than milk and are venturing into specialty products, e.g., yogurts and functional drinks to match the tastes of today's urbanites. The Chinese market is following the same trend, and thus dairy companies are seeking to establish multiple brands in different categories. As the companies grow, they secure both brand expertise—including manufacturing technology and practices—and product supply, not only in China but also overseas.

Lessons Learned

The dairy supply chain in China is a tricky business, as same major scandals made headlines with farmers "upgrading" their milk products by adding melamine to achieve a higher yield and price a few years ago. Such cases are also a reflection of the two-tier speed of social development between the urban and rural populations. In the context of establishing new brands and products to suit evolving customer needs, Chinese dairy companies are under considerable pressure to become global leaders in supply chain and quality management, and to ensure product safety.

China witnessed a significant milestone in its development in 2015, when for the first time the majority of its population became urban. This has sparked a fundamental change in the urban–rural relationship, along with changing diet habits that now include more Western foods. This shift has been accompanied by new foods, and no element has been more significant than dairy products.

Before the 1990s, China had little or no dairy industry to speak of. Even after EU involvement in building China's dairy industry during that period, the local dairy market represented consumption of only 1.25 million tons by 1998.

How things have changed since then! By 2014, dairy consumption had reached 26.4 million tons[1]—a phenomenal increase. Liquid milk alone represented 87% of that consumption.[2] Consumption patterns have also been changing, with fresh milk consumption being only 4.1 kg per urban household in 1981 and rising to 14 kg per urban household by 2012.[3] Euromonitor expects this to nearly double in value, from RMB 377 billion in 2015 to RMB 602 billion by 2020. At this rate, China will overtake the USA as the largest dairy market worldwide by 2017.

In the short term, imported milk is expected to play an increasingly significant role in the market. There are in total (both online and offline retailers) around 800–1000 imported milk brands on the Chinese market, 3–4 times as many as in 2010. Imported milk grew from 7000 tons a year in 2008 to 460,000 tons a year, with a CAGR of more than 80%.[4]

Instead of being driven by availability, the increase of imported milk is mostly driven by consumer preferences. Previously available through online retailers such as Yihaodian and Tmall, imported milk is gaining shelf space in hypermarkets and supermarkets as customers have become used to having both local and imported alternatives side by side. Locally manufactured milk products are also popular, but consumers increasingly tend to prefer the local product output of overseas manufacturers. This increased accessibility to foreign dairy brands serves to enhance consumer awareness and drives a constant temptation to trade up.

Further, there are some specifics and trends about the dairy industry that bear consideration. Reliant on small-scale farmers, whose incomes and margins are small, the dairy supply chain has remained highly fragmented for a long time, and this has created a situation in which supply-side food security can be significantly compromised. The most serious case highlighting this weakness in the supply chain was the 2008 melamine scandal, which resulted in six infant fatalities (from milk powder laced with melamine, used to bulk out poor-quality raw milk) and made 300,000 other children sick, with kidney issues caused by the contaminated milk powder.[5] Between September 14th and 20th 2008, during the Poisonous Milk Incident, the Baidu Index of melamine reached its peak at 47,373, while the average index for the word was generally below 1000.

It reminded me of the concern for safety at my own company. From my observations, Chinese people have always been concerned about the connection between food and health. However, when the melamine scandal broke, the issue of food safety, food dealers' behavior, and the safety of the entire value chain became one of the hottest topics in the country. I remembered what steps we had taken, testing products and regular checking with all suppliers. Anecdotally, when we moved into our new offices in 2010, I made sure we positioned our QAS lab on the same corridor as our main supplier meeting room.

My thoughts echoed those of Mr. Pan Gang, the Chairman of China's no. 1 dairy company. Pan's general observation was that the "purchasing power of the Chinese people keeps growing," yet he immediately added that "consumers pay more attention to health and nutrition."

While somewhat compromised by the safety issue, the infant milk formula market and its cross-border component represent an ongoing opportunity. According to RABOBANK, China's infant formula market grew at 16% by volume between 2000 and 2013, with international players capturing the largest share of this growth. This volume growth will be cut in half by 2020, but still growing by 7–8%, driven largely by income growth and improving distribution networks to lower-tier cities and rural areas. New onshore and offshore capacity expansion projects, invested in by Chinese dairy companies, account for 640,000 tons of new infant formula capacity annually, equivalent to 45% of the total market volume in China in 2015.[6]

We see, then, that China's dairy market is undergoing rapid diversification into one more similar to Western markets. Increasingly, there are specific dairy products for different functional needs, catering to health improvement, fitness, recovery, and sheer indulgence. From being an occasional essential to replacing soymilk, this sector has now achieved critical mass, becoming a major consumer favorite and fueling more and more consumption. It's exciting news for the industry, especially for companies that are combining the differentiating taste buds of consumers with a deep value chain.

Until recently, I hadn't realized just how big Yili is. It ranked no. 8 among the RABOBANK 2016 Global Dairy Top 20—making it the highest-ranking Asian dairy enterprise. As shown in Fig. 15.1, the key players on China's dairy

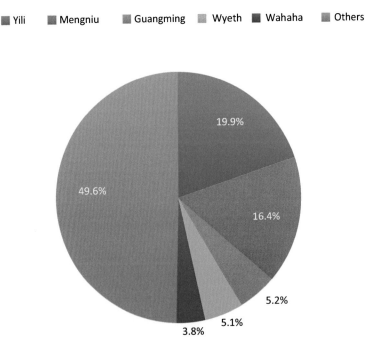

Fig. 15.1 China's Top 5 dairy players in 2016. Source: Nielsen (http://www.dairyreporter.com/Markets/Party-over-for-infant-formula-firms-as-China-s-remarkable-demand-slows)

market are Yili, Mengniu, Guangming, Wyeth, and Wahaha. The five leading dairy companies have a combined market share of nearly 50% (see Fig. 15.1).

With a year-on-year sales growth of 10.88%, Yili's net revenues in 2015 reached RMB 60.3 billion, exceeding RMB 60 billion for the first time in its history, with a net profit of RMB 4.65 billion. The company is vast with nearly 100 subsidiaries. Its four major business divisions include liquid milk, ice cream, milk powder, and yogurt. Albeit its revenues primarily come from milk (78% of its total revenues), it is now making more and more consumer products, including its growing ice cream business, which represented an 11% share of its revenues in 2015.

Mr. Pan confirmed that the company's initial growth stemmed from developing alongside the wider Chinese economy, as well as through the company's own efforts.

Yili was founded in 1956 as a cooperative dairy farm and was operated in a rather traditional way until major changes came when the company decided to restructure it into a joint stock company in February 1993. This is how the company became the Yili Group as we know it today. It was clear that the new course was set towards FMCG: In July 1993, Yili launched its ice cream division. The company went to IPO in Shanghai in March 1996, becoming the first listed company in the dairy sector and leading China's milk industry into a new era. By 2000, Yili ranked first in China's milk industry, both in terms of profit and tax. Five years later, one of its newer growth drivers, the yogurt division, was established.

There is little difference between the way Yili operates and that of international conglomerates. It has a clear mission, that is, to be the most reliable provider for healthy food. That "We Keep Innovating for Human's Healthy Lifestyle" is what the company advocates, which is an interesting reflection of our so-often repeated mantra that companies need to keep up with people's lifestyles and that following trends is essential for companies to stay in the market.

Given Yili's size and the company's shift towards diversifying into more and more (young) consumer products, I was keen to hear about consumer trends and market changes from its chairman, Mr. Pan Gang. Also, I wanted to know what competitors were doing and what role the Internet played in the dairy industry.

We kicked off with a geography lesson. "In the past Chinese consumers didn't have the habit of drinking milk. They often drank soybean milk and deep-fried dough sticks for breakfast. Drinking milk was not a custom in China due to geographical and farming restrictions," said Pan.

Geographically speaking, China is immense. The habit of drinking milk in larger quantities followed the country's economic development, which focused on the urban areas, mostly the cities in the Eastern belt and Southern China (especially Guangdong) and some areas in the middle. However, the dairy industry is mostly located in the north of China. Therefore, from the very beginning, the dairy supply chain and value chain were destined to be a challenge. In the past, milk products could only be kept for 2–3 days. It was common that, when dairy products from cattle in the North were shipped to consumers in the South, they deteriorated underway. Recognizing this gap, Yili introduced modern technologies from overseas to extend the shelf life of milk to between 6 and 8 months, making it possible to distribute high-quality milk from Northern China to consumers across the country, "especially the economically developed areas where consumers could afford milk consumption and cared more about health," as Pan explained.

To fit the needs of brand-conscious consumers in Eastern/Southern cities, Yili had to innovate and "learn branding" at an early stage. Also, Yili invested considerable effort into the education of consumers by promoting the benefits of dairy products.

As the company scaled up to cover the entire nation, it established manufacturing facilities in over 30 provinces. According to Mr. Pan, prompt delivery to consumers became one reason for its brand satisfaction, helping Yili become the leader in the domestic dairy market.

The journey to get there was one of learning about consumer habits arising from geographical differences. Mr. Pan feels that the market still has a way to go: "If you look at milk consumption per capita, there is still a big gap between China and overseas countries." Pan says China's annual milk consumption is only 20 kg per capita, while the world's average is over 100 kg and in developed countries like the USA and Europe, it is about 200–300 kg.

In Pan's eyes, the greatest potentials lie not only in the dairy market but also in the related FMCG market. "Juice consumption per capita is also much lower in China compared to overseas markets," says Pan, continuing, "Although Yili focuses on dairy products now, it aims to be a provider of healthy food in the future." According to Pan's study, Chinese people consume only 1/10 the juice per capita compared to their counterparts overseas. Pan believes there is still huge room for juice, health supplements, and health food to grow in the future.

As for the overall economy, Mr. Pan did not seem to be overly concerned: "As you can see, China's economy is facing a bottleneck in the short term. Due to impacts from the global economy, we can see that the economy is at a critical stage. It had been growing at high speed in the past and had gradually slowed to a steady rate over the last two years." In the past, China's GDP growth was never lower than 7–8%, and according to Pan, it will likely be set at around 6.5% in the 13th Five Year Plan.

Although I had not intended to ask anything regarding the current state of the economy, I was pleased to see such positivity and confidence on the part of Mr. Pan, who surely has better access to the inner workings of China than I.

Back to the food safety issue: in our business, we deal with food products every day. In fact, Chinese food quality laws and food safety regulations are very strict. In Pan's experience, the quality standards in China for the dairy industry are much higher than those in the USA, EU, or New Zealand. "We have a much wider range of quality indicators in China that require mandatory tests," says Pan. He remembers that when building the manufacturing facility based on the New Zealand standards, the company could not pass the quality tests required in China. "We had to source laboratory equipment from all over the world to upgrade the laboratory in New Zealand plant, so as to enable it to conduct the tests required by the Chinese standards before we could resume delivery to China," Pan recalls.

The Chinese government is extremely strict as a deterrent to forcing especially mid-size and smaller companies, which might lag behind in investment or mindset when it comes to food safety. Big companies like Yili, therefore, take pride in creating strong value chains, which is sometimes just the opposite of what I've experienced in China myself. The weak links are often in initial primary production and the mindset at basic levels of the value chain.

Pan is very conscious of food safety issues: "The industry chain of dairy production is the longest in the food industry." Yili needs to make sure every single part of the industry chain is well managed. Accordingly, in 2014, it implemented a comprehensive QA program dubbed the "3-2-1-0 strategy," which entailed QA ranging from management to processes, the goal being "zero food safety incidents."

Yili has made huge investments in the QA area. Due to its size and the risks on the Chinese market, Pan points out that the cost of quality management invested by Chinese dairy companies is much higher than that of foreign counterparts, quoting Yili's total QA costs at the end of 2015, which amounted to RMB 565 million.

I felt in the interview that presenting a fairer portrait of Chinese companies' efforts to ensure food safety was very important to Mr. Pan. While individual cases can be serious, there are food safety cases everywhere; yet due to the prevalence of social media, those that arise in China seem to grab both national and global headlines more immediately.

Pan emphasized what I have so often experienced with companies in China. The dynamics of the market, weakness in human capital, and sometimes resources have been making well-managed Chinese companies not just resilient but also better equipped to learn and adapt, sometimes leapfrogging technology or process steps.

Further, with most of them being cash-rich, Chinese companies can afford to invest heavily in the latest technology, especially since the payback due to high business growth is practically guaranteed. Therefore, Chinese companies are extremely adept and confident when it comes to technology. If we take Yili as an example, as it expands its manufacturing capacity to fit growing demand on the market, each new plant is equipped with the latest technology, allowing the company to stay cutting-edge. According to Pan, the company is equipped with robot manipulators made in Germany, product lines from Germany's Combibloc and Sweden's Tetra Pak, as well as Asia's largest three-dimensional storage system.

My observation has been that this process is much slower in the West, where markets grow more gradually. Pan summed this up nicely: "Since foreign market grows slowly, foreign companies are not in a position to keep technology and equipment up-to-speed." Pan is confident that "no company can beat Yili in terms of technological advancement and equipment" and explains that, "It is not because we are stronger than our global peers, but because, as we have kept building new plants in recent years, we were always the first to apply the most advanced technology and equipment in our factories."

The underlying point: As Chinese companies are growing fast, their short innovation cycles are rapidly pushing them to buy the latest equipment. Compared to the West, where replacement happens over years and after payback, Chinese companies could generally become more likely to have the latest equipment.

The company has also continued to focus on overseas growth, including acquisitions to ensure the milk supply and the evolution of their products. We talked briefly about the motives behind Chinese food companies making overseas acquisitions, and we both agreed the real goal here is not global market share but to either secure supply or (more often than not) to make better products for the domestic market.

In fact, Chinese companies are doing so to learn how to make safer products or how to improve the supply chain. Mr. Pan cited Yili's RMB 3 billion investment in New Zealand in 2014, which was well received after initial criticism from the local government. Yili combined the investment into manufacturing offshore there, which involved the use of New Zealand-made equipment and providing loans and support to local farmers. Pan proudly mentioned that now New Zealand wants Yili to build a second-stage plant.

I was keen to explore Mr. Pan's insights into the Chinese consumer in general, especially the sensitivity to spending. Pan believes Chinese consumers' behavior is closely linked to the social welfare system, "which was lagging behind in the past; as a result, consumers are worried that if they spend a lot, they will not be able to raise their kids or pay for their retirement." Over the years, China's social welfare system has improved, but the impact remains—Chinese consumers are not willing to spend extravagantly, even if they are wealthy.

"Chinese consumers care about not only their own lives, but also the lives of their children, including their jobs, housing, and living conditions. They are very family-centric and therefore only spend when they feel 100% confident that they are financially capable of supporting their family's future needs," Pan adds.

This situation is totally different than what is happening overseas, where many people are short of cash and are using up their money. Pan further explains that this is why people always say there are many opportunities on the Chinese market if the spending behavior of the still rather conservative consumer can be changed. "The government is now also driving the internal demand and encouraging people to spend," Pan confirms, making it official. From my observation, this process is already underway, and will develop exponentially once our GenMobile consumer generation moves higher up the salary ladder.

Therefore, Yili and Mr. Pan are extremely keen to keep pushing forward the value-added agenda and to pursuing product innovation. The company has launched Shuhua Low-lactose Milk, which targets the needs of Asian people, QQ Star for children, and the low-fat milk Byebye for younger consumers.

Premiumization is also a trend, with a growing awareness of the benefits of pro/pre-biotic products and consumers already showing considerable interest in ambient spoonable yogurt. According to a Euromonitor report, consumers believe this high-end yogurt offers healthier practical benefits, as it incorporates better quality bacteria and undergoes superior processing techniques.[7]

It is no surprise that leading players are seeking to launch new high-end products, such as Mengniu's Just Yogurt and Yili's Ambpoeial in 2014. According to Yili, by November 2016, sales of Ambpoeial showed a growth of 114% compared with the same period the previous year.

Yili also partners with international consultants and groups to explore what future model the company could use to generate better innovations. It is quite different from most large-sized companies I have met in China, which still think innovation takes place in laboratories. Yili seems to be a pioneer in terms of searching for ways to do things more in tune with modern times. It is currently developing an R&D center in Europe and a Sino-US Food Wisdom Valley in the USA. In New Zealand, Yili cooperates with local agricultural universities and institutions to build R&D arms. According to Pan, the company has ongoing collaborations with partners such as McKinsey, IBM, Roland Berger, and Accenture. In 2016, he even led a team to visit companies like Facebook and LinkedIn to absorb their leading operation philosophies.

Pan is convinced that, as the market situation keeps changing, only confident and well-organized companies with a good consumer understanding will thrive. "Through the integration of global institutional resources and information we make innovative progress in creating products that meet the consumer needs," says Pan. It seems there are no plans for Yili to take over the world, but plans to bring better products to China.

Almost as a given, Mr. Pan fully embraces the Internet and e-commerce. "The Internet grants us additional access to consumers and enables us to communicate and deliver products to them in a faster manner." In 2016, according to the company's own records, it covered more than 250 data sources across the online platform, thus enabling it to analyze 90% of the online sales.

We were nearing the end of our interview time and I was keen to ask a fundamental question, namely where Mr. Pan hopes Yili will be 5–10 years from now. While focusing on the core business, Mr. Pan also foresees some shifts and—as I interpret it—these revolve around superior product knowledge: "Now we have a new vision to be a leading health food product provider globally. This vision will lead us to expand from dairy products to food."

Currently, Yili is the eighth largest dairy company in the world and the number one in Asia. Mr. Pan's next goal is to become number five in the world. "It is quite challenging because of the changes in the macroeconomic environment of China and the fierce competition," adds Pan.

For Pan, the goal will be hard to reach if the company solely relies on internal growth. That's the reason Yili is also considering external growth, such as M&A to diversify the business. According to Pan, "In the meantime, we are also looking at other areas like vegetable protein drinks including soybean milk and walnut milk, etc."

In closing, Pan added a statement that is representative of what I keep saying to foreign companies who are not innovating in China—namely, that local companies will understand their consumer better and will follow their changing tastes better. As Pan put it: "We have had some new products already, which offer better quality and taste than import products and are a better fit for Chinese consumers' needs."

As for me, I would like to see Pan's dream—building Yili into a major food conglomerate in the future—come true!

Acknowledgment This interview has been published with the kind permission of Mr. Pan Gang.

Notes

1. National Bureau of Statistics of China, http://data.stats.gov.cn/easyquery.htm?cn=B01
2. KPMG, http://www.kpmg.com/CN/zh/IssuesAndInsights/ArticlesPublications/Documents/China-Milk-and-Dairy-Market-2015-201504-c.pdf
3. National Bureau of Statistics of China, http://data.stats.gov.cn/easyquery.htm?cn=C01
4. http://news.xinhuanet.com/food/2016-10/27/c_1119795134.htm
5. Forbes, http://www.forbes.com/sites/yanzhonghuang/2014/07/16/the-2008-milk-scandal-revisited/#6bed7f9b4428
6. http://www.cnagri.com/ruye/aigeshidian/20160429/381345.html
7. http://www.dairyreporter.com/Markets/Party-over-for-infant-formula-firms-as-China-s-remarkable-demand-slows

16

Supermarket Sophistication: Yonghui

Supermarkets—No. 1 supermarket chain—Zhang Xuanning, Chairman (photo with kind permission of Mr. Zhang Xuanning)

© The Author(s) 2018
C. Nothhaft, *Made for China*, DOI 10.1007/978-3-319-61584-4_16

Opportunity

The increased competition among supermarkets, combined with shoppers evolving as different segments, has created a need for innovation. Further, supermarkets are at the forefront of food safety concerns for Chinese consumers. To set themselves apart from the competition, the best operators work on creative new store and shopping formats (both online and offline), to get more in tune with today's consumers. At the same time, as consumers are highly aware of food safety issues, supermarkets are evolving their sourcing and supply chain capabilities to bring more brands and direct imports to China.

Lessons Learned

A mix of national and regional players is competing openly, with online heating up the game at all levels of the vast Chinese market. The game is intensifying and has turned into a veritable battle royal for market share. Consolidation is already happening (such as the joint venture linking CRE and Tesco), and this process will likely accelerate. Pure-play Internet models have shaken up the market, and now established supermarkets like Yonghui are developing ecommerce competence at scale.

I had heard that some of the billionaires in modern China were the founders of supermarkets and hypermarket chains, so I was eager to find out how many billionaires came from this industry. After consulting China's Hurun Rich List for 2014, I found that 52 of the country's 1271 billionaires had a retail background (the number increased to 67, though with a percentage drop from 4.1% to 3.6%, in 2015).

Taking a quick look at the supermarket chain growth rates in 2015, I saw that Yonghui was the second fastest growing company in the supermarket sector at 14.7% (year-on-year) based on an already large company with RMB 42.15 billion (US$6.1 billion) in sales. Before that, the company had maintained a year-on-year growth of more than 20% for 5 consecutive years. With that background in mind, I was keen to interview Zhang Xuanning, Yonghui's Chairman. While preparing for the interview I discovered that his was a real rags-to-riches story or could be called "from farmer to billionaire in 15 years." Mr. Zhang was the youngest chairman of a Shanghai-listed Chinese company when Yonghui (SH: 601933) listed in 2010, at a staggering PE ratio of 73.6! By way of comparison, Wal-Mart's PE ratio then stood at 13.43.

Taking a look at the share war between China's online retail market and offline market, it's no exaggeration to say that Yonghui has achieved a good

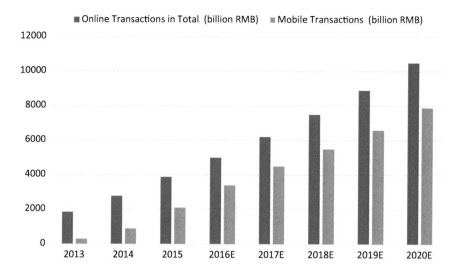

Fig. 16.1 Mobile transaction growing more popular in China. Source: China e-Business Research Centre (http://www.ebrun.com/20160520/176832.shtml)

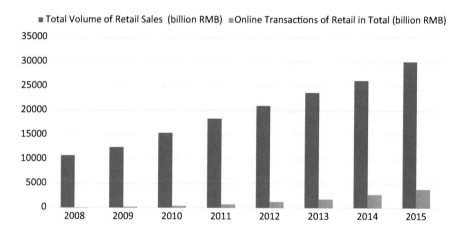

Fig. 16.2 China's online retail market is fighting for consumers. Source: iResearch, NBS (http://www.iyiou.com/p/24138)

score. China's online FMCG market, with a transaction value of 3.83 trillion in 2015 shown in Fig. 16.1,[1] is huge and growing fast (see Fig. 16.1). The top four players (Taobao, Tmall, YHD, and JD) cover 90% of the market.[2]

As shown in Fig. 16.2, the core of this war for market share is the new shopper acquisition and traffic building (see Fig. 16.2). In a recent conversation with an insider at one of the top online supermarket companies, I was told that, due to the high level of competition, the per-customer acquisition cost had risen from RMB 8 to RMB 90 in the past 5 years. The current battlefield is how retailers can bring goods to the consumer faster. In mature cities, supermarket companies now offer delivery within 1 hour of an order and often for free. With low average order value, it's no wonder that many companies lose money on almost every order. The current scenario is less "winner takes all" and more "last man standing."

The intensified competition for market share with different consumer groups explains in part why there has been the emergence of more sophisticated "high-end" supermarkets, which are segmenting supermarkets into different price bands and "lifestyle themes." Since 2008, the consumer market has shifted towards younger consumers, who are more open to and are in search of more lifestyle and branded items. The "boutique" trend has accelerated tremendously in recent years. Most locally run supermarket chains now have different brands, such as CRC Vanguard's Olé and Yonghui's Bravo stores, which they use to cater to different consumer clusters, including a more "modern consumer."

China has only taken about 20 years to arrive at a tipping point, where local competitors are in a stage of outperforming their foreign invested peers. How local companies got there is a story of avoiding foreign competition: in the 1990s, China saw the spread of all kinds of supermarkets across the country, mostly operated by state-owned enterprises. In the late 1990s, international chains moved into the Chinese market and set a clear standard based on huge product variety and aggressive pricing that local supermarket chains couldn't entirely match. Foreign players could establish these standards back then due to their more efficient business- and management methods, buying power, and supply/cold chain capabilities. Today local chains have acquired these capabilities and, therefore, the competitive advantage for foreign players has dwindled.

Local hypermarket and supermarket chains evolved privately. Instead of contending directly with foreign players in key cities, in the initial stage local supermarket focused on smaller and familiar provincial cities to gain size and market share. While foreign brands have expanded out from tier-one cities over the past 10 years, local chains have moved into tier-one cities and quickly adapted by diversifying into different formats, equipped with good knowledge and fresh capital.

The market is now experiencing some drastic changes. For white-collar urban residents who are shopping closer to home in smaller quantities according to their daily needs, shopping in hypermarkets is losing its luster. More and more people shop online to avoid the hassle in supermarkets or simply to save time or money. With the highly competitive price of most goods, online supermarkets also offer shoppers a range of choices including overseas brands, with some cross-border websites even shipping products directly from overseas.

On the other hand, hypermarkets continue to grow outside the major cities. As a good value option and comprehensive shopping experience, they continue to successfully pioneer into new, lower-tier cities and new residential areas. As mature urban areas become equipped with metro stations, I have also observed a trend away from hypermarkets in the suburbs and to supermarkets closer to home, such as mini-marts and convenience stores. Customers are less and less willing to spend time traveling a long distance to get to their shopping experience; instead, they want to be able to shop "around the corner" and in a sophisticated format.

The goal of providing better products to increasingly demanding consumers is, therefore, leading to globally integrated competition with a balance between product and distribution coverage. With China's food safety concerns at the top of consumers' minds, domestic supermarkets are increasingly looking overseas to buy food. This has even led foreign supermarket retailers such as Sainsbury's (UK) and Costco (USA) to begin selling food online without even having any stores in the country—and distributing from Hong Kong.

As a result, the best companies we see are in a race for better product supply, which means direct supply chains and cooperation with farmers and manufacturers not only in China but also globally. In my opinion, this could pave the way for the highly integrated discount formats we know from Europe. Discount may not be the main selling point at this time, but the trust that comes from integrated supply chains and manufacturers.

Yonghui seemed to have adopted this "bigger picture thinking" in 2014. With a payment of US$925 million for a 20% stake, the company took on Dairy Farm (HK: DFIHY) as an investor, which helped generate new insights and synergies with regard to supply chain and global sourcing.

It seems that the company has a more comprehensive offline and online strategy that the leading online retail platform JD.com (also the fourth largest Internet company in China) took a 10% stake in Yonghui at the same time with the Dairy Farm investment.

During my first meeting with him, I learned that Zhang Xuanning (45 years old) had left the running of the supermarket empire to his younger brother Zhang Xuansong and had taken some staff from the company based in Fujian to Shanghai to focus on a "new project." All that sounded mysteriously like a major plan in the offing, which whetted my appetite to meet this legendary chairman again in person to find out more about what was actually going on.

Mr. Zhang grew up in a village in Fujian province, where he helped his mother sell vegetables at the local market. While his family were originally farmers, Zhang's father had already moved into the construction industry as a general contractor—a typical example of the "moving worker" decade. In the 1990s, Zhang and his brothers started a business doing beer distribution. The business sometimes did well and sometimes not. It is important to note that Fujian has severe weather swings and is famous for typhoons. As a young adult, Zhang already realized that vegetable prices would, therefore, fluctuate and that farmers who were desperate to make a living would resort to all sorts of tricks including selling produce that is not ready to sell, especially at typhoon times. Mr. Zhang's "eureka moment" came in 2000 when Metro (Germany) and Wal-Mart (US) entered Fujian.

Zhang asked himself how these companies managed to have consistently good vegetables, while also keeping prices stable. Curious to figure it out, the Zhang brothers did two groundbreaking things: first, they sold their beer business to start two supermarkets and second, they bought Sam Walton's book to figure out how to run them.

Mr. Zhang admired Sam Walton from the very beginning. "Because his mission is to provide healthy, safe, and good-value-for-money products at a lower cost," says Zhang. "And he boosted the development of supply chains and provided so many job opportunities for people," Zhang explains.

Studying supermarkets, foreign invested companies, and the Wal-Mart model, the Zhang brothers quickly learned not only the basics but also the strategic thinking needed to build a supermarket empire.

During the founding stages of Yonghui, Zhang and his brother developed quality testing standards and processes for fresh products and introduced them into Yonghui's supply chain, including investment into testing at the place of origin, and distribution centers. Zhang prides himself in that "there has never been a food safety case in Yonghui for the past 15 years."

The Fujian government had been promoting the testing standards, especially when Xi Jinping became the local governor and launched a project called "stop pollution on the dining table and build a safe and reliable market" in 2001. Yonghui grew quickly in the brothers' home province of Fujian; the Yonghui model was then duplicated for cities in other regions such as Chongqing and Beijing, and, eventually, the rest of China.

In Zhang's opinion, the technology gap in the foodservice arena is small, but the gap in producers' minds and behaviors is much larger: "More and more companies now understand the need to build brand loyalty for their products, and product safety and quality are essential to that aim." He points out that many companies are still in the process of developing this understanding.

As Zhang sees the people managing the supply chain as the weakest link in achieving better food safety, he realized that staff attitudes and loyalty were crucial to success. Of course, this is also heavily inspired by Wal-Mart's people basics. From an early stage on, Zhang tended to share the company's successes with his staff as a form of motivation through joint ownership.

While there is a similarity between Wal-Mart and Yonghui, I found this to be a trait many companies in China possess. It's partially rooted in ensuring that everyone shares in pulling in the same direction and does his or her best. It is also because, as mentioned earlier in the book, local companies are cash-strapped in the early stages of development. So, sharing out ownership in return for hard work and in lieu of higher salaries can help to alleviate that cash problem, while also cultivating a strong sense of loyalty.

Further, in a market where talent is so scarce and competitors may offer double the salary to lure away your best talent (usually the key management who are hardest to replace), it's no wonder that companies have to go to great lengths to retain their employees. This is especially so at an early stage of company development, and almost all companies in China are in those early stages.

Even seemingly mature companies like Yonghui, which are only 10–20 years old, are still in a "startup phase" compared to more mature global companies like Wal-Mart (founded in 1962), Carrefour (1958), or Metro (1964). When companies start up in China, cash is scarce, and in order to speed up expansion and stay ahead of competitors, they have to reinvest any liquidity.

While employees are also shareholders in Yonghui, the company does demand high standards of dedication. For Zhang, commitment to the company mission means "providing healthy, safe, and high price performance products," which he follows that up with a clear growth goal, namely "to be the number three in retail."

That goal may sound odd, but it reflects the humble way that Zhang (a Buddhist) chooses to express himself. Here comes the interpretation: numbers one and two are Alibaba and JD, basically the eBay and Amazon of China. As such, being number three would mean being the real number one in physical retail.

To be clear, that would mean surpassing Wal-Mart and every other physical store retailer in China!

Today, purchasing volumes represent less of a competitive advantage since the competition between supermarkets' supply chain capabilities is increasing. As a result, most retailers now play on an equal footing. Competition isn't just about who has the best price, but who has the most exciting product range. To be more specific, it is not only about the local product range, down to any district's local fare, but also about who has the best range of international products.

For example, in contrast to many of its competitors, Yonghui has the distribution rights for Moutai (the most famous distilled Chinese liquor) and can sell it directly to the consumers. "Customers come for your products," Zhang kept emphasizing. His vision started there, and Yonghui is now sourcing globally. "Next month we will obtain the distribution rights for one of the best Australian wine brand," he elaborates.

After getting closer to local suppliers and partly eliminating middlemen, now the trend is to get agencies for foreign products. By doing so, Chinese companies could globalize without necessarily leaving the country, but by bringing international products to China, and most notably, directly from the producers. This recently emerging trend was partially triggered by leading (pure) online retail players gaining traction in categories via direct imports, such as milk, baby formula, and other similar kinds of perishable and nonperishable foodstuffs. With the Chinese supermarket retailers growing so quickly, and thus heavy competition, direct sourcing (to achieve competitive pricing) and global sourcing (to achieve brand positioning and differentiation) are becoming major new trends.

Retailers like Yonghui are putting considerable effort into staying at the forefront of global sourcing, snatching up cooperation and distribution rights away from distributors, and dealing with overseas manufacturers directly. One example is that the company is cooperating with Korea's CJ Group on its supply chain. "We are looking for more opportunities in global sourcing," says Zhang. As all things are increasingly going tech in China, Yonghui is already working on a global Internet buying platform.

During the interview, I realized there was a topic Mr. Zhang is very passionate about personally: his new business ventures. In 2012, he took 20 employees with him to Shanghai (the most competitive market in China) to set up a core team for business innovation. According to Zhang, "The driving force of future innovations will be the post-90s generation of consumers." This new team, therefore, will focus on this younger consumer group and new formats.

Zhang already had the GenMobile consumer on his mind. To attract these people to his innovation team, he rented space in the middle of Shanghai (Jiang An district where most young people like to hang out), in one of the trendiest office buildings. I did not ask him why, but it is clear that innovation in China is born out of market pressure and not in isolated R&D centers at the outskirts of the city. You have to be in the most competitive workplaces to attract the best talent.

The new company, Yonghui Cloud and Innovation (literal meaning), mainly focuses on three initiatives:

A new store format to evolve supermarket and retail formats to appeal to the higher-end customer. The new store, dubbed "Super Species," opened in Zhang's hometown Fuzhou in January 2017 with an area of 500 m^2. Yonghui presented its global sourcing capability with products from overseas including wine, beef, and seafood in the supermarket, as well as in the restaurants. According to Zhang, all aspects of this new-format supermarket have been reinvented, from customer positioning to products and to the way the store is run. The store boasts many new merchandising and lifestyle elements like flower studios, a live kitchen and organic food ranges.

The second focus is on supply chain and product development to adapt to globalization and to make more and more private label and customized products.

The third is on big data usage and its combination with stores. Zhang sees the Internet and the digital age, together with new consumer trends, as creating a chance to develop his retail business, embracing it as an opportunity. Yonghui already runs an online retail site, along with six apps to deal with sales and logistics, staff, and CSR matters.

The company once tried launching a Yonghui Wechat Mall, but didn't achieve the expected level of success. For Zhang, the former online platform was more like an experiment and preparation for the later Yonghui Life App, which now has more than 20,000 (together with JD Daojia) orders per day and daily turnover of RMB 1 million. "Unlike the single Wechat platform, the new content-comprehensive app can encourage consumers to spend more time with it and enhance their activities," says Zhang.

Mr. Zhang's vision for the future will continue as he plans to build 3000 club stores, backed up with screens to sell products based on customer data generated from the Yonghui Life App in Shanghai. Last year, more than 30 stores of this kind, with an area of around 200 m^2 each, opened there.

We ended the interview with a toast of German wheat beer, which he seemed to enjoy, and I wished him all the best for his future ventures. The waitress reminded us the German food buffet was closing. Too bad, I thought; that would be the end of our interview and learning about supermarkets and the future of the industry in China.

Trying to wrap up quickly, I asked Mr. Zhang a final question: "What do you want international readers to know about Chinese companies?" As expected, I received a humble answer. "I hope people from outside will better understand Chinese companies and their founders. I hope the book will inspire more communications and interactions." From my personal knowledge of Mr. Zhang, I'm sure he will continue his journey of learning and incorporating valuable lessons from others.

Acknowledgment This interview has been published with the kind permission of Mr. Zhang Xuanning.

Notes

1. http://www.ebrun.com/20160520/176832.shtml
2. http://www.bain.com/Images/REPORT_Winning-over-shoppers-in-chinas-new-normal-vol2.pdf

17

Urban Fast Food Formats: Gil Wonton

Fast food—No. 1 dumpling chain—Zhang Biao, Founder (photo with kind permission of Mr. Zhang Biao)

© The Author(s) 2018
C. Nothhaft, *Made for China*, DOI 10.1007/978-3-319-61584-4_17

Opportunity

As Chinese consumers become more sophisticated and concerned about food hygiene and want to eat Chinese fast food in air-conditioned, branded stores, new opportunities will arise for local fast food chains.

Lessons Learned

Chinese fast food chains are rapidly evolving, but it's a tough business, as companies have to constantly improve their core product and their store concepts—the market is very competitive with all sorts of issues, including copycats trying to get a piece of the pie from successful entrepreneurs.

In 1999, I had the pleasure of running my first company in China as Managing Director. It was a poultry processing plant in Weifang, Shandong province, which produced fast food products for sale outside China. The reason was that chicken could be reared and processed cheaply in China—even though the original chicken stock itself came from the USA, since the "Western" chickens were much meatier than the local ones. We also imported flavors and spices and contract manufactured for export to large fast food and supermarket chains in countries across Europe and Asia.

So, oddly enough, we made products for the Western fast food industry in a city that didn't have a single Western fast food outlet. In contrast, there was local fast food everywhere, literally on every street corner.

One day, a KFC outlet opened downtown, and I decided to take my colleagues there for lunch. We only got back to the office 3 or 4 hours later because of the unbelievable queue. Over the weeks, more and more colleagues had tried out the KFC, but they had various opinions on how the product tasted. However, they unanimously agreed that (1) the arrival of fast food meant progress, and (2) it was so clean and safe that everyone should aspire to go and "enjoy" it.

To put this aspiration into perspective, a senior worker at our factory earned around RMB 300 (approx. US$35) per month back then, while a meal at KFC cost between RMB 20 and 30, meaning a KFC meal represented about 7–10% of their monthly salary! Let me ask you: Would you pay US$200–300 for a meal at McDonald's, KFC, or the like?

Today, among the foreign fast food brands, only KFC has made a real breakthrough in China, due in part to its early entry and good leadership.

McDonald's has always been working to catch up with KFC, which is harder to achieve in a market where fast food prices are low and operating costs keep rising. Two major reasons for this success, besides timing, were operating capability and preferences. Chinese people love chicken (wild jungle fowl, from which all chickens descend, are native to southern China), while they had to first develop a taste for beef—Chinese people do love their local fare. As well as enjoying their local cuisines, they also love the local prices, which are "dirt cheap." As long as I have been in China, the local fast food market has remained one of the toughest to survive in. The following story concerns a man who took a local family eatery and transformed it into a 3000-store fast food empire.

The wonton (Cantonese pronunciation), pronounced *huntun* in Mandarin, is similar to the Western dumpling. The history of the wonton (something like a dumpling, but with a much thinner wrapper, and always served in soup) can be traced back to the nineteenth century. For many years, it was served by small, independent, family-run catering businesses.

Gil Wonton was the first fast food chain to come along and make the wonton its signature product. Founded in 1999, Gil Wonton had 3084 stores across China by the end of 2016 and sales revenues of RMB 1.4 billion. The company has positioned itself as a Chinese-style fast food chain targeting the younger generation with fresh, authentic (tasting) products at a fair price.

Mr. Zhang Biao, founder, chairman, and CEO of Gil Wonton, was the first person to respond to my invitation to do an interview, saying that he realized we both ran a chain of stores and both had a catering background.

Our conversation began with how he started the business.

"In the '90s, franchising became a good opportunity, because you didn't need to invest a lot, and other people would pay you franchising fees and royalties. I learned from the training I received, and gained a rough idea about how franchises work," Zhang Biao shared with me. "Among all the different types of Chinese dim sum, wonton is the one of the easiest to make, store and process. When our management capability was low, the product's inner strength helped."

Fast food chains are still expanding across China, but it's harder for them to make returns. Because they are capital-intensive, return years can be as long as five or more, which exceeds lease terms in most tier one or two cities. On top of that, operating costs have quickly skyrocketed, while competition has kept pricing low (including high VAT).

It is, therefore, hard to achieve economic scale. Many companies have failed to achieve critical mass, because even though China's cities are huge, the relevant density of affluent consumers is not yet sufficient to support multiple Western fast food players. In a way, KFC and McDonald's, along with some coffee chains, have (by default) cornered the market—for now.

To achieve economies of scale, local players especially need to create high store density in their local cities or provinces—often relying in part on franchising outside their core territory. That is exactly how Zhang started Gil Wonton.

Besides the franchising Zhang mentioned, the challenges posed by the Chinese fast food market are still hard to define, and there is little precise data available regarding how organized the market is, or which company holds which market share. So, as a proxy, we shall approach this from a more Western angle.

When the PRC was founded in 1949, the country underwent a three-decade period of planned economy administration, during which people were more likely to cook at home for survival, and rarely dined out due to a lack of disposable income and fragile interpersonal relationships. So, when the market opened up in the late 1980s, it was practically a blank slate.

After this initial period, the catering industry entered an era of rapid development, growing in total value from RMB 140 billion in 2000 to RMB 766 billion in 2014.[1] Over time, the industry gradually nurtured a few segments to serve different needs. There emerged, for example, premium brands mainly for business purposes; restaurants at all levels of pricing for social functions and private gatherings; and fast food, including small kiosks to fill the empty stomachs of busy workers who had no time to cook at home.

For any international player in the fast food industry, on paper at least China represents a greater opportunity for growth than the USA. However, these two markets are very different in terms of market maturity. According to Euromonitor,[2] the US fast food market enjoyed two good years of growth in 2012–2013, growing at 5% and 4%, respectively, yet China grew at 12.4% annually from 2009 to 2014, three times the speed in the USA.

If we take the date when the first McDonald's was opened in 1955 as the starting point, the US fast food market has been around for over 60 years, offering consumers food choices they are familiar with, such as burgers and fries. In China, although the history of food kiosks offering noodles or dumplings can be traced back over hundreds of years, the modern fast food industry did not arrive until KFC opened its first Mainland China outlet in 1987. With a culture of fine dining spanning thousands of years, will fast food (often criticized as junk food) be able to sustain growth once Chinese consumers' curiosity for the Western fast food culture has faded? The answer likely lies in the current post-2000 generation.

Urbanization and the related change in eating habits (often resulting in a change of diet over time) have been the key driver for the fast food industry. Aside from people taking homemade lunches to work, fast food is the next most popular choice. Perceived better hygiene is a big reason why people like branded chain-store fast food. During the 2002/2003 SARS outbreak in China, when people in many cities were subjected to a curfew to prevent the disease from spreading, many resorted to ordering takeaway from fast food restaurants because they could be confident that the food from such outlets was hygienic. Indeed, that year was significant for sparking more rapid growth in the market.

Structural changes to modern Chinese families have also played a significant role in the development of the fast food industry. In a traditional Chinese family, there are three generations: grandparents, parents, and children. Grandparents take care of the children and cook for the whole family.

As a result, the three primary consumers of fast food include:

1. Members of the working class (aged 25–44) who need to fill an empty stomach. The fast pace of urban life does not allow them time to cook. As they may be sharing an apartment with others, they may not even have a place to cook, thus choosing fast food for lunch. Convenience and low price are the key factors. Fast food edges out cooking at home by providing convenience, affordability, AND hygiene.
2. Young–middle-aged parents and their children (below age 16), who eat out as a family during leisure time, especially on the weekends. They tend to visit fast food chains such as McDonald's and KFC, especially the outlets equipped with a designated children's play area. In a way, Western fast food is often equated with casual dining in China.
3. Juveniles and youths for social gatherings or for hanging out after class to study. Young people value the dining environment, consumer experience, and value for money. Cleanliness and Wi-Fi are a must. An innovative menu, frequently updated with new products, and techy add-ons are great tools to attract their curiosity.

Generally, Western brands like KFC and McDonald's grab the headlines in part due to good PR work, as they are generally under "consumer scrutiny" with consumers having high expectations as to their food safety and professional standards. While the Chinese love their rice and noodles, of the top ten organized chains in 2013, only three offer Chinese food. Gil Wonton thus represents a good case study for the fast-food sector, being the Chinese industry leader in terms of outlets. KFC and McDonald's, and perhaps some similar spinoffs, cover the rest.

Zhang Biao and I met in 2015, during the period of a massive stock market crash in China. Zhang also shared his concerns about the economic downturn, and he saw the need to increase sales in his existing stores. "Due to the economic slowdown, competition in the industry has become tougher. We deal with more competitors in the same vicinity... So our understanding of consumers has had to change."

According to Zhang, "Today's consumers in China have a different understanding of life compared to the older generations. More and more consumers have shifted their focus from survival to living well." Now 40% of Gil Wonton's customers are under the age of 30. Instead of valuing price alone, "They have a greater demand for personality, personalization, self-awareness," Zhang added.

The ever-evolving customer in China always wants new designs and concepts. "Every five years you need to renovate your store, and introduce a new concept." During 2007 and 2008, Gil failed to inject new elements into the brand prior to increasing prices. The response from the market hit the company so badly that they had to close one-third of their stores in Shanghai. Fortunately, Gil managed to overcome this crisis by reinventing the store format. According to Zhang, the sixth version of Gil Wonton stores now has elements of street culture, appealing to young consumers.

"Strategy wise, when we face difficulties we cannot sit back and take a conservative approach, to cut costs, etc. Instead, we should invest more and be more assertive, which is the only way that can help us overcome the difficulties. Otherwise, it's just a matter of time [before you die]."

Brand building, an enriched consumer experience, and personal connection with the customer are important. Zhang said firmly, "I believe, in the coming years, the consumer behavior on the Chinese market will see an explosion of the pursuit of individualism and personality." Besides this, Zhang emphasized that the number one rule in dealing with Chinese consumers was to offer good value for the money.

For some industries such as footwear retailing, adapting to market changes is interpreted as multiple-brand management. Does this strategy also apply to the fast food industry? KFC expressed its interest in this idea, and in 2004 it introduced a sub-brand (Dongfang Jibai) specifically offering Chinese-style meals. The verdict is still out on this, and I asked Zhang for his opinion:

The market is big enough that I can expand my business by basically applying similar activities in other regions. If my market is Shanghai only, when my business develops to a certain stage, the room for further growth is limited, and I will then have to develop multiple brands. I would rather focus on one thing.

As to potentially expanding overseas, Gil Wonton has begun preparing for this by registering its trademark in Japan and the USA. However, Zhang is not sure, quoting food culture differences and management challenges.

> I think it will take another 5 to 10 years before more Chinese companies will expand overseas . . . Most of the brands and resources are now in the hands of my generation, but we grew up in a closed environment. Our language skills and limited contact with the external world were big restrictions on our ability to expand. When the next generation gets ready to take over the wheel, the opportunities for Chinese companies to go overseas will be much better. The Chinese people are hard-working and eager to explore new opportunities.

As part of this journey, he foresees substantial piloting of technology use (automatic ordering through QR code scanning, online payment platforms, etc.) to enhance convenience, increase customers' sense of participation, and promote take-out business. "As the take-out platforms like Ele.me and Meituan emerged quickly, we planned our own O2O system accordingly, at a relatively early time in 2015," Zhang added.

Whether he goes global or not, Zhang's biggest focus is on product quality, specifically food safety. Chinese people may love their local fare, but they consider local fast food to be "less safe" and assume that McDonald's, KFC, and the like are "safer" due to their high-tech approach, standardization, and professional management—in part because they come from abroad. The concept is somewhat the reverse of that experienced in the West, where fast food is often deemed less safe due to its long-term health effects on the body.

Food safety is like a sword of Damocles dangling above the head of anyone like Zhang who runs a food business in China. Being consumers' biggest concern, food safety can be turned into a symbol of quality assurance or unique selling point (USP) if it is well managed by a particular brand. Conversely, if a business fails to maintain consistent food safety, its business can face sudden death. For Gil Wonton, the focus is mainly on ingredients and running a central production of its products.

"(We must) Ensure that all materials come from the best growing land and the processing procedures should be as natural as possible." Zhang said now the company promises an MSG-free processing plant and direct delivery, which are parts of his objectives to "promote the best materials for the health of our customers."

Apart from food safety, intellectual property infringement is another major issue in the fast food chain industry (and of course other industries) in China. Although the Chinese government has gradually invested more and more effort into enforcing IP law within China, generally speaking, for copycats the huge return easily outweighs the cost of breaking the law. While Westerners tend to see the international aspects of IP infringement, the domestic challenges within China are being overlooked.

Zhang brought this up when I asked him about the number of stores he has: "We have 2000 fake stores. . . " Gil wonton now has 364 direct-sale stores and more than 2500 franchising chain stores. The copycats came from his previous franchisees, who at certain stages wanted to get out of the franchise system to start on their own. Zhang has a certain understanding for entrepreneurs who want to grow their own companies, but he is worried about IP—franchisees using his name and brand. "I will hunt them down relentlessly," said Zhang. This offers an interesting insight on the importance of IP from a Chinese company's perspective.

Undoubtedly, catering is a labor-intensive industry. Younger generations (post-1980ers, post-1990ers, etc.) are now entering the labor force and are starting to take on bigger roles. Many people from the older generations (post-1960/1970ers) complain about the generational gap between them and their young colleagues. Interestingly, Zhang holds a different view. He thinks that the young generations are easier to manage.

> They work for a better life, not for survival. Bearing this in mind, when you pay enough respect to their personalities, you will be able to understand their behavior.

Compared to the older generations, Zhang feels another reason young people are easier to manage is that their behavior is "more genuine, no matter whether in front of the crowd or behind the scenes."

Zhang described his vision of employee relationships as "another important innovation," and he referred to his staff as partners:

> In the first 10 years, our relationship was more about management and control. In the second 10 years, we have made 'goal setting and support' two important pillars in our relations with staff. In the meantime, I hope to provide them with other financial benefits beyond their salary and bonus.

Rounding out our interview, I asked Zhang if he would like to use this book to convey any message about Chinese entrepreneurs. His answer was as follows:

I hope it will show that the mid/small size businesses in China, without much support, have done a lot to demonstrate our traditional culture, such as [being] hard-working. We are very adaptive to changes and are willing to embrace them. Along with our rapid development, we are willing to take on our responsibilities as common citizens. I think these are the things many Chinese companies are willing to do, but sometimes at different stages of their development; when they are under pressure to survive, some companies may not be able to demonstrate it. But, in the future, I believe there will be a big change towards it.

Acknowledgment This interview has been published with the kind permission of Mr. Zhang Biao.

Notes

1. Source: KPMG/Euromonitor International.
2. http://www.euromonitor.com/fast-food-in-the-us/report

18

Better Booze: Jing Brand

Liquor and Spirits—No. 1 health liquor—Wu Shaoxun, Founder (photo with kind permission of Mr. Wu Shaoxun)

© The Author(s) 2018
C. Nothhaft, *Made for China*, DOI 10.1007/978-3-319-61584-4_18

Opportunities

Hard liquor producers in China are now under tremendous pressure, facing two major challenges, the first of which is an evolving society that has less of a drinking culture. Further, the change in government policies has put an end to expensive government entertainment and gift giving, shifting the market power to the real consumer, who wants to drink "healthily." In response, liquor companies are now rebranding their story and reshuffling the opportunities among the big players.

Lessons Learned

Health liquor companies could potentially fare better in weathering the storm created by customer habits—toward drinking less hard liquor—if they can improve their brand positioning. Health liquor companies could capitalize on the belief that health liquor has health benefits and could potentially market it to young consumers as a healthier and trendier product. A privately held company, e.g., the example here, has been able to weather the storm better as—being owner-driven—it can take a longer-term view on change management.

I still remember what happened to me during my first big corporate dinner at Watsons China. It was the annual dinner, in a concert hall in Shanghai with over 30 tables, and 12 people per table. As is Chinese custom, I (as the "boss") went around toasting each table and wishing everyone "Happy New Year." Having finished 30 tables without too much damage, I thought "ok, I survived that," but I had forgotten that each table had to then return the favor and come to my table to make a toast. I had also forgotten that each senior manager (there were more than 20) would also come over to toast. . . So, on and on it went. The rest you can imagine—a huge hangover! However, the reward for my hangover was that from the next day on, I was no longer a stranger in the office, and people started to warm up to me!

This is the so-called jiu wenhua (liquor culture) in China. Having worked in this country for more than 10 years now, I have learned to appreciate how important a role baijiu, Chinese liquor, plays in relationship and trust building among Chinese people. Nothing can work faster in bringing people together than sharing a few toasts. As a result, large quantities of baijiu and wine are often consumed at business dinners and private functions at company events. Unlike people in Western countries, Chinese people tend to measure the volume of liquor consumed as an indicator of the success of a function or the value of a relationship.

In the past, almost without exception, the more you drank, the better chances you had of building a relationship, and the more likely it was that you could create a business opportunity. This was especially true for our GenRed and GenRise generations. However, things have been changing rapidly, and GenMobile people now tend to see this habit as being a bit antiquated, and part of their parent's generation—and who wants to be like their parents anyway?

Despite this change, the alcoholic drinks market in China is huge, with over RMB 1.3 trillion in sales in 2015, and almost 40% of that coming from spirits and liquors.[1] Spirit sales in China enjoyed a "golden decade" of rapid growth from 2004 onwards. Especially in the period from 2005 to 2011, the industry grew at a CAGR of 13% annually, and the spirits market more than doubled in value, exceeding RMB 500 billion in 2012.[2]

This made major players in the market, such as Moutai, Wuliangye, and others, the new sweethearts of the capital market, with the prospect of continued liquor market growth. There are now 14 major alcohol manufacturers listed on China's "A" stock markets.

Unfortunately, this rapid growth was suddenly interrupted in 2012 and further deteriorated to become negative in 2013. What happened? The Chinese government launched an anti-extravagance campaign, which enforced strict controls on the use of public funds for entertainment purposes and to purchase alcoholic drinks from late 2012 onwards. This hit the spirit industry hard, especially the premium brands. The market size for spirits dropped by 1.7% in 2013, versus a year-on-year growth of 7.9% in 2012.[3] Far worse, in 2013 the total market value of 14 publicly listed liquor manufacturers fell by a staggering 40% (though it remained RMB 255.2 billion).[4]

Due to the sharp decline in demand for premium brands, the major players in the spirits industry had to shift their focus from premium brands for entertainment purposes to mid- and low-price range products. In fact, their primary customers changed—from restaurant owners to individual consumers!

Given this situation, interestingly, herbal spirits somehow recorded an upward trend, despite the dire situation on the spirit market in general. Herbal spirits traditionally tended to fit into the mid-range price group of alcoholic drinks. Due to their price position, they were not considered to be a premium gift choice for business-relationship-building purposes. Consequently, and because herbal spirits already had a large consumer base (unlike baijiu and wine), they largely escaped the anti-extravagance campaign. It is, therefore, no surprise that the herbal spirits market grew by almost 19% CAGR between 2009 and 2015 to RMB 20 billion and is expected to continue growing at around 16% to RMB 109 billion by 2019.

The history of herbal spirits can be dated back to the Shang Dynasty over 3000 years ago. According to traditional Chinese medicinal theories, soaking herbal ingredients in alcohol can help bring out their essence and activate their medicinal qualities. According to a consumer survey, 64% of respondents buy herbal spirits for home consumption, 16% for holiday gatherings, 10% for entertainment and relaxation, and only 9% for business banquets.[5]

As of July 2015, there were about 5000 herbal spirit manufacturers in China. Every year more than 200 new players enter the market.[6] Today, the top players in the market are Jing Brand, Ye Dao, Gu Ling, Moutai, and Zhi Zhong He.

Being the largest health liquor company in China, Jing Brand has reported double-digit growth for five consecutive years since 2011 and accounts for around 30% of total sales in the sector today. This stellar performance made Mr. Wu Shaoxun, the owner, Chairman, and CEO of Jing Brand a legend—and the perfect person for me to interview.

Jing Brand is located in the city of Daye, 110 km away from Wuhan, the capital city of Hubei province in Central China. Chairman Wu, though a bit surprised at a foreigner taking an interest in his brand, was delighted to invite us for an interview at his factory in Daye (a city I had never heard of before, but now will never forget).

The company was founded in 1953 and entered the herbal liquor sector in 1978. Its signature product Jing Jiu was launched in 1987, later becoming a household name in China. This single product not only made the company the number one in the herbal spirit sector but also the largest private sector tax payer in Hubei province—which has a population of 58 million people, and, according to SCMP, a GDP rivaling that of Belgium.[7]

Daye is a mining town of coal, metals, and non-metallic minerals and, as such, not necessarily the first choice to host a herbal health spirits company.

However, the Jing Brand factory campus is a world of its own. We arrived at around 4 p.m., just as more than ten coaches lined up on campus waiting to take employees off home. What a community service, I thought! Young ladies in uniform walked by us chatting and smiling, and everyone seemed to be in a great mood. The atmosphere at this industrial park was very different to those I had encountered in Shenzhen or Dongguan, which are full of bustling and stressed looking workers.

Following a tour of the campus, we were greeted by Mr. Shaoxun at the main entrance of his office building. Like his workers, Wu also wore a Jing Brand uniform. I wouldn't have realized he was the owner of business with annual revenues of RMB 8.5 billion (about US$1.3 billion, in 2015) if I had met him on the street.

Following retirement from military service in 1980, Wu was assigned to work in a local textile factory and worked his way to the top of the ladder. In 1985, he was sent to the regional Party School to study for 2 years. After graduation, he was appointed (in 1987) to be the head of a local state-owned liquor plant, which was the predecessor of today's Jing Brand. Under Wu's leadership, this small county-level plant grew into a national brand in less than 30 years.

The sales volume of its most popular product (the 125 ml bottle of Jing Jiu) is over 800 million bottles a year—or, to put it in perspective, more than one bottle for each human being living in Europe. What is the secret behind this amazing scorecard?

From reading this book, you might already have realized that, for successful companies in China, especially those focusing on the domestic market, diversification is not the key and quite the opposite is the case. Mr. Wu is a primary example.

In the past 27 years, we have focused on one brand (Jing Jiu), since it was designed in 1988 and launched in 1989. It has become the number one brand in the herbal spirit market in China. While Jing Jiu does produce some other product lines, it clearly allocates the main resources to Jing Jiu (and a new product, Maopu) as the core. We don't set any targets for the rest of the products and the resources allocated to them are limited.

I also felt that everyone we met at Jing Jiu was passionate about the product, and when I mentioned this to Wu, his eyes lit up: "We drink what we produce. If I don't drink my own product, who else will buy it?"

Wu continued to explain that—on the consumer side—Jing Brand has conducted an ongoing consumer research project for over 20 years, tracking the physical health of consumers, and Wu emphasized how it has improved after drinking Jing Brand products.

Suddenly, our interview was interrupted. An unexpected government delegation arrived. Mr. Wu had to excuse himself for half an hour to deliver a speech to the delegation, while we enjoyed some—to my surprise—freshly brewed coffee. The situation reminded me of my early days running a food manufacturing business in China. As general manager, you always had to plan spare time every day for unexpected government visits.

Meanwhile, Mr. Wang Nanbo, VP of Jing Brand to charge Sales & Marketing, explained their strategies to improve the company's product strength in response to the increased competition, due in part to new players from the traditional spirits business crossing over to health liquor. To my surprise, Jing Brand had a GenNet and GenMobile Strategy! I was keen to hear how such a traditional product would cope with the rise of GenMobile consumer who is, in general, less keen to drink when compared to, say, the GenRise/PC generation.

"Along with changes in consumer behavior, herbal spirits have become a trend representing nutritious, low alcohol content and healthy liquors," Me. Feng, Mr. Wu's head of international business, explained, and low alcohol versions of German beer popped up as the Western example in my mind. However, this is a more long-term opportunity, while the shorter-term one lies in growth in remote corners of the domestic market. The second largest opportunity lies in high-end orientation of existing products, and the third with developing more product lines at the higher end of the price spectrum.

Wu believes Chinese consumers are changing considerably. The first change he became aware of was their growing concerns about drinking alcohol, and its negative effects on health. Traditionally, the main market for hard liquor was among middle-age people, while herbal spirits were primarily targeted at seniors. But, with rising living standards, middle-aged consumers were increasingly looking for products that could offer the fun of drinking liquor, but without the risk of ruining their health, which has been Jing Brand's ongoing opportunity.

While I was initially a bit skeptical, I remembered a similar brand story from Europe. It reminded me of an old traditional product called Jägermeister, once a rather local German product that my parent's generation would drink after dinner, to settle their stomachs. When I left Europe 20 years ago, the brand was almost dead. Today, it's available in nightclubs and bars globally as a fun drink for young people—we could say GenPC and GenMobile. The analogy to Jing Brand's potential immediately became clear. When I mentioned the name to Mr. Feng, he immediately knew the brand and the case.

Wu and his team developed a new product called health liquor under the brand name Maopu, which smells and tastes the same as traditional hard liquor (baijiu), but claims to offer consumers further reduced potential for liver damage through the health benefits of four herbal ingredients. Also, it claims to promote lower blood sugar, lipids, and uric acid. Through comparison tests with the best-selling brands of baijiu, it was also proven that people who drank Jing Brand's health liquor the night before felt much less of a hangover the next day—although how one measures such things is still a mystery to me!

Coming from the non-premium end of the market, Wu confirmed that now it was his strategy to take market share away from premium brands. Since its pilot launch in 2013, Maopu has been doing very well in certain markets. Wang and his sales team expect this product to contribute the biggest volume of sales increase for the next 5 years. According to Jing Brand, the most loyal customers are in the 36–55 age group, accounting for more than 60% of the total consumers.

While focusing on Jing Brand's core consumers, new ranges are being sold at smaller volumes in anticipation of new demand and consumer shifts. Wu has observed that younger people are more in favor of low-alcohol-content drinks. "It may take a longer time to get young people interested in healthy liquor, and most of them will not try it until they turn 30," Wu said. His R&D team is now focusing on developing products that can meet such needs. This strategy is based on Wu's history of successfully investing in herbal spirits in the early years and slightly outrunning the competition while the product gradually became trendy, ultimately making him the market leader.

Chinese liquor companies are gradually saturating the market, while consumers' drinking frequency is declining. Despite the core business as healthy liquor, Jing Brand has to face competition from all baijiu brands. Armed with brand strength and cash, Jing Brand is now expanding into the baijiu producers' territory by creating a new subcategory: healthy baijiu, which combines baijiu with Jing Brand's health aspects and "healthy image."

Focusing on one product for 27 years doesn't mean Wu and his team rely on only one recipe. During the car ride, Feng told us they update the product continuously. Wu values the integration of modern technology and cultural heritage behind Chinese spirits. This plays an important role in managing a brand especially for the GenPC consumers (the current key consumer group in China).

Learning from the Western liquor manufacturers when it comes to brand building, Chinese liquor manufactures have invested heavily in promoting the heritage and culture of their products. For Jing Brand, Wu believes there should be more to it than that. He also follows pharmaceutical manufacturing standards to produce his herbal spirit and he keeps reiterating the need to be a technology leader in making the best health liquor.

In aligning with traditional Chinese medicine (TCM) companies, research institutes, and universities, Jing Brand has evolved the technology and techniques of TCM extraction and purification to its liquors. Wu is convinced that: "More and more people will get to know TCM and its benefits."

While many producers of spirits have focused strongly on the retail shelf, over the decades Jing Brand has built a leading position in the "on trade" business, i.e., a strong position with restaurants and bars, as well as small restaurants. It appeared this "on-trade network" was Jing Brand's main strength, beside the product itself. It would also allow the company to drive new trends pro-actively and to keep ahead of its competitors.

Just as in other industries, e-commerce is also sweeping through the spirits industry. For Jing Brand, online still only accounts for 0.4% of sales. But the plan is for online sales to grow to 4% within 5 years. To make that happen, Wu has already doubled the size of the e-commerce team to 67 people. Despite the investment required to meet this ambitious goal (4% represents over US$50 million), Wu has some conservative views, too:

> Liquor products are different from other FMCG products. In the short term, e-commerce cannot replace, or even threaten, the traditional channels such as restaurants and hotels where drinking takes place.

In their plans for the future, the Jing Brand team emphasizes O2O with the delivery of online sales taking place through their distributors and community stores, to reduce logistics costs. To avoid conflicts with the existing distribution systems, Jing Brand has separate, exclusive online products for shipping directly from the plant to consumers. "Liquors bought online are mostly used as gifts for friends and families, and thus differ from those bought offline, which in most cases are used in restaurants," Wu explained. 20% of online customers surveyed would now buy Jing Brand's products again.

And, clearly, Mr. Wu sees Internet business as just one distribution channel, with the core business still being the product itself: "I don't believe the Internet platform can do anything meaningful without the best products. The Internet helps with brand building, but it cannot steal the show."

He would rather focus on his own products and brand. Wu emphasizes that he has learned hard lessons from diversification, with investments he made in the past merely consuming a great deal of his time.

> Chinese companies have grown very large in recent years, but not strong enough. The main reason is that they lose focus due to diversification. When a crisis comes from the outside, the companies that have diversified will be more vulnerable.

Wu believes that no less than 50% of the companies existing now may not still be around in 10 years' time.

Mr. Wu had given me much of his time (and let us extensively sample his products, too), so I wanted to wrap up by getting a glimpse of his grand vision for Jing Brand and for himself as an entrepreneur. The sales of herbal spirits in China account for only 2% of the total alcoholic drinks market.[8] Being number one in the herbal spirit sector won't satisfy Wu's appetite. His dream is to earn a seat in the tier-one group of liquor brands in the next 10 years, competing with the likes of Moutai and Wuliangye.

Going global is another objective. Wu believes that the best chance for the Chinese liquor industry to do so lies in herbal spirits and companies like Jing Brand. Rooted in traditional Chinese medicine, herbal spirits are a unique product that China can offer the world.

As with other entrepreneurs I met, Mr. Wu also has a philosophical side. In fact, he has a clear hierarchy as to "what comes first," which in fact, by Western standards, would frighten any shareholder/investor. According to Wu, at Jing Brand, he values the stakeholders in the following sequence:

First, customers—how we keep improving our products and service to satisfy their needs; second, staff—how I can help my staff to work and live well; third, the world—how we can make a more beautiful world alongside the company's development, how can it contribute to the surrounding community, the nation and the world; and lastly, shareholders' interests. If there is a fourth party, shareholders' interests will always be the last priority.

Mr. Wu, the billionaire from Daye, is in the enviable position of being the sole shareholder. So he can set the above priorities, which, if everyone followed suit, would indeed create a better world.

Unfortunately, he finds it common among the business world that business leaders consider the shareholders' interests to be their first priority, rather than the last. As Wu aptly puts it: "People don't understand that, when the skin is gone, there is nothing left for the hair to grow on. Without customers or citizens, how can an enterprise or a nation survive?"

Acknowledgment This interview has been published with the kind permission of Mr. Wu Shaoxun.

Notes

1. KPMG, Euromonitor.
2. Ibid.
3. Ibid.
4. http://news.xinhuanet.com/finance/2014-05/19/c_126515529.htm
5. http://www.emkt.com.cn/article/591/59134.html
6. KPMG, http://www.tangjiu.com/baojianjiu/news/12830.html
7. SCMP.
8. http://www.emkt.com.cn/article/591/59134.html

19

Turning TCM Classics into FMCGs: Guangzhou Pharma

Pharmacy—No. 1 pharmaceutical company + No. 1 Non-carbonated drink—Li Chuyuan, Chairman (photo with kind permission of Mr. Li Chuyuan)

© The Author(s) 2018
C. Nothhaft, *Made for China*, DOI 10.1007/978-3-319-61584-4_19

Opportunity

The government's current policy is to gradually open the medical sector more and more for private companies, and as the pharmaceutical industry matures, it will open up even more. With more private doctors emerging, the sector of prescriptions received from private doctors and also OTC products is likely going to further grow, shifting more decision-making power over to the consumer. Retail growth will create new means to sell more products of higher value. Online retailing including to-your-door delivery services is now flourishing in the key cities and is thus a major area of growth. Traditional Chinese Medicine (TCM), traditional Chinese health foods, and "functional drinks" like Wanglaoji are a potential market not only in China but also across the globe.

Lessons Learned

Although the Chinese pharmaceutical sector is now (in part) open for foreign investment, the Chinese government is wary of too much privatization and therefore slowly giving up control, learning from some Western markets where pharmaceutical products have become extremely expensive, which would not benefit the Chinese people. Further, medicine supply through hospitals is prevalent and enables a stable revenue stream to keep hospitals going.

Consequently, pharmaceutical companies operate within boundaries—balancing a higher social mission (inexpensive medicine) and a practical political agenda. Having used their distribution while developing the nonregulated consumer-oriented side and nonmedical side of the business, some companies have succeeded in growing beyond their framework. The business case here, Guangzhou Pharma, is an example of how a pharmaceutical company used its distribution system and customers' faith in TCM to make a Chinese herbal tea into the best-selling soft drink in the country.

To appreciate how interesting this business case is, can you imagine Coca-Cola, the most popular soft drink in the USA, being produced by the US's largest drug company, (currently) Pfizer? The story here is exactly that. It is a story of a TCM remedy creating an opportunity for China's largest pharmaceutical company to make the best-selling soft drink nationwide. It is also a story about what a company needs to do in connection with its role in society, and what it can do with its capacities.

Before digging into the Guangzhou Pharma story, it might be useful to know more about the necessity of the reform in the Chinese pharmaceutical sector.

When it comes to the medical sector, government influence is particularly significant for pharmaceutical players, as the Chinese government is in the midst of a push to reform healthcare coverage, spending, and insurance, trying to determine which economic model is best for the future of the country.

The Chinese government is especially focused on keeping hospital costs down, partly through professionalizing the domestic healthcare equipment and device industry and relying less on imported, expensive foreign equipment, which, again, would defeat the purpose of making health care more affordable. Hospital bills in China can be just as costly as in the West, and state healthcare insurance only covers basic costs—the rest comes out of people's pockets. More often than not, a longer hospital stay could bankrupt an entire family.

Here is one of my related personal experiences. In 2011, after an exhausting trip, I went to a hospital in China with a severe bowel obstruction that required an emergency operation. It ended up with me paying US$50,000 for a 2-week hospitalization. I sent a copy of my bill to a relative of mine in Germany who is a skilled surgeon, and he said in Germany, it would have cost only one-third as much. The price was likely inflated by the cost for the value chain of importing medicines, routine devices, and equipment.

The current healthcare reform plan began in 2009 and entered its final developmental stage in 2016, as part of which hospital pharmacies will no longer be the primary distributor of drugs. Currently, public hospitals account for 80% of drug sales.[1] In other words, the market share ratio between retail pharmacies and hospitals was 1:4. In China, this has been traditionally used as a way to fund hospitals.

In China, drug companies face price capping on most of their products to keep the cost of medicines as low as possible and ensure that as many people as possible can afford them. Because of the low-value volume sales of cap-priced drugs, the pharmacy retail business is not highly profitable. Our company in Hong Kong has a pharmacy in every store, but it has none in Mainland China. This is because the cost of licensing every store in China would be outweighed by the poor revenues made from selling drugs.

Therefore, instead of focusing on volume sales of generic medicines, the pharmaceuticals business is likely to concentrate more on specific, value-added drugs in the future. It would appeal to a younger consumer audience who is more open to new ideas and potentially more likely to go to a private doctor rather than to the hospital, as is customary today.

Picking the best parts of healthcare and hospital management models from overseas and keeping a close eye on the activities of international "big pharma" companies and their profit models in this country, the government is moving forward to achieve the reform goal.

There is no reason for international companies to neglect China's pharmaceutical market, as it is currently the second largest in the world after the USA. It reached a value of about RMB 1.22 trillion in 2015 and is expected to reach RMB 1.8 trillion by 2020.[2] The period of the fastest development in the industry was between 1980 and 1999, when the number of pharmaceutical companies increased almost tenfold from 680 to 6357.[3] According to the National Bureau of Statistics (NBS), there were only 3301 pharmaceutical companies with annual sales revenues of RMB 5 million or more in 2000; in contrast, there were 7108 companies with annual sales revenues of over RMB 20 million by 2014.

Pharmaceutical market sales maintained a CAGR of over 20% between 2005 and 2010,[4] and with an annual output of 800,000 tons of pharmaceutical ingredients, China has been the world's largest active pharmaceutical ingredient (API) manufacturing and export source since 2012.[5] While the growth of industry output slowed to 8% in 2014, CAGR is expected to recover to roughly 10% throughout the period from 2015 to 2020.[6]

Despite a slowdown in growth, the Chinese pharmaceutical market remains attractive for both multinational pharmaceutical giants and domestic players. It is also attractive for the following reasons.

China has the largest elderly population, as well as one of the most rapidly aging populations in the world. The average life expectancy of Chinese people rose from 68.6 years in 1990 to 75.5 in 2013.[7] The United Nations estimates that, by 2050, there will be 2.02 billion people over the age of 60 in the world, among which nearly one quarter (480 million) will live in China. This alone is more than the total population of the USA.[8]

Healthcare and pharmaceutical costs will climb dramatically as people get older. Along the way the Chinese are also getting wealthier, with average incomes continuing to rise. As such, they have become increasingly able to pay for better medicines, which is driving growth on the market.

China is also likely to see an increase in the frequency of "lifestyle" diseases, as the quality of life has improved. More people have become victim to chronic diseases such as obesity, heart disease, liver disease, and diabetes. There are also ailments linked to pollution, and mental health issues brought about by a fast-paced life and mounting pressure. For example, globally there were 1.8 million new cases of lung cancer and 1.59 million deaths in 2012, one-third of which were in China.[9]

The market remains appealing, though China still has lower per capita pharmaceutical expenditures compared to countries with comparable levels of GDP, such as the USA, Germany, and Japan.[10,11] Health spending in 2009 accounted for only 5% of GDP in China, of which the share of drugs was as

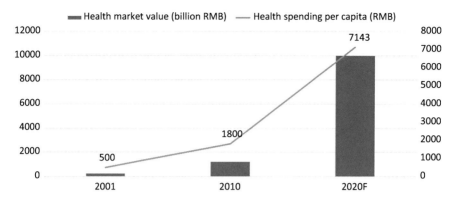

Fig. 19.1 Chinese health spending expected to grow. Source: KPMG, Chinese Academy of Science and technology for Development

high as 50%, compared with only 13% in the USA.[12] As shown in Fig. 19.1, in 2001, the total pharmaceutical market in China was worth RMB 240 billion, representing a spending level of RMB 500 per capita across the urban population. By 2010, when the total market valued at RMB 1206.5 billion, that per capita spending level had more than tripled to RMB 1800 (see Fig. 19.1). The urban population, however, is growing at less than 2% a year, so per capita spending will need to continue to rise significantly.

Seeing the immense potential, both international pharmaceutical giants and thousands of local domestic companies are in fierce competition to carve out a place in the market. In the "top 100 Enterprises in the PRC Pharmaceutical Industry of 2015" list, the threshold for candidates increased from annual sales of RMB 1.4 billion in 2010 to RMB 10 billion in 2015. This indicates that the pharmaceutical industry in China has been enjoying a rapid growth in recent years. Among the ranking, the Guangzhou Pharmaceutical Group (Guangzhou Pharma) is number one.

Besides its leading position in the market, the company also caught my attention because of the centuries-old heritage brand it owns, which is also one of its most popular products in China—Wanglaoji Liangcha (Wanglaoji). Founded in 1828 under the name Wong Lo Kat, Wanglaoji is based on Liangcha—an herbal tea from the Guangzhou (Canton) area. Cantonese people believe it can rid the body of unhealthy, "toxic" heat. People commonly drink it after eating anything spicy such as chili or BBQ sauce, or when they are suffering from sleep deprivation.

Following the establishment of the new China, Wanglaoji became a state-owned business and later a subsidiary of Guangzhou Pharma. In recent years, Wanglaoji expanded out of the Canton area and became a household name across China, with an annual sales volume of six billion cans.[13] Does that mean the average Chinese person drinks about five cans a year?

We met with Mr. Li Chuyuan, the Chairman and President of Guangzhou Pharmaceutical Group for a rare interview. We met on a beautiful autumn day in his office building, which I later learned was where my company Watsons had operated from 100 years ago. Coincidently, it was also the day before Li's 50th birthday, which gave us plenty to talk about, as I had also just turned 50 a few months earlier.

"Guangzhou Pharmaceutical has a 415-year history. The reason we've survived so long is our good genes." We both chuckled as Li continued to talk about the corporate culture at Guangzhou Pharma. "Mexico, Egypt, India, and Europe are rich in culture. But visitors don't go there only for the heritage. They also are attracted to the innovations and new things there." Besides corporate culture, Li emphasized the importance of ongoing innovation as another key factor to success.

According to Li, as the company values health, anything that can benefit human health can be an area for innovation. Wanglaoji is an example of how the company keeps developing new products in the health beverage category. The company launched two new premium types of Wanglaoji in early 2016—sugar-free and low-sugar variants—to cater to younger consumers. Though the product appeals to all age groups due to its cooling function, 70% of Wanglaoji drinkers are between 25 and 35 years old.

"Another example is new prescription drugs for cancer and vaccines. Every category is important to me. It is hard for me to identify the areas for innovation. We cover the whole industrial chain," says Mr. Li.

It makes sense to me now, as a large SOE must cater to the currently planned direction of the government, which sometimes can be clearly defined by social needs, e.g., focus on certain health aspects. At the same time, it needs an "open door" to develop strong sectors according to the current needs and opportunities in the consumer market.

Having expected to encounter a state-owned style of management, I met a sharp-witted, open-minded, and very forward-thinking CEO. I just imagined how he must have spent every day translating his thoughts to government officials, as well as to more traditionally raised employees, to get the company to where it is today. This is a real skill—combining management, diplomacy, and politics all in one. Mr. Li is also a representative of China at the Davos summit meetings.

Though benefiting Guangzhou Pharma, TCM would seem to be the last industry you would expect to see innovations. However, Li didn't see things this way. Guangzhou Pharma applies modern scientific technologies to bring out the best in TCM, the company's priority.

As an industry leader, the company established full integration starting from standardized herb-planting bases, continuously innovates with new cooperation models, and has conducted a series of research projects on herb-planting techniques. Consequently, from 1998 to 2015, Guangzhou Pharma established over 40 standardized and industrialized herb-planting bases across the country.

"We will play not only the role of promoter of TCM, but also that of a major driving force and executor, as well as ultimately one of the beneficiaries of industrial development," says Li.

As for the Internet, Li does feel it is gradually putting pressure on the pharmaceutical industry, causing "massive disruption" to existing models.

Guangzhou Pharma, however, is very active in the Internet. Launched in 2014, the company's Jianmin e-store was the first e-commerce platform in China that accepted payment using the health insurance cards issued by the Guangzhou government. It offers a one-stop online shopping experience from price inquiries to transactions, to payment, and to delivery.

Further, Guangzhou Pharma is one of the few successful prescription medicine portals in China. The country's e-commerce market for health products, especially prescription drugs, is still under development. Regulations keep evolving as business models in this sector tend to be ahead of the regulatory environment.

In January 2015, the company introduced Jack Ma's (Alibaba) Yunfeng Investment as a strategic investor. Through this partnership, Guangzhou Pharma managed to cooperate with Alibaba's AliHealth subsidiary in developing pharmaceutical e-commerce, hospital prescriptions, and healthcare services. The ultimate goal is to create a new Internet business model that covers the entire medicine and healthcare industry, which, as shown in Fig. 19.2, has already achieved dramatic growth in the past few years.

In May 2015, Guangzhou Pharma reached an agreement with Jiuzhoutong, one of the largest pharmaceutical distributors in China, and Saibailan, a digital marketing solution provider, to create a joint venture for O2O sales of Guangzhou Pharma products through a cloud-commerce strategy. "We are now promoting the tradition of our century-old brands and optimizing the existing industrial layout," Li stressed. The current China pharmaceutical e-store picture is shown in Fig. 19.3.

I was keen to find out what was brewing in terms of acquisitions, as the company is currently working on its 13th five-year plan (a holdover from its state-owned heritage!) There are two strategic directions in Li's plan:

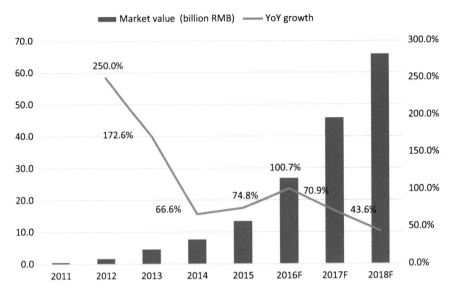

Fig. 19.2 China's pharmaceutical e-commerce market. Source: Analysys

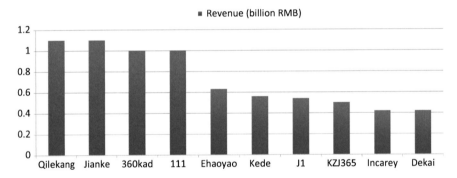

Fig. 19.3 China's Top 10 pharmaceutical e-stores 2015–2016. Source: China Pharmacy
(http://www.ydzz.com/zgyd.php?col=22&file=56581#)

capitalization and expanding abroad. Since Guangzhou is a public company, Li is committed to maximizing returns for shareholders through continuous innovations.

Expanding into the rest of the world is part of this direction. To me, a frequent consumer of the drink, Wanglaoji has the potential to go global. Guangzhou Pharma is now focusing on three major aspects: product export, culture export, and capital export. Also, the introduction of global talent and integration with global resources are other important aspects. Global cooperations are already shaping up, but Guangzhou Pharma has not yet set any priority among the overseas markets. Market readiness is the key factor to consider.

"The goal of globalization is to bring our products out of the country and form global partnerships," Li says, citing the example of investing in a plant in Indonesia to produce Wanglaoji for SE Asia. The company is also establishing new partnerships in India.

Li then explained that the value of an overseas market is subject to how much value it can produce for the company from two perspectives: profitability and helping to improve human health.

Wanglaoji will likely be a vital part of the company's globalization strategy. Originally coming from drugs, Coca-Cola and Wanglaoji share a lot of similarities in the development process. In today's China, Wanglaoji is sometimes jokingly referred to as China's Coke.

Wanglaoji has already completed its global trademark registration and is now available in over 60 countries and regions. Recently, Wanglaoji and a Nigerian company signed an agreement to enter the Western Africa market. The beverage's sales on the African market are expected to reach hundreds of millions of yuan in the future. Li has a dream that the Wanglaoji brand will be transformed from a "Chinese symbol" into "the world's Wanglaoji" and become the world's number one herbal tea brand.

From a broader perspective, the globalization of TCM is another goal Li and his team are pursuing. At the government level, the 18th Party Congress report particularly emphasized its support of TCM's development. Li believes that through the spread of Chinese medicinal culture, the world will come to recognize the theoretical system of TCM and accept TCM standards. The company has made some progress in recent years. Huatuo Zaizaowan, a TCM product, is now listed in Russia's Basic Drug Directory. Its export sales have ranked top nationwide in the Chinese traditional patent medicine category for more than ten consecutive years.

To advance TCM development through cultural exports, Guangzhou Pharma plans to build herbal tea museums around the world in the future. With such "global ambitions," I had to ask Mr. Li which companies he admires.

Coca-Cola, Siemens, and Hutchison are on his list. "Coca-Cola was a cold remedy in the beginning, and was then turned into a popular beverage that makes people feel good. It created a fashion in drinking and dining. With a historical heritage and a low price point, Coca-Cola makes consumers grasp a sense of American culture," says Li. Now the role of "exporting culture" made sense to me, since Wanglaoji is a symbol of Chinese culture. For him, Coca-Cola has been very innovative in spreading culture, health, and fashion.

Mr. Li believes Siemens represents German and European innovations. Hutchison Whampoa stands out because its business reaches every corner of the world. It has done an excellent job regarding operation and management. In Li's view, these companies represent the three areas he feels are critical to a company's success: excellent management, risk control, and being innovation-driven.

In the company's 13th five-year plan, Guangzhou Pharma has set a goal of becoming one of the World's Top 500 Companies within 5 years (by 2020). I asked Li how he would achieve this goal. His answer: "With a 1-2-3 strategy." The first goal is to achieve several hundred percent growth, multiplying revenues to RMB 100 billion in 2017; the second is to devise strategic paths to achieve its capitalization and globalization goals, and the third is to strengthen the three main pillars of the strategic plan: management, risk control, and being innovation-driven.

Such rapid growth sounds ambitious, especially in light of China's GDP slowdown and Guangzhou Pharma's already huge business volume, RMB 88 billion in 2016. However, if we look at the potential of the healthcare market in China, we may not need to worry about the company's ambition. According to research, pharmaceutical sales in China will reach RMB 3649.5 billion by 2020.

Through all these efforts, Guangzhou Pharma is planning to achieve RMB 150 billion (about $21,654 million) of sales by 2020 to become one of the world's Top 500 Companies. Yet as shown in Fig. 19.4, it still has room to improve competing with large global pharma companies (see Fig. 19.4).

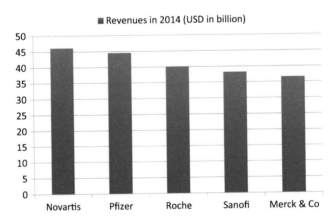

Fig. 19.4 Top 5 global pharma companies 2015. Source: GlobalData (http://topforeignstocks.com/2015/09/19/the-top-50-global-pharma-companies-2015/)

At the end of the interview, I asked Li what he would like the world to know about Guangzhou Pharma and Chinese enterprises. His response:

> Although Guangzhou Pharmaceutical Group has a history dating back more than 400 years, I feel we're still young. Our goal is to build a millennium business. To do so, we must preserve the best genes from the past, and innovate in response to market changes.

As far as Chinese companies are concerned, Li recognizes that, compared with Europe and the USA, China only developed a market-driven economy very recently. Therefore, the average age of Chinese companies is younger. But there are still quite a few traditional businesses and heritage brands in this country, which he feels are representative of Chinese culture and the China story.

I can tell from Li's response how proud of and confident he is about Chinese companies. That confidence stems from his understanding of the Chinese market, the pharmaceutical industry, and Chinese consumers. I look forward to seeing his dream to come true—which would also be a good reason for another interview!

Acknowledgment This interview has been published with the kind permission of Mr. Li Chuyuan.

Notes

1. http://www2.deloitte.com/content/dam/Deloitte/ch/Documents/life-sciences-health-care/ch_Studie_Pharmaceutical_China_05052014.pdf
2. http://www.yigoonet.com/article/22336364.html
3. http://www.cfr.org/china/chinese-pharma-global-health-game-changer/p36365
4. KPMG, Euromonitor.
5. http://www.cfr.org/china/chinese-pharma-global-health-game-changer/p36365
6. KPMG, Euromonitor.
7. http://www.worldlifeexpectancy.com/country-health-profile/china
8. http://news.mydrivers.com/1/439/439579.htm
9. http://www.yuqinge.com/zxxx/1407115874170362.html
10. http://www.cpema.org/gjdt/1506/1ezmz09t36ojuqlw_1.shtml
11. http://www.yuqinge.com/zxxx/1407115874170362.html
12. KPMG, Euromonitor International.
13. http://www.iwshang.com/Post/Default/Index/pid/243716.html

Part V

Fun, Entertainment, and Leisure

Another stereotype I sometimes hear about Chinese people is their supposed lack of humor. They are often perceived to be "constantly working." Yet, while Chinese people do work very hard, that is in part due to the fact that as the economy has continuously evolved, they have had to work hard to make a living or simply to support their personal development (studying late at night and working during the day). This situation is a current priority in Chinese society, whereas other societies experienced it a generation or two ago.

So, yes, you will see a lot of determined faces out there in China.

However, as you will find out quickly when you live here, especially when you speak the language, Chinese people can be very fun-loving and humorous. Chinese people as I know them really like to have fun, especially the younger generation who are less worried about mere survival. They are the ones who are now making the consumer decisions. And they share their funny moments on social media, especially on their main communication tool, WeChat.

Chinese consumers are increasingly traveling and seeing the rest of the world, not just their own country—which is itself the size of Europe. They especially like to hang out together and enjoy company. They also like movies and going to exhibitions and to theme parks. All of these areas are currently underserved, which means they have massive room to grow as incomes improve for the younger generation.

I came to Asia in 1996 and began setting up chain restaurants in various Asian countries around China including Korea, Singapore, and Indonesia (during its upheavals following the Suharto regime). Back then, China was still a black box; nobody could tell me if it was a viable market or not. So one winter day in 1996 I took a trip with our designer and some investor friends from Hong Kong to see what could be done.

The taxi ride from Shanghai Hongqiao airport was a bumpy one; there had been road construction, mainly concerning an elevated road called YanAn Road, which seemed ambitious, since there weren't many cars but mostly bicycles and—yes—donkeys. We asked the people with us if the road construction project was perhaps a bit too ambitious, but their response was: "We will need it." And today, that road is one of the main arteries through Shanghai and is constantly jammed—so they certainly proved me wrong.

As my company was in the leisure business—restaurants, cafes, and food products, including the world's best ice cream (at least if you ask me), hotels, and other leisure facilities, local government officials wanted to meet us to see what we planned to do in China. The government officials were talking big and about "lifestyle" and rebuilding Shanghai back to its greatness. However, I needed a lot of imagination to picture this given the state of the place back then. My impression on my first day in China (forgive me) was that Shanghai had three types of populations: local visitors from other cities who came to gawk at the Oriental Pearl tower; construction workers working, living, and cooking everywhere; and local residents, who seemed rather lost between the half torn-down buildings and the early signs of a skyscraper-filled metropolis.

I couldn't identify a single lifestyle, but all the people I talked to were confident that in a few years Shanghai would be like Paris. In fact, after a day or two I started to believe them: with so many optimistic people around, the statistics spoke for themselves. So, young and energetic, I tried to sell my bosses on investing in China early. The idea was to put up hotels and restaurants, as they would be booming industries. But it was a tough sell based on a gut feeling: we had one hotel in Beijing at the time, and it was giving us plenty of trouble. Even though the government would finance us a building in a swamp next to the Oriental Pearl tower, our company decided not to struggle with the potential difficulties (the fact that this area, called Lujiazhui, has since become the Manhattan of China in terms of real estate still drives me to tears). So, much to my frustration, China was a no-go and in the end we missed the boat.

In my personal observations, the Chinese—except for different looks, language, and food—are not that different from Westerners when it comes to leisure. As mentioned above, most of the Chinese people I've met work a lot, but they also know how to have a good time. Often portrayed as serious and therefore misperceived in the Western mind when it comes to enjoying things, they in fact like the same things as Westerners—going out, discovering, traveling, and hanging out together. In some cases, these traits are even amplified: as Chinese society values engaging in activities together as a family, all generations would enjoy their leisure. Whereas in the West you would probably see parents taking their kids to a theme park, in China, chances are that the grandparents will be there, too—which explains why you sometimes see 70-year-olds on the rides at Disneyland!

As urbanization has intensified, people have flooded into the cities. The life of the average Chinese urbanite is growing more stressful due to competition at work and inflated prices for apartments and food. So people increasingly enjoy short escapes, be it a trip to the countryside, an afternoon on the golf course or on the mountain, or a daily trip to the café to escape the bustle in the street.

Western and especially European lifestyles are something the Chinese are curious about—and they're constantly learning. Many people study various aspects of Western lifestyles through social media, even books or courses. The number of people I know who are endeavoring to learn a European language or have taken French cooking classes continues to grow. The same applies for Korea and Japan in terms of food, clothes, hobbies, fashion, and travel.

This chapter highlights some great companies that have succeeded by tapping into customer lifestyle trends.

We begin with the maturing travel industry and Ctrip, a paragon company that draws on two major trends: the Chinese love of travel and the emergence of mobile connectivity, which allows everyone to show off their "travel trophies" as a new status symbol. Fun and peer pressure, combined with one of the most competitive societies in the world and one of the most populous nations, have given rise to the world's largest travel market.

Chinese like their traditional food flavors (just like Westerners). But recently, as a younger and more fun-loving consumer society has evolved, more and more people have come to appreciate innovative forms of food preparation and different environments in which it is served. We'll be taking a look at Haidilao, the number one casual dining chain, and see how traditional hot pot cooling can evolve with time. Will a themed casual dining industry arise, one similar to what we've seen in the US and other markets? We'll also look at the typical difficulties operators face as costs in China continue to rise and the service industry becomes less and less attractive as a workplace.

A common misconception that I hear from foreigners is that Chinese don't really need cinemas, since DVDs are so cheap. But that idea can be easily dispelled in light of the booming cinema industry. Chinese urbanites love the big screen so much that companies are now investing huge amounts of money to break into the value chain of the movie industry. Considering the scale of China's future movie industry, some companies, like China's Wanda conglomerate, are now deservedly aiming for a top market position globally. This chapter provides some logical explanations to why, in a few years' time, Hollywood and US entertainment giants will face global competitors from a place they would never have expected 20 years ago.

Asia in general and rising China in particular is home to consumers who embrace consumer technologies. If their budget allows it, Chinese consumers ideally change television sets and gadgets with every new trend that emerges (that's about one upgrade per year). As devices' technical features become less important and product differentiation comes more and more from software-based functions, the next battlefield will be the integration of devices and content. The last chapter in this section presents TCL, one of the world's largest consumer electronics manufacturers. The company's story demonstrates how companies have to go beyond their normal frameworks, forming alliances, buying out other companies, or integrating new services to keep up with their evolving consumers—worldwide. It can also be seen as the evolution from manufacturer to local brand to global player in a disruptive industry.

20

Curious About the World: Ctrip

Travel Industry—No. 1 travel agency and operator in China—Fan Min, Co-founder (photo with kind permission of Mr. Fan Min)

© The Author(s) 2018
C. Nothhaft, *Made for China*, DOI 10.1007/978-3-319-61584-4_20

Opportunity

With 59 million overseas trips and 2.2 billion domestic trips in the first half of 2016 alone, China's travelers are shaping the future of the global travel market—and will do so for years to come. While Chinese overseas travel is what makes the headlines, what the consumers are longing for is a tremendous opportunity, especially if those trends can be converted into some domestic business.

Increasingly individualized travel and adventure travel mean that people are making their choices on the Internet, thus putting online agencies at a huge advantage. On the business side, the market is moving towards integration between travel agents and operators, which means the leading companies could achieve a dominant market share through consolidation.

Lessons Learned

Large e-commerce and offline agencies have democratized and "disrupted" the Chinese market by competing for the local consumer. The game is no longer just about travel booking and improving related services. Companies are now looking into cross-investments inside the travel value chain in an attempt to create new experiences or secure part of lucrative sectors like cruises or specialist travel.

Every few months I fly back to Germany—not because I miss it much, but more to keep up with my relatives who live there. At some point I realized that a significant change had occurred over the course of those many trips: the people I sat with on the plane.

Over the years of flying with Lufthansa, I mostly met German business people and tourists visiting China, or returning home. I would shake my head at the tourists cramming all the overhead baggage compartments full with traditional farmer hats, rolled-up paintings, and cheap faux Ming vases. Sometimes I amused myself by asking them what they had bought and how much they'd paid for it. The fun was in knowing that a local would have probably paid a tenth as much. I was always torn between telling them the truth (about what they should have paid) and ruining the satisfaction they enjoyed with their hard-won souvenir.

Now things have changed. More often than not, today I usually sit next to Chinese travelers—not business travelers, but tourists. They are not corralled into groups wearing identical baseball caps; they are FITs (Free Independent Travelers) or families, and they sit in business class. This means fewer problems with the overhead luggage compartment on the way out from China to Europe, but more challenges on the way back: bags of Hugo Boss, Gucci, and even German glassware and kitchen knives! More often than not, I end up having a conversation with my seat neighbors about their experience in

Europe—which places they visited and (interestingly) how much money they spent. They will gladly tell you without much asking, because they are proud to put a number on how much they can afford.

Usually, I ask them if they would like to come back. The answer is usually "yes," and they plan to either bring friends or do something specific and individual, such as climbing a certain mountain, spending a week in a particular city they liked on this trip, and . . . doing more shopping.

That's a significant change! My experience reflects the dynamics of the Chinese travel industry in recent years. It used to be that the dream of going overseas was only available to a few élites like the top brass in government agencies or state-owned companies. Travel was seen as a huge reward for someone and probably the most "face" one could give someone.

With the "Regulation on Chinese Citizens' Overseas Travel" in 2002, the government began relaxing the requirements for Chinese tourists to go abroad. In response, the number of Chinese traveling abroad for personal reasons has soared from 5.6 million in 2000 to 120 million in 2015.[1] The Chinese traveler suddenly became a global one.

Accordingly, in the following we'll look at the domestic and international market separately. Today, the domestic travel market is worth RMB 3.42 trillion[2] (about US$0.5 trillion), versus the US$0.95 trillion domestic tourism revenues in the USA in 2015.[3]

With this market size, China is nearly the largest single travel market in the world. According to the WTO, it is anticipated to become the number one by 2020. Between 1994 and 2014, the number of trips undertaken domestically soared almost sevenfold, and travel expenditures rose nearly 30 times in the same period.[4]

What happened? Chinese have been traveling for decades for trade, and, most notably, for the annual home visit during the Chinese New Year holiday. Though Westerners travel a lot for Christmas, the annual Chinese New Year home visit, combined with visiting relatives at home or other cities, amounted to a staggering 1.38 billion trips during the first half of the 2016 Chinese New Year travel rush alone.[5]

China's domestic market began taking off in 2005 (following the Beijing Olympics), when the new GenPC and GenMobile consumers began establishing travel as part of the new, aspirational modern lifestyle. Judging from my tour of around 50 cities a year, the market continues to grow steadily. Figures 20.1 and 20.2 reflect both a substantial growth in volume and a trend toward higher per-trip spending.

As a result, there may be some upsides in the making: cities have already started competing for tourists by developing their infrastructure, landscapes, and

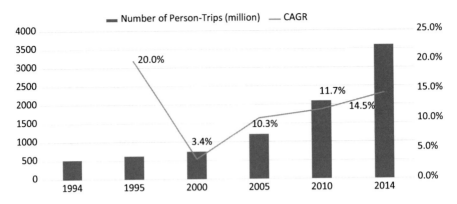

Fig. 20.1   Domestic travel in China: increasing people. Source: KPMG, NBS (KPMG, National Bureau of Statistics of China)

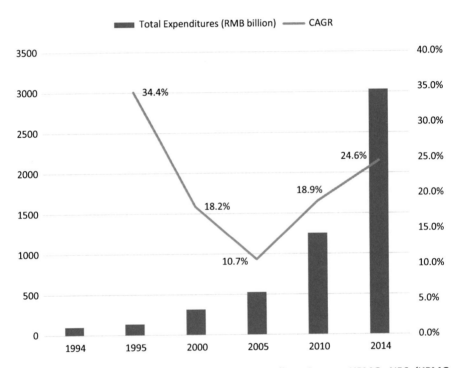

Fig. 20.2   Domestic travel in China: growing spending. Source: KPMG, NBS (KPMG, National Bureau of Statistics of China)

offering newly created tourist destinations, usually in the form of theme parks or shows for tourists. Twenty one new theme parks were opened in 2015, while another 20 are under construction, including Disney (Shanghai), Lotte, Eastern Hollywood, Universal Studios, and four other "world-class" theme parks.[6]

New travel trends are also helping foster a new found interest in heritage and eco-tourism among local consumers, such as biking in the mountains of Yunnan. Social media has also played its part in allowing people to chat about their trips, posting boastful selfies in front of "must-see" sites, and thus triggering in others the feeling that they need to "keep up."

The "stiff" competition brought by the Chinese is also affecting every other corner of the world, as overseas travelers from China are one of the most dynamic areas of the consumer market. Less than a decade ago, ticking off the list of obvious "world sites" such as the Eiffel Tower, Empire State Building, and Coliseum would send people into awe, but now travelers are chasing more exotic places on their "bucket lists," queuing up to scale Mountain Everest or crowding onto ships bound for the Antarctic. According to the International Association of Antarctica Tour Operators (IAATO), the number of Chinese tourists visiting Antarctica has grown significantly over the last 10 years, from 37 in 2004 to 3328 in 2014, placing them third behind American and Australian tourists.[7]

As the single largest source of tourists in the world, it's no surprise that China is worth studying. The World Tourism Cities Federation (WTCF) and Ipsos conducted a nationwide survey, distributing questionnaires to over 100,000 Chinese overseas tour customers, and 3170 valid respondent reports were selected for further analysis.[8]

In a nutshell, the findings were as follows:

- While Asian destinations are still preferred, destinations afield are rapidly growing in interest due to accessibility.
- From the GenPC and GenMobile generation, Chinese travelers tend to be young and travel surprisingly frequently.
- Chinese tourists primarily travel to see sights and natural beauty.
- They spend a great deal of their travel budget on shopping, thus maximizing savings on transport and hotels. But they still want quality hotels.

The favorite destinations for Chinese travelers are shown in Fig. 20.3.

A key trait is that they like to spend when traveling. According to the WTCF and Ipsos report,[9] 40% of respondents said they spend RMB 10,000 or more just on shopping, 53% spend more than RMB 20,000 on food,

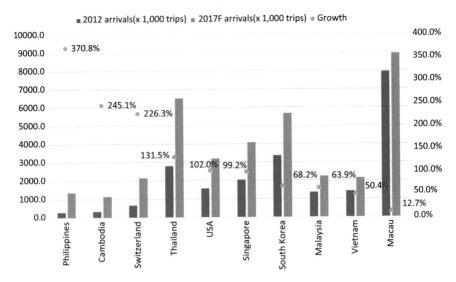

Fig. 20.3 Top ten fastest growing countries for arrivals (×1000 trips) from China 2012–2017. Source: Euromonitor (https://skift.com/2013/09/03/top-25-most-popular-des tinations-for-chinese-tourists/)

sightseeing, excursions, and shopping during each overseas trip, while 11% claimed they spend over RMB 30,000 and 8% more than RMB 40,000!

When the Internet began taking the travel market by storm, it was the harbinger of the Chinese travel industry's success. It allowed customers to make flight and accommodation decisions independently, inevitably leading to a rash of new online travel agencies, all trying to catch the most hits on search engines. As much as information and ease of booking, what consumers wanted were dependable recommendations and ratings.

There are hundreds (perhaps even thousands?) of travel-related websites in China. In 2015, the online travel booking market was worth RMB 409 billion, having more than doubled since 2012. The leading company in this market is Ctrip. Home to more than 30,000 employees, the company had a gross transaction value of US$50.5 billion in 2015, with a sales volume of US$1.66 trillion in 2015. By democratizing access to hotels and cheap flights, Ctrip quickly established its domestic market position and has now begun branching out overseas, acquiring tour operators and integrating new business markets.

The Ctrip Group consists of several sub-brand agencies: Tours for Fun specializes in travel services to North America; ezTravel in travel services to Taiwan; Joint Wisdom provides a hotel booking service; Wing On Travel specializes in travel services to Hong Kong; Tie You is a train ticketing service; Tu Jia is China's version of Airbnb; and HH Travel offers premium travel services. The Group also integrates further services through acquisition, including a restaurant booking service for secretaries. Today, the company's core competence lies in its 250 million-member database, its 12,000-seat call center, and its technologies.

Ctrip is one of those companies in China that was founded by a dream team. With Neil Shen (the legendary Chinese investor from Sequoia Capital) being one of the founders, the second was James Liang, who came from Oracle and is highly tech and business application savvy. The third founder was Ji Qi, who operated his own IT training business and had vast experience in growing companies. The fourth co-founder was Fan Min, who joined in to provide the travel expertise—both in terms of travel agencies and hotel agreements.

When asked about his role at Ctrip, Fan Min simply replied: "They needed somebody who knew the travel industry." At the time, he was the general manager of both a travel agency and of a hotel. Especially in Ctrip's initial stage, Mr. Fan had a wealth of experience and expertise that dovetailed with that of the other founders.

I met Fan Min at a humble coffee shop in Ctrip's large Shanghai offices. It was a Friday evening, and I was quite run-down after a long week including four flights. However, once we started talking, I found Fan's energy to be infectious. Fan Min is famous for telling his managers not to work over 50 h per week, which is practically impossible in China, where executives easily average 60/70 h or more. We shared our similar views on the need for employees to be efficient. Also, we found that we share a love for detail when it comes to execution and good service—both of us having a hospitality background.

Ctrip was founded in 1999 and went IPO (NASDAQ: CTRP) in 2003. Timing was critical to its success: nearly all the major Internet companies were launched between 1998 and 2000, including Alibaba (1999), Sohu (1998), Netease (1997), Tencent (1998), and Baidu (2000).

This was also the time when business, personal, and shopping travel really took off in China. When people wanted to buy a ticket in China in the 1990s, they needed to have official reference letters written by a certain level of government or state-owned company; only then did they receive a permit. Twenty years later, everything has changed. As Mr. Fan succinctly puts, it, "It's been totally dismantled, reorganized, and rebuilt." Mr. Fan and his co-founders at Ctrip saw an opportunity to be part of a growing market and to transform it. In those early years, according to Fan, more than 300 companies tried to position themselves as Internet travel companies, but "most of them later disappeared."

During 2000 the travel industry—along with many other areas of business—experienced turmoil as a result of a financial crisis in China. Ctrip could have easily gone tumbling down, but it was in the right place at the right time in terms of its business model, access to capital, and management team. In my opinion, it survived because it diversified early on, expanding away from just offering ticket sales or leisure travel, but also focusing on business clients' travel needs.

Above a certain account size, Ctrip provided a dedicated travel manager, who handled the client's travel arrangements directly, creating "marquee customers" who provided the company with stable revenues at an early stage. (I guess the modern language for this business model would be O2O!) I told Mr. Fan the story of his company representative sitting at my office for hours, just so he could pass on his business card and "be allowed to" continue our already-established business relationship. Fan seemed to think that was normal and part of good business-building to maintain or gain marquee customers.

Another important strategic element for Ctrip was having steady sales, which helped the company to avoid over-reliance on the full mass market, allowing it to make money and lead to a stronger financial situation. This is especially difficult in rapidly growing companies that are used to acquiring customers and burning money. In Fan's opinion, most of the Internet companies at that time focused on marketing, trying to burn money to get more attention. "Not that many people thought about how they could make money in the short term." In the very beginning, instead of gaining attention, Ctrip found the most important aspect to be a sustainable business model, one that would put the company on a highly profitable path.

With technology being an important aspect but not necessarily the focus in the early years, Ctrip acquired customers using traditional methods like sending sales people to train stations and airports, distributing Ctrip business cards. The Internet wasn't that well established back then, so Ctrip established a model that didn't solely rely on the Internet, but also (and predominantly) on its call center. However, now less than 40% of the air ticket booking business is processed by the robot system used in the call center.

In addition, the company pioneered some elements that we take for granted today: a toll-free telephone number, which only very few travel agencies had in 1999, and 24-hour hotel booking, which most companies didn't offer, due to a lack of staff and the high costs involved.

Coming from overseas, I was particularly interested in how Ctrip was building its international business. Instead of focusing on local hotels to capitalize on the booming domestic business travel market, Ctrip initially scaled up international business through B2B agency partners and other website operators, which notably included booking.com.

A few years ago, Ctrip began penetrating the value chain with more direct cooperation. For the Asian and ASEAN countries, Ctrip signed with hotels directly, with agencies and branches there. For most of the European and American hotels, the company cooperates with booking.com, while also signing with all the hotel chains. "By contracting with the hotel chains and partners like booking.com we can cover nearly all the hotels in the world," says Fan.

Today Ctrip serves a wide variety of customers. In the fierce competition for the constantly evolving new consumer, Ctrip has to constantly innovate and "invent" new products. This is crucial to maintaining consumers' loyalty to the brand in China. "I think that's why, for the past many years, we have accumulated customer recognition." To cater to the most promising consumers in the country, who were born after the 1990s, Ctrip has launched services such as a small loan service with installment payments, VR technology for room selection, an intra-city express service, etc. The company also has a plan called "Baby Tiger" in place to promote in-house innovation.

Assuming Ctrip (like my company Watsons) would have good customer data, I was eager to learn more about the different customer segments, especially the differences between generations like the post-1980s and post-1990s, etc. According to Mr. Fan, the post-1980s are still highly website-oriented and focused on word-of-mouth. They enjoy being FITs (free, independent travelers), but also traveling in tour groups. In contrast, the post-1990s are more independent, use more mobile services, and are interested in more diversified products. The differences seemed to be quite significant. And for Ctrip—just like other companies working hard to cater to the Millennials—doing business via mobile is becoming more and more important. According to Mr. Fan, Ctrip's mobile app has been downloaded more than 200 million times in China, with 21.2 million MAUs (monthly-active users).

Fan believes that, in the future, outbound travel may ultimately be always the best tourism industry. "No matter whether the world experiences a financial crisis or widespread prosperity, outbound tourism will enjoy double-digit growth for the next 10 years." The omen for this judgment is that 5 years ago the leading travel pattern was in tour groups, while right now more and more people tend to buy package products, not only in Asian countries but also in Europe and the USA. "I think in the near future, people will be more interested in independent travel. They'll just book flights and hotels and then travel by themselves," adds Fan.

In my opinion, Chinese travelers are quickly moving further afield, looking for more exotic destinations and growing increasingly independent. Their travel behavior is becoming more refined as more people are choosing self-guided tours and package products (flight + hotel + local transportation, etc.).

As the Chinese are already the number one consumers in most countries, Fan also sees a continuation of the trend that Chinese travelers enjoying shopping while abroad. As he further explains, "Sometimes people buy goods while traveling not only for themselves but also for their relatives in China. This market will be very lucrative in the next 10 years."

With such a bullish attitude, it made sense to me why Ctrip (and its founders) were in a position to cherry-pick the best opportunities in specific growth segments of the travel industry and invest in them. Ctrip founded a joint venture with Royal Caribbean in 2013 to launch Cruise ships under the SkySea Cruise Lines. According to Fan, less than a million of the more than 100 million outbound travelers have used cruise products in China. This percentage is quite small compared with that in the USA or European countries—where at least one-tenth or one-sixth of outbound travelers use cruise products. "So the market potential is huge. Even if one twentieth or one thirtieth of Chinese outbound travelers wants to use cruise products, you will need a lot of cruise ships in China. Not to mention one tenth," adds Fan.

Another reason Fan expects the cruise business in China to boom in the near future is the country's aging population. Cruise products are good for elderly people, and thus for family tours. "Ten years from now, cruises will be one of the best choices for people born around the 1960s," says Fan. He predicts that China will soon become the second-largest cruise country, and the number one in 20–30 years.

I knew Mr. Fan had another meeting to get to, so before we were through I wanted to be sure to get some tips on what it takes to start a company successfully. His answer was the "VIP principle" that he adheres to:

Vision: You should have very good vision, plus passion. You should know which direction to go. For Ctrip, this consisted in building the most feasible model.
Insight: You should have very good insights on the industry. You have to know what is technically possible and what is strategically possible, as well as how you can move forward, month by month and year by year.
Persistence: You should be very persistent.

It was clear that Ctrip's success is no coincidence, but the product of knowledge and insight. All the founders value good service and detailed figures upon which to base decisions. And this is what Fan Min recommends for

Chinese companies as they move forward: staying focused and sticking to those businesses and industries that they understand how to run.

Acknowledgment This interview has been published with the kind permission of Mr. Fan Min.

Notes

1. http://news.china.com.cn/2016-01/05/content_37457113.htm
2. http://www.cnta.gov.cn/zwgk/lysj/201610/t20161018_786774.shtml
3. https://www.ustravel.org/system/files/Media%20Root/Document/Travel_Economic_Impact_Overview.pdf
4. KPMG, National Bureau of Statistics of China.
5. http://news.163.com/16/0214/05/BFOUNR3G00014JB5.html?bdsj
6. http://fj.winshang.com/news-514804.html
7. https://thenanfang.com/chinese-tourists-antarctica/
8. http://en.wtcf.travel/download/report201409en.pdf
9. http://en.wtcf.travel/download/report201409en.pdf

21

Eater-tainment: Hai Di Lao

Casual Dining—No. 1 casual dining company—Zhang Yong, Founder (photo with kind permission of Mr. Zhang Yong)

© The Author(s) 2018
C. Nothhaft, *Made for China*, DOI 10.1007/978-3-319-61584-4_21

Opportunities

The casual dining market growth is brimming with opportunities, now that more young consumers are dining out and given the increasing number of shopping malls. There is a window for more branded and better organized casual dining chains to enter China, provided they are well organized and can scale up quickly, while also flexibly adapting to changing Chinese tastes.

Lessons Learned

There is a demand for casual dining establishments that appeal to younger consumers. However, the jury is still out as to whether or not foreign casual dining concepts can be successful on a larger scale in China nowadays, since the Chinese do enjoy their traditional dishes. In addition, managing expansion and labor costs is increasingly becoming a challenge, forcing companies to go to great lengths, seeking to manage costs and staff to become more competitive.

It might take some time for Chinese restaurant chains to go global, and, initially, they might depend on Chinese communities in foreign countries, since (naturally) they are successful in appealing to Chinese tastes.

The restaurant industry has undergone an interesting development over the past 10 years, and I have observed tremendous changes from the day I first arrived in China in 2007. We have seen the industry become more and more organized into chain stores. This trend has simply been driven by entrepreneurship and the emergence of professionally managed shopping malls becoming the place where young people especially like to hang out, stroll, and have fun.

Interestingly, apart from the two fast food giants KFC/Pizza Hut (in China they are run by one company) and McDonald's, not many other restaurant chains have attempted to gain a foothold in China. One reason lies in the fact that the Chinese simply enjoy their own cuisines, especially for dinner with friends. However, as young people, who are more adventurous, like to hang out together, it will inevitably create new opportunities in this "hot" casual dining sector.

However, given rising labor costs and rents, managing a restaurant business isn't easy, and it is becoming increasingly difficult to retain staff. Hai Di Lao's story demonstrates how companies are now tackling these challenges. As the number one in China's casual dining sector, Hai Di Lao had its hotpot soup ingredient supplier YIHAI INTL go public on the HK Stock Market (HK: 01597) in July 2016.

Before we dive into the founder's "rags-to-riches" story, let's have a quick look at the big picture first.

With a 13.33% growth in per-capita consumption from 2014 to 2015 and a shift away from traditional dining, casual dining provides growth opportunities, especially with young consumers, as formal and salon restaurants offering lavish dining aren't as appealing to a much younger crowd that enjoys hanging out together in the evening.

One of the most important things for foreign brands to understand about casual dining is that nobody has to be converted in China regarding food. Offering a lot of varieties and focusing on basics like fresh ingredients, Chinese cuisine is probably one of the best in the world. Those who are familiar with China's culinary culture know that there are about eight main culinary traditions in China: Anhui, Cantonese, Fujian, Hunan, Jiangsu, Shandong, Sichuan, and Zhejiang. They range from very mild flavors (Cantonese) to very spicy (Sichuan). And, of course, every city or town has its own special twist on food, resulting in hundreds of different culinary directions and eating habits across the country.

Chinese people don't like to eat alone. Dinner is an especially social occasion, which may also be the reason the "lazy Susan" was invented there—a turntable that allows dishes to be rotated around the table so that every dish can be shared!

Chinese consumers have very high expectations when it comes to service, so restaurants have to work hard to gain a reputation and maintain it. Sometimes, standard Western restaurants fail to do so.

Managing staff in the service sector is a struggle, and the key driver is the difficult living situation for lower-earning personnel in cities where their dreams of saving for and buying an apartment are growing farther and farther beyond their reach.

As the market is characterized by fierce competition, to remain competitive and to gain economies of scale on small margins, many restaurants are open 24 hours a day. The operating partner of a large private equity company told me that the common space for catering in shopping malls had grown from 15% of the area 3 years ago, to an average of 30% by 2015. That means, right now, more players are getting into the game. Fun dining with many varieties and choices is becoming mainstream—both on the supply side (driven by malls) and on the consumer side (driven by 1990s consumers hanging out).

On the chain store side, there have been mixed results for some of the operators who were inspired to join in the fray by the success of KFC. In fact, KFC was an exception to the rule in the dining industry due to its early market entry, operational excellence, and a reputation from a time when Chinese consumers considered foreign operators to be technologically advanced in terms of food safety. For most chain store players, the truth is, costs are rising and payback terms tend to stretch beyond 4–6 years, while lease contracts tend to be for 5 years, offering little help. It is, in the end, hard to establish "national leaders."

As for the consumers, from my observations, it is the GenNet generation that has given rise to casual dining. But they may now be busy raising families, and working pressures have likely tightened their schedules. The development of casual dining concepts goes hand in hand with more open-mindedness on the part of the consumer, as well as a younger consumer generation with higher expectations from the start.

As the new customer generation evolves, casual dining has become part of a lifestyle where especially GenMobile people like to hang out with friends, away from home. This provides a fresh new opportunity for the catering industry, and many casual dining restaurants are now opening in response. As they strive for professionalism and brand distinction, some companies have attempted to buy overseas brands. For example, the Chinese investment house Legend Holdings acquired the UK chain Pizza Express in 2014, and Fosun became the second largest shareholder in Secret Recipe of Malaysia, also in 2014.

Hai Di Lao, with its 166 stores across 31 cities and 2015 sales of RMB 5.05 billion, is not a small company in China's ever-changing consumer economy. They are large restaurants, with some boasting over 1000 m^2 for each floor area, most of them over 1500 m^2.

The cuisine is based on Sichuan's hotpot, where customers cook their food around big dining tables with hot broth full of spicy flavors. It is a highly social form of dining and good fun!

Mr. Zhang Yong, 47 years old and once a factory worker in Jianyang, Sichuan, founded the company in 1994. When we met, before work in Beijing's Jockey Club, it was 07:00 am—perfect, since neither of us minded getting up early. "The early bird catches the worm," we both joked, using an old Chinese idiom. I wanted to know right away how he got into the restaurant business. The answer was somewhat of a surprise: "So that I could buy an apartment!"

"The first motivation to start up the business was to change my life status. Not like the current China market, in which there are so many opportunities, there were no other possibilities in my small town, so I started as a street vendor. It was a good fit for me, since I could work in the factory in the daytime and run my night snack business on the street in the evenings. I just wanted to buy an apartment to improve my living conditions. All human beings should have a dream," he told me.

In my view, Hai Di Lao is successful because of four factors: (A) a focus on the young consumers with a product that people already like; (B) a focus on fun and using technology to connect with young consumers; (C) building a reputation on service; and (D) being highly competitive and cost-focused.

Sichuan hotpot is a very traditional dish, usually eaten in colder periods of the year and more likely in West China, due to its cultural roots. However, eating hotpot with friends can be very entertaining, especially with a group of friends. Somehow this hits the trend of being "social" among young consumers.

Zhang Yong: "For the restaurant industry, mainstream customers are in their 20s or 30s. Hotpot is, by its nature, a good fit for young people." He adds with a smile: "It doesn't make sense to explore whether or not a dish is too spicy for consumers over 80."

Hai Di Lao is famous for entertaining its young consumers. Each restaurant has entertaining staff, including noodle makers who juggle noodles, and waiters who occasionally sing. It's like a food circus!

These elements have gained it a reputation for focusing on the consumer. Technology is now a new driver to attracting and retaining young consumers. Hai Di Lao has introduced social digital games to its restaurants, allowing customers in the restaurant to communicate and play games with each other while waiting. The winners are awarded coupons. Seventy percent of post-80s and post-90s take part in playing the games when they wait in the queue, and fewer post-70s, as Mr. Zhang highlights.

Hai Di Lao even introduced some new gadgets in a newly opened store in Beijing, including a cooking range hood above each hot pot table, as well as wireless recharging stations on the table. I am always amazed how Chinese entrepreneurs always like to be at the forefront of tech! Going much further, the company talks about using things like face recognition and other technologies to provide unique and efficient service to its customers, especially those with a membership card. This idea particularly amazed me, having grown up in a country where data privacy is practically a religion.

One of the toughest struggles food service companies face when scaling-up is ensuring consistent food quality standards. Even the large and very experienced Western companies struggle with their food safety. There have been several cases over the years that have made the headlines, most recently an "expired meat" scandal in 2014 that affected McDonald's supply chain, and the antibiotics case in 2012 surrounding KFC's suppliers.

The biggest challenge remains the supply chain with farmers and producers and monitoring the origin and handling of the produce. For Zhang and his team, improving the situation through automation, professional storage and handling, material processing, and supply chain management is a daily task.

Zhang mentions that, in the eyes of the Chinese public, brand owners will always take the blame, even if the root of the problem is somewhere much farther upstream. Therefore, though the company "only" has 166 stores across China, Hai Di Lao has already gone to great lengths to take control of its principal product supply chain—building seven distribution centers, an ingredient manufacturing facility, and a meat processing plant to sustain its network.

Because competition in the restaurant business is fierce, I quickly come to understand why Zhang downplays his success and focuses on the daily tasks at hand. As he succinctly puts it, "Modern commercial civilization is built upon competition."

Hai Di Lao has become a standard business case in China in light of its customer orientation and staff management. Even my team has studied the "Hai Di Lao management ingredients." We realized that the frontline execution is backed by rigorous people management, and I discovered something of a "Jack Welch" element in how Zhang manages his teams.

In terms of staff management, Zhang believes in competition. "I believe that if I outperform you, I will be promoted and rewarded with a better salary and benefits. Moving up step by step from junior-level to middle-level positions requires you to constantly do a better job than your colleagues. If you cannot perform as a store manager, I will demote you to a lower position without any hesitation. In China, the laws and the public perception allow me room to do so. It's accepted as a reasonable practice."

In China, competing and outperforming your neighbor is par for the course, not just at work, but also in many other areas (including "jumping the queue" at airport check-ins). Therefore, Zhang's practice is perfectly acceptable in this country, both professionally and socially, even though Western readers might be a bit shocked.

"We see the cruel reality that a store manager may forget about all the hard times he went through after having started as a waiter. He may abuse his power and treat subordinates badly. This could happen among our leaders. Our solution, though most likely not scientific, is a mandatory 'bottom out' system," Zhang explains.

Interestingly, Zhang sees these methods as a temporary necessity. He believes that, as society evolves and the level of education—and with it, the sophistication of leaders and middle management—improves, these methods will eventually no longer be necessary.

Costs in China are rising, and companies in all industries, especially those that have a high labor and rent component, are innovating to compensate for them. Mr. Zhang is currently experimenting with paying waiters not by the hour but based on their efficiency, in fact per number of "items delivered."

Zhang draws a comparison to Western markets: "In Europe and the USA, there is no need to manage waiters. It surprised me to learn that pretty blond girls and handsome boys are willing to work in restaurants, for tips. However, in Asia—in China, Japan, and Korea—customers don't have a tipping culture."

"I found we could instead pay per items delivered. The pay is calculated on the number of customers served, the number of items delivered, or the number of dishes washed," Zhang explains. He is convinced that this promotes competition among frontline staff and stores, the goal being: "When they voluntarily compete, the quality is guaranteed."

This is an interesting approach in a country where tipping is something customers don't do and are most likely not going to start doing in the foreseeable future.

One reason that Zhang tried this approach is that, throughout the service industry, staff are crucial to the business. The bottom end of the Chinese labor market is extreme, as people often have to change jobs to keep up their salary. In addition to pay based on the number of "items delivered," Hai Di Lao has also gained a reputation for buying or organizing bulk purchases of apartments for its staff. This is rooted in Mr. Zhang's original dream, to one day own an apartment despite being a lowly factory worker. As he says, his goal is to give people who "work hard with their hands" a platform that enables them to change their lives. Zhang explains the circumstances of a typical migrant worker:

According to Zhang, the children of our frontline staff are left behind in the villages, and their spouse may work in a shoe factory or toy plant in Shenzhen. In the early years, migrant workers from the rural areas needed a temporary residence permit to work and live in cities. Zhang was committed to helping his staff with that and in return creating a culture of worker loyalty.

"Although I'm not able to provide everybody with a good life, I can help some of them (the outstanding ones) to live in relative dignity," he claims. "I made a calculation, and found they need to earn RMB 5000 or more a month to buy an apartment, but in reality this amount of money is not that easy to earn." He found the salary of his frontline staff was about RMB 3000–4000 at best.

For Western readers, it might be necessary to explain the burden of financing an apartment purchase in China:

An apartment (not in the city center) in a smaller provincial capital or tier-2 city would cost roughly RMB 8000 m^2. In tier-1 cities like Beijing and Shanghai, the price can be three to fifteen times as much! A well-paid worker would make around RMB 4000 a month, before taxes. Applying a savings rate of 30% (on the high side), they can save around RMB 1300 per month. A small 50 m^2 apartment for a family of three costs roughly RMB 400,000 in a tier-3 city and at least RMB 2 million in a tier-1 city.

So we are looking at 25 years (in tier-3 cities) of repayments on an apartment without a mortgage. The conclusion is that achieving ownership of an apartment, if you work in the service industries, is a dream that can only be realistically pursued outside tier-1 cities and most likely with the help of multiple generations of your family.

But there are some catches:

– RMB 3000–4500 is a good salary for manual work in today's China.
– Costs in China are going up a lot, and a one-third savings rate at the lower end of the salary scale is becoming less and less feasible.
– An air ticket home between a tier-2 city and another city in the middle of China costs about RMB 2000, which represents one of two fewer repayments per trip home.
– Most of all, property prices have been soaring over the last 10 years, so in the city center, where the good restaurant (or retail) jobs are, such properties are no longer affordable. They are in fact 30–50% higher than the number given above, which would mean a repayment period of closer to 40 years. In my company, we have been paying some staff who work in inner city stores a transport allowance, because they simply can't afford to live close by, or even within a 10-km radius.

Therefore, while the rise in property value has driven GDP over many years, and has made many people rich (especially developers and owners in tier-1 and tier-2 cities), for the bulk of the population, owning a piece of property means a lifelong struggle, and also limits their ability to spend. So, property prices, especially for younger consumer generations, can significantly impact the consumer industry, somewhat negatively in the long term.

That's why Hai Di Lao emphasizes that it is a place where you can move beyond a college graduate's salary by performing well, even if you were untrained before. This matches the staff's dreams with the company's need to be highly competitive and service oriented.

As Zhang proudly states, "I'm glad to share with you that in the recent bulk purchase of apartments in Xi'an, over 200 employees signed up." In 2015, 23 employees in Xi'an purchased apartments with a price of between RMB 5200 (hardbound) and 7400 (rough) per square meter. These prices are slightly lower than the market average, and the company also provided a small amount of money for each employee who purchased an apartment, to be used as a furnishing allowance.

We have already seen how Hai Di Lao is pursuing greater connectivity with consumers, partly with the help of new technologies. As the company expands, the market grows even more competitive, and rents keep rising, Zhang (like many other entrepreneurs) needs to constantly build and rebuild in a very competitive environment.

For example, Hai Di Lao is now pursuing a strategy to develop smaller sized neighborhood stores to be closer to its customers, or more specifically, to become a "neighborhood store." The main reason behind the move is that Zhang found too many consumers waste their time on the way to the restaurants due to traffic jams. In response, he decided to open more stores, but in a smaller size.

> I think the strength of Hai Di Lao is that we are willing to do small things for customers. With much smaller stores, our staff (who are ready to serve customers' needs) are closer to the customers. I hope my restaurants and my customers can build a strong relationship, such as that between residents of a small European town and the owner of the local café. My efforts are based on this purpose, instead of improving the space efficiency through smaller stores.

Hai Di Lao has now also launched some overseas stores with a focus on Chinese communities. "We always start with the overseas Chinese." While Southeast Asia is the main focus, Hai Di Lao opened a store in Tokyo in September 2015 and now has four in Singapore and two in Korea. There are also two stores in the USA, with a third in progress.

However, Zhang finds it harder to penetrate non-Chinese ethnic groups. "Different tastes may be a factor. We may need to find a way to improve the participation rate of non-Chinese. That's why I don't want to enter Europe. So far, I haven't figured out a way to attract Europeans to the hot pot." There is no specific expansion plan in Europe but to my delight, Mr. Zhang claimed he wouldn't mind having a store in Germany in the future.

In Mr. Zhang's view, each country is a wholly new challenge. His view on expanding in a foreign land is rather cautious: "I'd rather pilot in a given place and observe it for 3–5 years. Once I am more familiar with the local market, I will then open more stores." To achieve its overseas goals, Hai Di Lao now co-operates with English training institutes to offer classes for store managers.

After learning so much, I was keen to get to know Mr. Zhang a bit better as a person—but it proved not to be so easy. Though he seemed extremely relaxed, I could sense that this was in part a cover for a high level of commitment and competitiveness. According to Zhang, he doesn't even have his own office. He also claims to work little and to focus more on talking to employees and thinking about better ways to develop Hai Di Lao.

He stressed the importance of making sure strategies are clearly communicated to every employee. He sees this as the most important aspect of any strategy: making sure everyone grasps it. He also sees "safety" as one of his main responsibilities as a leader.

Since most of these tasks can't be attended to from an office, he therefore insists on not having one. "None of my main tasks can be handled during official working hours." Interesting logic!

The interview was drawing to a close, so I slipped in my final question, namely, what he wanted the rest of the world to know about Chinese entrepreneurs. Zhang shared an interesting perspective on how he sees Chinese entrepreneurs.

> Entrepreneurship and the pursuit of financial success is the character of the Chinese ethnic group. Chinese people are willing to sacrifice their health and many other things for business and money. Some very successful entrepreneurs even claim that Chinese families are born for business success. But I'd like to remind entrepreneurs that life is multi-dimensional. Everyone has a life of his or her own, with all of its dimensions. It doesn't make sense to invest all your energies into achieving success in just one area.

Zhang has apparently been developing a strong philosophical bent from his work and overseas travel. He concludes: "Human beings' pursuit of a good life is a universal constant, no matter what their religion, skin color or gender. Ultimately everything will be unified, including language. I believe that China will be connected with the rest of the world."

Acknowledgment This interview has been published with the kind permission of Mr. Zhang Yong.

22

Chinese Hollywood: Wanda

Entertainment Industry—No. 1 global cinema owner—Wang Jianlin, Chairman (photo with kind permission of Mr. Wang Jianlin)

© The Author(s) 2018
C. Nothhaft, *Made for China*, DOI 10.1007/978-3-319-61584-4_22

Opportunity

Chinese consumers have embraced being entertained during their leisure time, which has led to a booming entertainment industry, especially cinema. It is also anticipated that the government and companies will have to give staff more vacation time in the long run. The young consumer generation in China wants to strike a balance between having fun and working hard. So, companies in China are now making substantial investments in the entertainment sector: in shopping malls and even entire theme parks to create local, regional, and even nationwide attractions into the movie industry.

Lessons Learned

Local companies in China are very good at execution and are determined to expand the entertainment industry. International global players will find great opportunities in China, but might end up taking a backseat, as local companies are willing to take longer-term bets with lower initial returns. At the same time, the size of the Chinese market will naturally make Chinese companies some of the largest players in the entertainment industry globally, which may garner them a seat at the table of the global markets, e.g., "Hollywood Inc."

Wanda is a real behemoth of a company. Originally founded in the port city of Dalian in northeast China, the company moved its headquarters to Beijing in 1988. I can remember well the first meeting and dinner together, when their management team moved to their new Beijing office to form a strong "command center" literally overnight.

Wanda's business is high-profile, given its size and exposure to various sectors. The company was originally a pure real estate developer, using a model of building inner city shopping malls with attached apartment complexes. It is China's biggest shopping mall developer, having opened 122 new malls in the past 4 years (it's closest competitor opened only 22 malls in the same time). As time moved on, the developments became bigger and bigger and also followed the consumer trend by integrating entertainment areas and cinemas into the shopping centers to attract residents and shoppers alike.

Over time, Wanda's core competence grew beyond real estate into what are now its core business pillars—commercial properties (residential real estate and shopping centers) and culture industry (entertainment/cinemas, etc.). The Wanda Cultural Group, established in 2012, operates 292 cinemas across China, mostly in Wanda shopping malls. The Group has made a number of high-profile acquisitions overseas—including the world's second largest cinema operator AMC cinemas for US$2.6 billion in 2012 and Odeon & UCI Cinemas Group in 2016 for US$1.2 billion, as well as its US$3.5 billion investment in Legendary Entertainment in early 2016 (though the deal was later suspended). And the latest was the acquisition of Nordic Cinema Group, the largest cinema chain in northern Europe, for US$930 million in January 2017.

The company also added a finance division in March 2015, aimed at providing one-stop financial services to retailers and consumers, rounding out its strategy with a third pillar.

Our company has been working alongside Wanda for the last 9 years, and our stores can be found in all of its shopping malls. Though I personally always found Wanda's shopping malls huge, somehow they have the power to attract enough shoppers and fill them well; as a result, all of my shops there have been successful. To be honest, I am happy with that—Wanda's shopping mall portfolio now comprises 187 shopping malls across China's major cities.

Wanda also owns 102 hotels in China, and this business is expanding internationally. The company has also developed a ski resort in Changbaishan, near the China–Korea border. I paid a visit there years ago, while it was still under construction, and was not convinced it would work—looking back today, it clearly does, and I wonder just how much of a skiing craze we'll see after Beijing hosts the Winter Olympics in 2020.

I met Wanda's founder Wang Jianlin for the first time sometime around the 2008 Beijing Olympics in Dalian, during a shopping mall meeting. We had a separate reception to hear about Wanda's expansion plans together with a handful of local executives, and embarrassingly I was—as often—the only Westerner in attendance. Though to me—then a newbie in China—the plans seemed overambitious, I could clearly sense the ambitions the CEO, previously a platoon commander in the Chinese People's Army, had for his empire.

Every year, Mr. Wang receives a number of national and international awards; among many others, he was appointed to the "Most Influential 50 in the World" by Bloomberg and ranked 37 and a "Top 10 Global Self-made Billionaire" by Wealth-X (he was the only Asian entrepreneur on the list). Maybe one of his most prestigious achievements was topping Forbes China's list of Chinese Philanthropists for 2014, and one of the most significant and recent accolade is his being dubbed the "Top One China-Hollywood Chairman'" by Hollywood Reporter in November 2016.

One early morning, we arrived at the Wanda headquarter, and I was delighted to hear that Mr. Wang remembered me and wanted to have lunch together in addition to the interview. The lunch we had included a good business update, with some insights into Mr. Wang's personal vision for the company, and it set a relaxed atmosphere for the interview. There are many stories and views about Mr. Wang, China's richest man (at that time we interviewed him), and I expected him to potentially be a complicated person, but from the first few minutes of our talk it became clear that he was simply very straightforward and very goal-driven, yet also very human-value-driven.

I had to cut to the chase right away and ask him why he places so much emphasis on the Cultural Group. One reason clearly is the consumer trend, in the course of which China will transform from a manufacturing economy into a consumer economy. Mr. Wang provided a simple yet convincing answer: the growth in the proportion of consumption in the total economy is faster than the growth in GDP.

Wang sees a fundamental change in the economy in the making. He concludes: "In the future, China will definitely become the largest consumer market. Whoever makes the first move into this market will take the lead." This rationale makes his heavy investment into entertainment a sensible one.

I realized Wang had included family and kid zones in his malls. Wang explained that he looks at a broader age group and seeks to serve all levels of customers. "I look at a broad base. The Wanda KIDSPLACE is designed for kids age 2–8, followed by Wanda City and Wanda Plaza, which aims at families." The company currently has about 15 ongoing large-scale projects to build theme parks within Wanda Plaza and ride the wave of entertainment in China.

While the real estate business is fairly clear-cut in China, and Wanda has performed remarkably in terms of getting good land and mass-producing huge projects at a staggering rate of roughly 50 malls plus residential a year, the entertainment business is multi-layered. Surely, at least so I assumed, getting to know and developing the sector must have its fair share of challenges. Wang agrees that the theme park business is different from that of movies and entertainment. "You can enter the film industry very quickly, but the opportunity to get into the theme park industry didn't emerge until the past 2 years." Wang explains that the rise in the average personal income is what makes a day at a theme park affordable.

As always in China, once trends become part of the government's "desired sectors," it is easier for businesspeople like Wang to rapidly enter and develop the sector. Wang elaborates that the government recently announced new guidelines about tourism promoting the annual leave mechanism among the government departments. Wang is convinced that government will encourage people's spending in the tourism and entertainment sector using peoples' holidays and leisure behavior as a driver.

And here is the long-term upside: A government officer has about 15 days of leave per year—about half or even less than in more developed societies, so as holidays might be extended as society develops, the potential for this sector will grow. Wang believes now is the time to get into the game early and at scale—domestically as well as internationally—by securing the best brands, concepts, and know-how. Further, Wang sees theme parks in China soon offering a wider range of services, e.g. indoor entertainment and integration with residential projects, creating synergies with Wanda's real estate and malls.

Sometimes I picked up news about Mr. Wang in the Wall Street Journal and on TV, and I realized Westerners had somewhat of a hard time understanding why a Chinese real estate businessman would spend heavily on cinema chains and building a cultural group.

While on the one hand, Wang explained all the investment rationale, I still felt there was some personal background here—his personal desire to promote Chinese culture across the globe, with movies being the key to doing so.

In illustrating his strategy, Wang claimed that China is missing some components in the ecosystem of movie production, and that this motivated his overseas acquisitions. "China has its movie businesses, but not a complete film industry," he said, adding, "We have movie shooting and movie playing, but not film production." According to Mr. Wang, China doesn't have the film production capability or the talents, and that's why film production is still all about Hollywood today.

Wang believes that film production creates the most value in the industrial chain and higher profits, and that this sector is totally in foreign hands when it comes to the global market—which clashes with the fact that China will become the largest movie market in 2017. As a first step toward changing the situation, Wanda committed to invest US$8 billion to build what is—according to Wang—the world's largest and most comprehensive filmmaking industrial park in Qingdao, the Oriental Movie Metropolis. He believes this will only mark the start for the industry in China, with other facilities sure to be developed in the future. In Wang's vision, sooner or later the Chinese people will master the core technologies of filmmaking, including sound effects, dubbing, and animation.

The same week we met, it was announced that Wanda would acquire Odeon for US$1.2 billion (Britain's largest cinema chain with near 250 cinemas and more than 2000 screens). Everyone around Wang looked very proud when I brought up the topic, asking about Wanda's cinema strategy and if there were more deals in the pipeline.

Wang hopes to get a seat at Hollywood's table of power brokers by acquiring a sizeable part of the value chain. "The Chinese movie business is feeble and doesn't currently have a say in the world market," says Wang. He feels it's hard to penetrate the content production industry, but there are good opportunities to penetrate the industry through M&A by moving downstream and approaching the consumer the same way that cinemas do.

Wanda then came up with the idea of entering into the chain from the distribution channel by acquiring AMC (second largest cinema chain in the USA with more than 5000 screens and near 350 cinemas), Carmike (fourth largest cinema chain in the US with around 3000 screens and 276 cinemas), Odeon and Nordic (North Europe's largest cinema chain which owns 68 cinemas and around 460 screens in seven countries). And Wang emphasized that more deals would follow: "In addition to the European market, our next targets will be Asian countries, such as Japan and Korea."

There are numerous film-related companies in the world, but only six studios have the ability to distribute films globally, and they are all in the USA. According to Wang, Wanda aims to be the first non-US worldwide film distributor. His strategy is to control cinemas, the end outlets of the film industry chain, to penetrate the film distribution channels in the long term, thus enabling Wanda to influence the upstream parts of the value chain—production and distribution. And the fact that Wanda cooperated with Legendary on the 2016 Matt Damon film *The Great Wall* is one example of that.

By acquiring these US and European cinema chains, Wanda now has a market share of nearly 20% globally. Wang believes Wanda needs to be large enough to successfully enter the "circle of distributors" and achieve a global market share of 30%. Wang is confident that Wanda will become an exception as the first non-US player to penetrate the sector at scale within the next 3–5 years.

For Chinese companies, cross-border M&A can be a tricky business. Wanda seems to do M&A at pace and must have found ways to manage takeovers well. I wanted to know Mr. Wang's secret recipe—which he boiled down to two main points:

1. Talent localization. Among all the Wanda overseas acquisitions in sports, entertainment, tourism, and real estate, the company hasn't assigned a single manager from China. "We always keep the management team of the company we bought," Wang says, elaborating that, although there might be some replacements in the management team, they all come from where the business is located. He believes a cultural difference between different countries does exist, so it's difficult for people from one country to manage people in others. "That's why we value local talents," Wang concludes.

2. Effective incentive system. Wang's approach is to let the management share in the success of the newly acquired company. "We always offer the management team individual shares of the company to also make them shareholders." According to Wang, Wanda has also changed management incomes to a more performance-based model, which effectively makes the management team the owners of the business.

This part of the conversation really resonated with me. I frequently attend meetings with brands in China run by foreigners, who get sent to manage businesses that were bought and taken over. More often than not, I have seen foreign takeovers fail when the local management gets replaced—not just in China, but also in other countries. However, Chinese companies interestingly tend to maintain the local management and instead place staff in other positions, where they can learn from the local operating environment. Our group is also such an example—over 10 years ago we acquired several companies in Europe and never changed the management—on the contrary, we incentivized performance more, and the local management improved over time.

Since we were on the topic of cross border M&A, I wanted to ask Mr. Wang if he feels Chinese companies are treated unfairly when trying to engage in overseas M&A activities. Wang claimed Wanda had never been treated unfairly, which he attributed in part to its high brand recognition, as well as Wanda's approach to keeping the local management after acquisitions. While he was talking, I remembered how our group acquired many drugstore players overseas in Europe, and part of the success has been because we run these companies independently, following their local CEOs' strategies.

Wang also believes that cross-border M&A from China is new for both parties—the target companies as well as the Chinese acquirers. In general, Wang thinks there is still a gap between Chinese companies as acquirers and Western companies as acquirers. "It takes time for the businesspeople in the US and Europe to regard Chinese entrepreneurs as a respectable group and welcome capital from China."

There is a long way to go before Chinese companies truly become global companies, according to Mr. Wang. "For example, you'll hardly find any Chinese CEOs in the non-Chinese global top 500 companies." (He is one of the few). "This gap indicates that Chinese entrepreneurs as a group are not yet recognized by the Western countries." Overall he believes Chinese entrepreneurs may need more time to play an active role on the world stage and be acknowledged by the rest of the world.

We circled back to the topic of the consumer market in China (my favorite field) and interestingly, Wang feels the market system is not fully developed, especially when it comes to transparency or a full set of market rules. "That's why foreign companies find it hard to manage here," he concludes.

Consequently, Wang sees Wanda as a platform for introducing new things to the Chinese consumer across multiple categories, e.g., food, drink, play, and fun. However, the market is extremely competitive, and brands need a major competitive edge or stand-out quality to win. As Western companies in highly branded areas like fashion need to rely on building a brand image locally, and this calls for a deep understanding of consumers, only a few are ultimately successful. Good examples are those with a high degree of talent localization, like Uniqlo, whose CEO in China is a local.

Wang's advice to any Western company entering China is clear and straightforward—to form a completely Chinese team. "Don't rely on a few foreign expatriates—it will be extremely difficult (to succeed)," says Wang. He emphasizes that the local team needs to be given real authority to make decisions. "In some companies, the internal control chain is very long, and making a single decision requires multiple levels of approval. Then the market opportunity is usually lost before the decision can be made," Wang concludes.

I felt a bit awkward at this point, having built a local company into a giant, but being a "foreigner." However, perhaps Mr. Wang's definition was based more on behavior than on skin color.

On the subject of which products and services are more likely to succeed in China, Wang also had a clear view: "I think the US and European products that offer consumers a satisfying experience are more likely to do well in China." He then cited the Perfume and Beauty sector, selective delicacy stores, and specialty food stores. Today a 100,000 m^2 Chinese shopping mall is usually home to between 200 and 500 brands, whereas in the USA it would be double the number. Wang believes, "The market is still in its early stages of development," and that China still has a long way to go regarding the number of brands and products.

I wanted to explore Wang's dream for Wanda. He is very open about his ambitions to build Wanda into a world-class multinational corporation with assets of $200 billion, a market capitalization of $200 billion, revenues of $100 billion, and net profits of $10 billion by 2020. According to the 2016 annual report, Wanda has achieved assets of about RMB 796.1 billion (US$115.7 billion), which means it is already more than halfway to reaching its goals.

Wang is convinced that he can achieve them and wants Wanda to someday be "the world's number one in every industry it enters." He then claimed, "We are already number one in the real estate industry as well as the movie industry. The next areas in which we aim to be a world champion include sports, travel, and children's entertainment."

Wang also wants Wanda to become a global household name like Microsoft, IBM, Apple, and Coca-Cola in 5 year's time: "I created an excellent organization, and it will soon be recognized by the whole world—that is my dream!" However, he knows the path to success is a difficult one, with the biggest worry being transformation—just as the other entrepreneurs in this book have recognized. For Wang, the particular challenge is to find the right talents, especially to run the new businesses outside real estate. "We keep hiring externally through headhunters. But it takes time for new hires to adapt to the Wanda culture. Both the company and the new hires need time to adjust."

Mr. Wang's favorite Western companies are Apple and Google. He favors Apple because it grew from a small, poorly performing company to an outstanding global player, deriving its power from superior products in an already highly competitive field. At the same time, he respects Google's grand vision and focus on the future, including research and pushing the boundaries of new areas, e.g., driverless cars and AI. "The investments they make today are not intended for immediate returns, but in the next 10 or 20 years. That's why I admire these two companies," Wang concludes.

Wanda wants the world to know that it is a friendly business—in terms of the environment, its workforce, and in its CSR work and charitable donations to local universities and museums in the USA and the UK. Wang also emphasizes that profits and cash made elsewhere are not being taken back to China but reinvested locally. "Wanda is a friendly business, rather than an aggressive competitor who comes over to take jobs away," he explains.

Lastly, I tried to engage Mr. Wang in an East-meets-West conversation, knowing he'd be quite open about what Western companies need to learn in order to cooperate better. Mr. Wang had one special message for Western media and entrepreneurs: "With regard to Chinese companies as a whole, I hope the Western media and entrepreneurs can clear up the misunderstandings that, for example, Chinese entrepreneurs only know about relationship building, under-table deals, and corruption, but lack capabilities and global vision. I hope to change their impression," and knowing Mr. Wang well over the years, I believe he will do so.

Acknowledgment This interview has been published with the kind permission of Mr. Wang Jianlin.

23

Home Entertainment: TCL

Electronics—China's No. 1 home electronics Company—Li Dongsheng, Chairman (photo with kind permission of Mr. Li Dongsheng)

© The Author(s) 2018
C. Nothhaft, *Made for China*, DOI 10.1007/978-3-319-61584-4_23

Opportunity

Simultaneously challenged by their current market position and encouraged by national policy to rejuvenate and upgrade manufacturing, more and more Chinese manufacturers are now going through a transformation process. Therefore, huge potential arises for overseas companies with smart technologies and intelligence to participate in this evolution or to be bought out by Chinese companies. While manufacturing itself is experiencing a renaissance, the evolution of the consumer market is also forcing manufacturers to think about convergence between product and content or services, so as to reposition themselves as solution providers rather than equipment manufacturers.

Lessons Learned

Traditional manufacturing companies may find it complex and difficult to directly transform into integrated solution providers, or to offer consumer services like Netflix. As such, these companies may choose different forms of cooperation, including buyouts, to accelerate.

Cross-border M&A is often viewed with skepticism, so I was keen to find a company that has had a history of using M&A to maintain or boost its competitive edge. One of the early movers in consumer electronics manufacturing is TCL, which gained attention 10 years ago when few other companies (in fact, the only other company was Lenovo) dared to step up the pace and engage in overseas M&A. When TCL's leader Li Dongsheng, a veritable legend in China, accepted my invitation for an interview, I was ecstatic. I expected TCL to offer a great example of how a large and already successful Chinese company does strategic M&A, and personally I was hoping for an expert's view and exclusive insights into his own experiences.

In the highly competitive Global LCD TV set market as shown in Fig. 23.1, with a total of 290 million TV sets worldwide in 2016,[1] TCL launched an M&A-based international strategy by acquiring Thomson TV and Alcatel (both in France) in 2004. In 2005, the company became the Global Number One in terms of volume for TV sets, and in 2010 it invested massively in flat-screen TV production, securing its global no. 3 position among flat-screen TV producers, which it still holds today.

The company has a long history of diversification into fields related to its manufacturing capabilities, as well as some efforts to invest in areas close to the consumer market, i.e., the acquisition of Palm (a former Hewlett-Packard PDA brand) and investing in a smart household company, both in 2015.

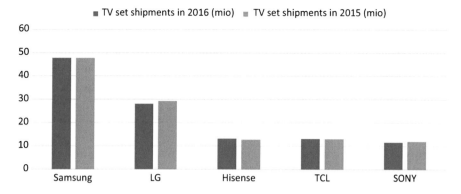

Fig. 23.1 Slowdown in shipments for global TV manufacturers. Source: WitsView (http://weibo.com/ttarticle/p/show?id=2309614074135230793533&sudaref=www.google.co.jp&retcode=6102)

TCL is also another incredible story of a Chinese company that went from its fixed role in a planned economy to become an industry leader by evolving rapidly through privatization. Originally, it was founded as an SOE in 1981 and became a Sino-HK joint venture in 1985, with a focus on manufacturing telephone equipment. Between 1992 and 1999 it diversified, expanding into TV sets (its primary business today), computers, batteries, and software. It went public in 2000 (in Shenzhen) and started its international journey 4 years later.

As mentioned above, I was very excited to garner an interview with Li Dongsheng, another legendary CEO in China who was famously dubbed the Best CEO of Chinese Public Companies in 2013—a great example, contrary to the common misconception that SOE leaders are more politicians than business or industry experts. Mr. Li, born in 1957, started as an engineer at the company in 1982 and led it through numerous transitions, successes, and crises. Under Li's leadership, TCL grew from a small workshop in Huizhou (the manufacturing belt of the Pearl River Delta) with 43 staff in 1982 to sales volume of RMB 104.58 billion and 13,000 staff at more than 160 sites in 2016.

I'd had some previous dealings with TCL. In 2007, I was the head of Hong Kong's largest electronics retailer. We were their key customer in Hong Kong and worked with them regarding private label products. Arriving at Li's office in Huizhou (a second-tier city with population of 4.6 million adjacent to Shenzhen) it was no surprise to see the atmosphere: even though the company was a market leader, everyone was quite informal and very open, probably also reflecting the innovative character of the industry.

We had a cup of coffee with the management team while waiting for the chairman to arrive, and I was a bit preoccupied because at that time Midea, another Chinese giant, was in talks to take over Germany's Kuka, a major robotics manufacturer. With costs in China surging, China had to some extent lost its original position as the workbench of the world, so I thought. What would TCL's approach be? Also, as there was more and more convergence of devices worldwide, would TV sets soon be replaced by tablets, now that phones had become cameras and vice versa?

Mr. Li led us to his office, and it was clear from his demeanor and style that we would find clear answers to our questions. I was looking forward to getting into it right away.

However, I also found Mr. Li's career very representative of the transition period in the Chinese economy in the 1990s. As such, allow me to tell you his story in a bit more in detail:

Mr. Li's generation still hails from a time when jobs were assigned to graduates, which was standard practice in the planned economy era. He had graduated as an engineer from South China University of Technology in 1982. His only choices at the time were to either work for a business or start down the government career path. As Mr. Li succinctly put it, "I didn't feel like working for a government agency." As such, he chose to work for a business and ended up joining a company called TTK, at the time a small cassette maker in Huizhou with only 42 employees.

Mr. Li worked his way up the ladder, from being a good engineer to being the head of the factory, and in 1985 even became the General Manager.

Even from an early stage in his career, Mr. Li remembers he always had to take on new responsibilities, which was typical for qualified graduates at the time, as higher education was not so common then. For example, in 1984, 2 years after graduating, Li was assigned as the General Manager to establish a facility for cassette tape coating. It was then a RMB 500,000 investment in CAPEX (capital expenditures), a gigantic project in Huizhou or even Guangdong. For the company, cassette tape coating was the latest segment, and Mr. Li tried very hard to get the products designed and manufactured for the first year. Nonetheless, sales were poor, so Mr. Li decided to step down as GM and focus on a supporting role that entailed traveling between Hong Kong and Huizhou to represent the company and the Huizhou government towards its partners and investors in the electronics industry.

This was the time of China's opening up, which attracted many foreign investors. As Li remembers: "I participated in establishing 11 joint ventures and accumulated a lot of experience." These projects included JVs with Philips, a number of large Hong Kong manufacturers, the USA, and Japanese companies. These projects earned Mr. Li director positions at a staggering ten companies.

Enriched with this experience and international acumen, in 1990 he found an opportunity to return to TCL and take on management responsibilities, becoming the GM of an audio system company.

In 1992, the TCL Group's focus shifted to the TV business, and around 1996 it became the core of the company. This was when disaster struck, as the founder of TCL's HK joint venture partner for the TV business died in an accident, and his widow put his share up for sale, nearly putting a part of TCL into the hands of a major competitor. With his competitors bidding for the shares in his JV, Mr. Li managed to create a new company to produce and sell TV sets with the help of another HK investor with manufacturing capabilities, thus avoiding what could be seen as a hostile takeover. The new company turned out to be successful and IPOed in Hong Kong in 1999 as TCL Multimedia (HK: 01070).

However, over the years, the Alcatel acquisition was Mr. Li's greatest challenge, due to its high-profile international nature. During the interview, Li vividly recounted how the President of France conferred him the State Medal of Honor of France: "I was very much in the spotlight when the deal was made in 2004." The real challenge came after the acquisition, when the venture reported huge financial losses in 2005 and 2006. "The financial loss in 2005 nearly killed me," Li remembers all too well, explaining that the entire company suffered, and that it was a major blow to his usually high confidence. Mr. Li told me it was the most difficult year in his career, prompting him to write a book about it called *"Rebirth of the Eagle."*

I wondered how he eventually got out of this dilemma, and what lessons he learned. The turning point came in 2006, when Li and his senior management team spent nearly half a year reviewing and adjusting their strategies. For me, it sounded like a "going back to basics" approach. Li and his team adjusted strategies in a down-to-earth manner to increase competitiveness, while also ensuring cash flow and funding. Eventually, the team overcame the difficulties and business improved gradually in 2007 and 2008.

As a manager I have tried to build everything we have at Watsons from scratch, rather than thinking about buying other companies, even though we had that option in our market. But I guess as a global player, M&A plays an important role for not only the market entry but also increasing market share even in the home market by leapfrogging know-how, capabilities, and potentially benefiting from a new brand's reputation (an aspect we've discussed in previous chapters).

So, needless to say, I was eager to hear about Mr. Li's lessons learned from his M&A activities.

Li believes preparation before M&A and especially in the post-M&A stage is a key ingredient. As he puts it, "Globally, M&As are more likely to fail," Therefore, Mr. Li's view was and is that it's better to first explore whether there are other ways to achieve the same goal, including joint ventures.

The challenge—besides the transaction itself and market behavior before and after the transaction—is how to generate synergy effects with the new company. For Mr. Li, the core question for any transaction is "whether it can create more returns than what you would gain if you invested in building from scratch on the overseas market." Further, he emphasizes, "You need to ensure the M&A's synergy effects and returns can justify the price."

As for further advice on M&A, Li believes having the right team to run the business ready in advance—or ideally taking over the "old" team and letting them run the business—is the key. In 2004, TCL closed two M&A cases, Thomson TV and Alcatel mobile. Mr. Li feels the Alcatel merger was more successful than that with Thomson, partly because he "managed to retain the Alcatel management team and relied on them for the overseas business." In the communications division, the overseas revenues contribute 85% of the total. According to Li, in France TCL-Alcatel is viewed as a local company by the customers.

Another piece of advice Li shared, especially for Chinese companies, is to be prepared for financial challenges and the need for more funds than originally predicted for an M&A project. Wrapping up the topic, he says, "You need to maintain a financial buffer."

Like many other companies discussed in this book, TCL is facing changes regarding the technological evolution and in terms of what customers want. There are significant challenges from new market entrants that focus on direct sales channels and online distribution, such as Xiaomi (value handset brand built on direct Internet sales), as well as those using content-driven business models, like LeTV. The underlying trend is a new business model with brands (often Internet companies) offering very cheap or free hardware, while charging for services.

Li also sees a growing convergence of hardware and services and is determined to transition his company from selling appliances to serving users. According to Li, TCL has now sold more than 300 million home appliances over the years. "But there is no link between you and the customer the moment you finish the sale. We must transition from focusing on the sale to concentrating more on service."

Therefore, TCL entered into Internet applications and services for smart TV and mobile phones very early. From 2010 on, TCL set up a service-oriented company to support Smart TV and applications. And in early 2014, it launched the "double +" strategy—combining smart + Internet and product + service to herald a new era of convergence. Subsequently, Li restructured the company into a multi-category conglomerate, consisting of seven product divisions and three service divisions, plus one capital company.

The seven product sectors include multi-media electronics, communication technology, optoelectronics, household electronics, audio and video, commercial systems, and components and materials. The three service segments focus on Internet applications and services, sales and supply chain, and finance. In addition, the venture capital investment mainly aims to develop new technologies and services.

The restructuring was done to accelerate growth. As Li says, "In the long run, the three service divisions will grow faster," adding that TCL will invest enormous resources, particularly in the area of Internet application and services. The goal is to ultimately create roughly 20 project companies to provide solutions for TCL's smart TV, mobile communication terminals, and O2O business models. The first signs of this strategy became apparent with LeTV in May 2016, with LeEco's investment of over 2 billion HK dollars (RMB 1.87 billion) in TCL's smart TV business. And Li is open to doing more such deals, practically extending an invitation: "We are open to cooperation with other companies like LeTV."

For TCL, the main focus is on smart TV and mobile terminals—not just products, but also services. For example, Li mentions Go Live (a.k.a. Global Broadcasting), a product similar to Netflix, which allows consumers to watch the newest movies from home as if in the cinema. Revenues can be generated from video-on-demand and advertisement. China Merchants Securities estimates that in 2016 Go Live had 15 million active users. Thanks to the cooperation with LeTV, the Go Live service will also be available for LeTV users.

When we met, Li told me he was also planning the restructuring of TCL's mobile telecommunication terminals business. "The point is that we have to change our business model," he explains. According to Mr. Li, in the past few years, the management team came to dislike the publicly listed status, as disclosing all the details every quarter did not prove beneficial for them.

As of late September 2016, the privatization of the mobile telecommunication sector had been accomplished, and the company now plans to re-list in the next 2–3 years. At the end of 2016, the mobile telecommunication company announced a layoff and moved its marketing center from Beijing to Shenzhen. "What matters is the transformation, not which stock market it will be listed on," Li emphasizes.

Will all the new efforts be more focused on dealing with the local market in China? That was what I assumed, but Li stopped me right there: "In fact, we will continue our global expansion. Overseas acquisitions and investments continue to move forward, including those in the Internet application and services sector." Mr. Li's 10-year vision for TCL is to be "a global manufacturer of smart devices and Internet application and services provider." He emphasizes that, in the end, service and content depend on the hardware. According to Li, TCL's aim is to become a global leader in two to three product categories, for example, smart TVs, smart mobile communication terminals, and LCD panels: "We want to at least reach the top five in each of these three categories."

Further, Li hopes to grow the overseas business, which had revenues of RMB 47.2 billion in 2016, rapidly, so that it surpasses domestic revenues (RMB 54.3 billion in the same year) in 2–3 years. When it comes to growth drivers for overseas expansion, Li feels smart technologies, including industry intelligence and smart products technologies from the USA, Europe, and Israel hold considerable potential. With regard to Internet applications, services and technologies may come from the USA and some European companies that are doing very well.

Now that TCL's basic strategy for international markets was clear, I wanted to move on to the hot topic of Midea's acquisition of Kuka—the negotiations were heating up at the time of our interview. I wanted to know if Li thought it was a smart move. As it turned out, Li saw it as a good opportunity for Midea, because Midea had been very successful in the home appliance industry. "Smart manufacturing and automation will be the core competence of the Chinese home appliance manufacturers in the future. Germany is very strong when it comes to smart manufacturing technologies."

At the time of our conversation, there was some controversy in my home country (Germany) over how fast technology transfer to China should proceed, and whether it was a good thing that a technology leader like Kuka would be taken over by a foreign country, especially China, with such a huge future market for smart manufacturing. Li revealed more of his thinking on how to "go overseas" and explained that he can to some extent understand why overseas companies try to avoid full takeovers.

"I prefer joint ventures when I invest in the USA, Europe, Israel, etc.," he states, adding, "The headquarters should stay local. But I would expect the new JV to establish a plant in China." This dovetails nicely with the Chinese government's Made in China 2025 concept, a 30-year blueprint for upgrading China's industries, especially manufacturing.

Consequently, developing Chinese companies' capabilities in the areas of automation and smart manufacturing has become a "national task" in connection with global manufacturing competitiveness and in light of the rising wages and costs in China.

Joint ventures are a smart and less capital-intensive method of achieving know-how transfer, allowing Chinese companies to learn alongside their JV partners, while—as the local player—maintaining control of distribution and sales. In my view, while in the past know-how transfer was a means of gaining an edge over a local competitor or opening new segments, it is now, in the age of global players, literally vital for huge companies like TCL if they want to ensure their future competitiveness regarding quality and cost.

Li outlines the expected impact for TCL with a simple example: "The average size of TCL's factories ranges from 1000 to 10,000 workers. Five years from now, I hope to have cut those numbers in half. I believe the first companies that can make this happen will come out on top."

I was trying, as I had with other company founders, to get a feel for which companies he considered to be role models. "In China, it's Huawei," says Li, explaining that Huawei did an excellent job in its markets both domestically as well as globally. Among the global companies, Apple, Google, and Microsoft from the USA are Li's role models. In Europe, it would be Mercedes and BMW from Germany. As for Asian companies, he admires Mr. Li Ka-shing's (he owns the company I run in China) empire, and the fact that he runs the business well and keeps innovating, despite being in his 80s.

I was also trying to learn which companies he felt did the best job in terms of management. He mentioned that he'd learned a lot from GE's Jack Welsh, and that Japanese companies had previously been strong when it came to management techniques. "But it used to be difficult to learn from Asian companies, since they usually don't openly share their management process."

However, as the world continues to change, many companies are moving away from their traditional origins and towards new forms, and TCL is no exception. Transformation is at the top of Li's mind, concerning management. "We come from a traditional industry, and the "engineer culture" is deeply rooted in our corporate management. It's not an easy task to change it."

In the past 2 years, Li had found that the TCL team needed to make a significant number of changes involving various aspects, including the workforce and management, to make the transformation work. "I have a stronger and stronger feeling that we cannot count on the existing team to make these changes. On the one hand, we need to cultivate young leaders internally, say,

Gen-X and Gen-Y. On the other, we will externally recruit Gen-X and Gen-Y who are capable of becoming our future leaders." The layoff in the mobile telecommunication business mentioned earlier is one example. This challenge is something most companies I met in China are trying to tackle right now.

Even at my company Watsons, I am working on this—on blending in a new workforce that can rejuvenate products (for younger consumers that are their age), bring in fresh ideas (i.e., in consumer marketing), or directly transform a company or parts of it for the e-commerce or—better said—mobile commerce era.

Li is working hard to achieve this—more than half of the managers in the three service divisions came from external companies and were recruited in the past 2 years. "The management risk is indeed very high when you have so many new hires. But I have no choice; we must do it."

Having seen a dramatic shift in electronic products away from Japanese and US brands towards Korean and now more and more Chinese brands (even globally), I had to ask Li if he believed the current big conglomerates from Japan and other countries would still be around 10 years from now. According to Li, this will depend on where the companies invest and on how open they are for change: "Companies must enter new areas of business rapidly and invest in new segments." As such, he concludes that some prominent Japanese brands might face serious difficulties or even disappear.

Among the largest players, Li thought Samsung might be an exception. "They put a lot of money into building infrastructure, for example, semiconductor chips, TFT (thin film transistor) LCD, and LED, etc." Li believes that by investing a huge amount of money and building a solid foundation in technologies, Samsung will have the edge over Chinese companies for at least the next 5 years, with Chinese players potentially catching up in 10 years.

We were nearing the end of the interview, so it was time to ask Li what he wanted the world to know about TCL and his team. His response was quite humble: "I want the Western readers to know that TCL is a global company from China striving to grow."

The Chinese economy has grown at an unprecedented rate over the past 30 years, allowing many private Chinese companies to enjoy significant development. Li firmly believes the Chinese economy and Chinese companies will play a bigger and more crucial role in the future world economy. "There are many outstanding people among Chinese entrepreneurs. In their future development, these entrepreneurs will follow a similar path to the one their counterparts in the West did," says Li. His view is that Chinese entrepreneurs will develop a broader global vision and take on more social responsibility.

Li is also critical of how some Chinese entrepreneurs have handled their success. "I have to admit that there are some upstarts among these entrepreneurs. They give the world the impression that they shop everywhere, with suitcases full of US dollars and euros." He hopes that Western readers can view China's economy and entrepreneurs from an objective perspective. "We are friendly, not aggressive or dangerous."

In fact, Mr. Li has a hard time understanding how China can be portrayed as an aggressor: "The Chinese people haven't invaded another country for thousands of years. In the past 100 years, we have always been the loser in wars with other countries. Even going back 2000 years, when China held a very powerful position in the world, our idea was to build the Great Wall to protect our wealthy country. At the time China was powerful enough to invade and occupy other countries, yet our ancestors only wanted to protect their belongings, not to interfere with the affairs of less developed countries."

From what I've seen here as a guest in China, I couldn't agree more.

Acknowledgment This interview has been published with the kind permission of Mr. Li Dongsheng.

Note

1. http://www.199it.com/archives/561847.html

Part VI

Made for China: The Future

24

Made for China: The Future

Our foray into China's consumer-economy companies took nearly a year to complete, mostly because it happened on weekends and "we" are all busy here building our own brands and companies.

We found many companies that were moving forward, rapidly adapting their business, transforming their business model, or upgrading their products. Essentially, the customer is now in the driver's seat, with companies playing catch up—which is creating tremendous opportunities on the Chinese market and globally.

Working alongside and competing with Chinese companies in the domestic market, I have seen their potential in terms of not only adapting their business model but also evolving it. I have also witnessed some of their challenges. Nearly all of the companies here have the ambition to evolve their brand globally or at least to a global standard.

So, as the conclusion of our journey, here I'd like to summarize my thoughts and observations about Chinese consumer companies. I will take the angle of pointing out the differences that most outsiders can't see. I will also share my views on how and in which fields they will appear on the global stage. As I have been working in the market for some time now, I will also try to add some value by summarizing which opportunities I see for companies outside of China to engage with Chinese companies and the Chinese consumer.

According to BCG data, US nominal private consumption will be roughly US$15 trillion in 2020, which is an increase of US$2.6 trillion from 2015.

© The Author(s) 2018
C. Nothhaft, *Made for China*, DOI 10.1007/978-3-319-61584-4_24

Germany and the UK, Europe's two largest economies, will have a combined nominal private consumption value of approximately US$4.3 trillion in 2020, up from about US$0.8 trillion today.

In China, by 2020, private consumption will be worth about US$6.5 trillion, which means an additional US$2.3 trillion on top of the US$4.3 trillion now. The additional US$2.3 trillion represents nearly three times the increase expected for the UK and Germany combined and is also more than Germany's entire projected consumption of US$2.2 trillion in 2020.

The recent political developments, including newly emerging trade protectionism at the global scale, will surely change some of these numbers. However, when it comes to the consumer market, the size of the Chinese market will not reverse, and even at lower growth rates, that size makes it a tremendously attractive market in absolute terms.

We must also assume that China's urbanization trend will continue, that more of the rural population will be able to afford an "urban lifestyle" and that the Chinese government will do everything in its power to keep incomes growing to "keep the population satisfied."

So, for me, the Chinese consumer market literally represents the single most important growth opportunity in the world and could reshuffle the cards for the balance between Chinese companies and global ones. In my view, in some sectors the best Chinese companies may come out on top. The battlefield won't always just be about market share in China, but as we can already see in some stories here, will in some cases be for a share of the global consumer market.

Interestingly, when spending time in my home country (Germany) or overseas, I still get questions from the angle of China being a "market to export to." However, since China's domestic market is a good opportunity if you are fast and you can evolve to keep up with local trends, becoming a strong brand in China with local expertise (and preferably local manufacturing) is what I recommend. I also strongly recommend, especially for service businesses, capturing the Chinese market internationally/overseas. Germany had more than 30,000 Chinese students and nearly 360,000 Chinese tourists in 2015, and the UK had roughly 85,000 Chinese students and more than 270,000 Chinese tourist trips in the same year.

Consumer Power Is Changing the Rules of Business in China

When talking about Chinese companies, many people seem to assume these companies have the competitive advantage on the ground. In conversations, people often "remind" me that this is because Chinese companies are being helped by the government or that they understand the rules of the game better, etc. I'd like to put forward a different perspective on this. When I ran my first business as a Managing Director in China, a food manufacturing business producing high-end poultry products for supermarkets and fast food companies back in 1999, I spent more than half of my time keeping trouble or vested interests away from the business or ensuring we maintained our permits and export certificates. I did feel then that local players (who often failed to comply with the law) didn't have to spend so much time on these things and consequently had more time to focus on sales and building their actual business.

Things have improved dramatically since then. Now, as customers in China enjoy transparency on what's available, the decision-making power has dramatically shifted to the consumer, who decides which product or service excels, giving better products and services a good chance to succeed. As such, my job as CEO of a company that has branches in over 450 cities in China has less and less to do with handling government relationships ("guanxi") and avoiding legal disasters, and more and more to do with figuring out what the consumer wants. Today, the drivers of the consumer market are twofold: a rapidly evolving consumer—with different consumer generations that have extremely different viewpoints on brands—and local competition. And local means local, i.e., today our company's main competitor is not a national chain but a bulk of tens of thousands of local competitors.

Therefore, to grow business in China, now for a consumer business like mine the main task at hand is to figure out what consumers want and to give it to them faster than anyone else. We have moved from being a competitive market to one characterized by hyper-competition!

At the same time, I have to stress that China has made great strides by establishing clearer rules to make the playfield more "fair," by reducing government departments and their involvement in companies' day-to-day business, and by tightening up their courts (yes, we do generally win when we are in the right, which was more difficult when I first started working here).

But local companies (luckily my company is one) do enjoy certain advantages here in China. Here are some essential aspects:

Distribution Capability

Let me say it again: In my understanding, the number one spot when it comes to advantages local companies enjoy is not "consumer understanding" but a "superior ability to bring things to market quickly (and then adjust to keep up with the changing consumer)." Over the years, Chinese companies have developed distribution capabilities that allowed them to outrun and outperform their competitors. The root lies in the fact that most owners aimed at quickly building national players or at least regional players. Product availability/showcasing across multiple channels including muscling out competitors by cornering channels is how most brands have been built here, which is no different to what happened on today's mature markets when they were at an earlier stage. Those that had built their distribution well and cost efficiently were able to build strong national brands. There are many good examples in this book that prove this point—including Haier, Suning, Liby, and TCL, as well as JD, which is taking its market share from Alibaba thanks to its focus on logistical capabilities.

As indicated in some chapters in this book, this situation may now be changing. First of all, more and more companies have efficient distribution networks across China; even third-party logistics companies have grown, covering huge territories efficiently and cost effectively. More importantly, with a shift to e-commerce and mobile-based e-commerce as shopping channels, distribution and "nationwide shop window advantage" are becoming less important. So, in a nutshell, most companies need to find a new main competitive advantage or main skill; they need to acquire new strengths to compete. Many of these strengths have to do with truly consumer-centric approaches.

Cost Efficiency: Price Advantage

Being price competitive is even more of a make-or-break factor in China—the market is so vast, the territory is so complex and diverse, and the competition is so fierce (you have seen many examples by reading the interview chapters). Further, Chinese consumers are so price-sensitive (they have small wallets, are smart shoppers, and they like to compare prices and research which brands offer discounts). No matter what you do with your brand here, the basic game is delivering a superior product at a lower price (than your competitors). The art then is to trade up over time, as consumers increasingly trust in your brand (but remember that trust can easily be destroyed by competitors at any time, since the consumer is immature and more prone to switching). Local players with high capacity, lower unit costs, and lower distribution costs continue to have an edge in terms of acquiring new consumers and keeping them.

E-commerce has to some extent become the new face of distribution in China. While in the past, large and integrated companies—with high-volume manufacturing capacities and low unit costs combined with vast distribution networks—were at an advantage, e-commerce platforms and their vast ecosystems have since leveled the playing field for smaller companies. In fact, as customers now want many brands to choose from, e-commerce ecosystems are better at providing them more choices at scale.

E-commerce is also becoming the new face of how customers find information and shaping their expectations regarding customer service. Non-Internet companies have been struggling for years to provide good service in China—since service staff in general are not yet very efficient and often lack simple behavioral norms, managing service in China remains a challenge. As examples in this book (like Ctrip and GreenTree Inn) show, now that customers are used to procuring services from a computer, it is much easier to provide this service—in a more standardized way and at a lower cost.

Speed to Market

Another important competitive advantage that Chinese companies enjoy here—and this one holds true especially in the Internet age—is speed to market. Chinese companies are simply faster than foreign companies when it comes to turning an idea into a product, bringing it to market, and adapting it to follow trends. More often than not, their higher speed to market is not due to a superior customer understanding, but to an array of operational factors. To start with, Western (and Eastern/Western ones, like when it comes to Japan and Korea) companies are more risk-averse, and the cost for them to develop new products is high. Local companies in China simply take comparisons to overseas brands AND take risks on trends at an early stage, often backed by the owners' gut instinct. Since the owners often wholly or partly control the distribution here, they can more directly monitor the launch of new products and can make corrections at an early stage. We have included some great examples in the book, including Daphne, Toread, and Jing Brand. Chinese companies aren't afraid to try new things; nor will they hesitate to stop a product or project quickly if it doesn't pan out.

Single-Boss Management

Throughout the interviews, I often got the feeling that the bosses were familiar in detail (at least in simplified terms) with the purposes of their brands and which customer needs they currently catered to. In fact, I see this more often in Chinese companies than among the top management from Western companies I meet with.

Speed to market and agility are facilitated by the fact that in China even larger companies are still run by a single boss, without too much debate or the involvement of boards. In most cases, they have built the company from the ground up and therefore know the market inside and out. More mature companies from the West tend to believe in science and market research, and their decision-making processes are often much longer. As a result, they often get to the party late when it comes to trends. At the same time, if a Western company's project fails, it might continue to burn money for years, because the management can't bring themselves to press the delete button or decide upon necessary adjustments quickly (and consequently creating the fear of a "black hole"—since many companies have lost money in China, and the losses were massive—for the Chinese market in Western boardrooms). Chinese companies, which are often helmed by a single first (or second) generation entrepreneur, are better suited to the experiments and entrepreneurial approaches needed in this market. By their nature, they are more successful at speed-to-market races like the consumer market "dogfight" we're seeing right now. However, as the market grows more complex, consumers "become younger," companies expand, and technology becomes a more essential factor in scooping up consumers; the single-boss approach will gradually change due to the complexity of decisions required.

For most companies, having seen many of the owners at work, I find nothing wrong with this approach. Companies here are learning and constantly face a lack of talent as well as management experience, so it is perfectly understandable that entrepreneurs consider themselves the heart of the company and play close to the vest. Also, even in large companies, many decisions here are highly entrepreneurial in nature and therefore involve taking risks that concern the entire company.

On a side note, as the reader can imagine, succession planning is currently a major topic at Chinese companies, given their rapid growth and size. Owners still hold a significant share and influence in big companies, and in many cases, the "second line" still has to mature.

Chinese Customers Want Choices

I have observed that Western companies often bet on a limited selection of their global products in China. They tend to believe in rationalizing what's on offer and focus on the evolution of their best products. Apple's story—becoming much more successful after narrowing its focus—is a good example; Nike's core focus in terms of designs could be another.

However, Chinese companies believe in offering the consumer more choices, and often offer more choices by default, since there are so many different consumer types (generations, local preferences, and wallet sizes) in China. I clearly recall the vast showrooms at Haier city—as a national manufacturer for 1.3 billion people with monthly incomes ranging from US$100 to several thousand; this is somewhat the mindset. And I have stopped viewing this approach purely as a "lack of focus" and belittling it, considering the fact that they intend to cater to China as a nation. While in the West we might say "less is more," given China's geographies and demographics, this is only possible for niche and—in my experience—very expensive brands.

In general, national brands do need to offer variety, and that is their strength over Western brands.

That being said, recently this has begun changing a bit: E-commerce, which promotes low-cost market entry, has proved a great opportunity for "less is more" brands by piling many of them together in a search engine, thus creating what the consumer wants—more choices! However, I can also see how international brands are now rapidly creating more choices through multi-branding. Adidas is a good example (they are now outrunning Nike by pursuing a multi-brand strategy built around Adidas Sports, Adidas Originals, and Neo). We also heard some stories here (including Daphne, Jing Brand, Yili, and GreenTree Inn) about companies implementing similar strategies.

As a strategy, providing more choices for Chinese consumers is harder to understand for Western marketers like myself. When entering new markets, we tend to rely on bestsellers. But I like to remind Western marketers who are sometimes encouraged by the early success of their bestsellers that they may be limiting themselves by focusing too much on low hanging fruits and might be underestimating the total potential their brand could unlock if they brought the entire business with all its choices here. The idea of betting on bestsellers from overseas has limits in China, where having many items available is often a sign of brand strength and quality in the eyes of the consumer. Also, when a new brand idea is brought to China, the new entrant may quickly face a situation in which a local brand takes the trend and presents it to multiple wallet sizes and different consumer groups (like GenPC and GenMobile) in different designs. Anyone who has ever compared Jack Wolfskin's or Columbia's range vs. what's on offer at Toread will know what I mean. Chinese brands understand this game of choice and segmentation much better than the Western companies operating in China (though the latter are now learning).

Local Brands Primarily Focus on Dynamic Evolution

When it comes to brand message, I find the approach used to position brands on the market is quite different between Western brands and Chinese brands (after working with both over the years). Western companies see their brand message as more or less "static," i.e., fixed over a longer period. They are constantly trying to find new ways to bring the message to the consumer and are more or less happy to burn through money on doing so. While the advantages of global scale are clear, the disadvantage of investing heavily and a high risk of total loss has been seen and felt many times.

Chinese companies often "design their brands" during the sales process, using customer requests, distributor feedback, or input from the celebrities they use to develop their brands. This process, albeit not so typical in the West (except perhaps with startups), has some merits of its own, especially in a market like China where society itself is evolving.

However, I can also see some challenges when it comes to building long-term brand strengths and brand image—which conveys what a brand stands for and what not. Recently, especially as consumers continue to become more diversified, competition is getting more intense, and marketing money is becoming scarcer, while the importance of social media messages continues to grow, more and more brands in China are learning from the Western approach of making it clear what their brand stands for and then pursuing their customers using e-commerce and social commerce via mobile to go wide in their customer acquisition strategy. We are currently at a stage in the market development where the two strategies are converging and Western companies can make a contribution in terms of how to create clear brand messages.

Can Chinese Companies Innovate?

Another question I get asked a lot is: Can Chinese companies innovate? This is an interesting one but not so difficult to answer if you can let go of the picture we Westerners have in mind when we talk about innovation, the one we know from mature markets. So, yes, Chinese companies can innovate, but so far they haven't really needed to—at least not in the sense that we Westerners understand it. It comes down to China being a young economy in a huge territory that has its own challenges, to consumers with evolving needs, and to a manufacturing base that comes from being the "workbench of the world." Therefore, the lack of visible innovation "as we know it" may not actually tell us much about Chinese companies' capabilities. Again, making products affordable, building wide distribution, defending against competitors (through price), and offering more choices for different consumer groups and wallets had been the "market game" here.

My foreign visitors often say, "Chinese companies can only copy." Generally, I ask them in return, "What does innovation mean to you, and do you think Chinese companies need to pursue it NOW?" If we understand that building distribution in China to reach more consumers has always been the priority, initially the need to innovate may have been less of a priority in general. I say "in general" because many companies here have built their business on innovating or on using their overseas exposure to learn about products they could make considering the local circumstances, because, at an early stage, most companies had to use most of their cash to build wider distribution, allowing them to outrun their competitors and build a national brand. In China, there are simply too many sharks in the tank for that not to be a priority! So, when it comes to building distribution over a vast territory at low cost, Chinese companies tended to innovate quite a bit. We can see how advanced these distribution networks are in the beverage sector (Jing Brand is an example) or in the FMCG sector (where Liby serves tens of thousands of small shops in remote areas), or in the tens of thousands of outlets and repair services that Haier and Suning manage. These companies had to innovate extensively to make that happen in an environment where innovation is often more about people management than the latest technology. China's e-commerce ecosystems and large parts of today's shared economy have evolved out of that and that's why, compared to other countries, China's e-commerce often has incredible service offerings. Even in remote cities, today I can order my lunch from one of a hundred different companies at 11:30 and have it in my office at 12:00 due to a well-organized logistics backbone consisting of motorcycles, bicycles, and even couriers on foot. In many cities I can sit in a restaurant without a wine list and can pull out an app and order wine from a nearby merchant to arrive in 20–30 min, as the merchant is happy to make this part of his business. I can share car rides if I want to save money, and so on. Most astonishingly of all, I can do this in an ever-growing number of cities.

Generally speaking, these business models and services innovate and disrupt traditional channels and thus create further pressure to innovate. In my company, we are now working out how we can bring cosmetics to a consumer in 1 h in 200 cities across China. Both online and offline companies are working on services like delivering diapers in 30 min, fish in 60, and drivers arriving on electric skateboards to drive you and your car home when you've had one too many (not that I need this service on a regular basis).

Again, this is currently a focus when it comes to innovation in China. Innovating the value chain intensifies competition, which again drives innovation. In the end, once all the logistics and distribution options have been more or less maximized, the innovative pressure will go back to improving the product itself. We are at that stage now. I can see this everywhere, including our company here. In our business, a retail company, I am now headhunting some of the best "product making brains" from global brands to help us innovate our original brand products. The reason is to have better products, more choices for more consumer generations AND to catch more and more of China's market-specific trends such as TCM (Traditional Chinese Medicine) and the latest consumer demand trends.

Combining this with superior social network marketing capabilities, and the loyalty programs that retailers like us can offer, has increased speed to market. Is this in itself innovation or not? Similar questions are being asked at thousands of Chinese companies right now. This type of direction is what most company owners here are thinking about. It will make it very hard for late market entrants in China to grow. It will create new business models and integrated companies—potentially faster than in other countries, where common thinking is based on "industry structures" or "professional sectors."

Product Innovation

As for product innovation itself, can Chinese companies innovate right now?

Again, yes. Over the last 5 years or so, I have seen how Chinese companies often launch product innovations that were on the market much faster than their foreign competitors, and they were also more successful, since the locals were smart enough to invest marketing money early to build a brand before their competitors could do the same. From what I can see, most products were not major local breakthroughs in R&D, but rather good and fast-tracked translations of trends that local entrepreneurs had spotted overseas. The local companies developed products that made those trends hot and affordable in China before mainstream global companies ever arrived. I have seen this over and over again, and as a retailer, we benefit greatly from such high-speed trend conversion. Essentially, we can ride the same trend twice: once when it's done by the local products, and once more when it's done again by foreign companies. Now, these business cycles are also accelerating, as companies seek to combine the core competencies of product innovation and speed to market through distribution and digital marketing.

To sum up: business innovation in China often implies a practical improvement in the application of a product's function or an improvement in the going-to-market strategy rather than huge technological breakthroughs.

Innovation in E-commerce and Services (and the Role of Big Data)

The same holds true for Internet products, especially services that cover needs that have arisen due to the customer's development stage. A classic example is how AliPay and WeChat pay have quickly filled in the gap that should be owned by consumer banks when it comes to managing cash, including the ability to send it to relatives and friends for shopping, or how microfinance companies have filled the void as banks failed to focus on small businesses or consumer credit. Another good example is online services, e.g., health advice or social networking apps that connect people through shared interests (e.g., running, beauty products, or even raising kids) and which have since become commercial enterprises. Shared economy services are extremely popular right now in China, often offering a digital version of existing businesses, e.g., shared cars or—a very hot topic recently—shared bicycle services.

We need to wait and see how these innovations will pan out in the long term. Currently, as China's VC market continues to be red-hot with too much money floating around looking for companies to invest in, many of the service business models or shared economy models exist because with so much liquidity in the market looking for investment, many businesses are allowed to burn cash for extended period of time during the startup phase. Or, as my smart boss put it to me recently: "Because nowadays in some industries it's ok to hand over shareholders' money to the consumer directly." In the long run, those innovations that have a revenue model—which means customers find the service so useful that they are willing to pay for it—will become the real innovations.

Especially, Internet-based service innovations exemplify a need for services including simple things like the need for information. China, in my view, is leading the pack in quite a few of these areas and innovations, probably even globally. When it comes to the nonconsumer sectors including transport, medical technology, or AI, I hear there is plenty of innovation happening in China. However, I cannot comment here, as they're beyond my field of expertise.

When it comes to inventing new products, my feeling is—with very large companies like Haier being the exception—so far the main challenge has been to build manufacturing capacity and to continually innovate manufacturing equipment to keep up with overseas standards. This has produced some Chinese companies with extremely high manufacturing standards. We shouldn't forget that many consumer companies here come from or are somehow related to OEM, or have maintained collaborations with international companies around their core capabilities. In some fields where China has continued to buy the latest equipment, many factories might be ahead of their aging global competitors' average factory standard. An example here could be Yili's facilities or some of the warehousing facilities I have seen across China including at Suning or GZ Pharma.

For smart Chinese entrepreneurs, innovating their product itself may have had a lower priority than the goal of becoming a better manufacturer. But now the market and especially the rapidly evolving GenNet and GenMobile consumer are pushing them to do so.

The Market as an Innovation Lab

We can also say that competition between niche brands, international brands coming in from overseas via cross-border R&D in consumer products areas, and branding have now found their way to the Chinese market. With entrepreneurs launching many products quickly and adjusting them as customers buy or choose not to buy them, the market has become the experimentation lab. As manufacturers that came from SOE thinking, the initial mindset in big companies would have been to open a research department or to cooperate with a university to develop new products. The downside of this approach is obvious—it, too, is geared towards manufacturing capability, but not necessarily towards understanding what consumers want or how to turn a customer interest into a need-fulfilling, functional product. What is changing this now: big (consumer) data and companies that truly operate closer to their consumer in the domestic market. Again, hyper-competition is forcing the issue.

The current stage is interesting. We can clearly see players becoming more consumer-centric. Almost every entrepreneur in our interviews talked about using "big data" to understand consumer behavior. Practically everyone here was aware of how social media impacts consumer needs and how important it is to understand what consumers talk about and what they don't buy from China because it's lacking there (cross-border business). I have observed how this is now on many entrepreneurs' minds, and how well understood it is by most of them.

More importantly, I can see how this is sparking new types of innovation—more focused on how to capture consumers' chatter, than on trends and then needs to churn out new products suitable to those trends and Chinese wallets. In a way, innovation has moved from the lab to a "real-time" market environment. Many companies here are now reinventing themselves in a shortcut process: between the first generation market entrepreneur (who is generally not restricted by boards or a company mission that is carved in stone) and the consumer.

This would explain why many companies—including the majority of Chinese companies—have no problem with using cash or organizing it from the market to invest into new "stories" for their brand. Often this is a reaction to a trend or perceived trend and an attempt to get a head start.

We have seen many examples here, including Yonghui's ongoing innovation program or Hai Di Lao's founder deliberating radical steps to improve service; examples like Jing Brand using traditional health liquor to strike a chord with younger consumers, BYBO's efforts to educate consumers on what good dental hygiene means, Grace Vineyard's efforts to educate younger consumers on quality, and Jing Brand having a global Jägermeister image in mind. These are all brand innovation stories. Some companies acquire overseas or in China to get the building blocks for protecting or deepening their core business. Some of the companies examined here have done so, e.g., Haier, Liby, Wanda, and so on, while others, like Kuka and potentially Jing Brand, are planning to do so.

Even shopping formats are re-branding: The latest trend is Alibaba Group starting to take over ownership of physical retailers and vice versa.

Some companies want to move downstream in the value chain to become more integrated providers, delivering customer experiences rather than products, e.g., Suning looking for content for their TV business and Wanda looking to directly invest in customer needs that it could cover at its malls, e.g., education centers and cinemas (in the latter case, astonishingly writing a Global Story of its own). These are bold moves at scale for companies that are relatively young and still in a learning stage when it comes to their core business—which can perhaps be explained by the fact that Chinese entrepreneurs are not particularly rigid when it comes to "industry sectors" as we know them. It is easier for them to step out of the framework of "how industries should be structured" to create something of value to consumers. (After all, attracting even only a tiny fraction of 1.3 billion people would mean a new market and might be worth the risk).

In my view, this is all a form of innovation—product-related, but most of all, business-purpose-related.

By now, some readers might agree that this is happening faster in China than in other parts of the world. In our rapidly evolving world, globally established companies are struggling with major disruptions, including some industries becoming totally automated or obsolete. Industries can disappear or change dramatically; industries can merge. In the age of total consumer power, I don't know whether the term industry even still exists or if "solution to consumer demands" might be a better term. Maybe the Chinese entrepreneurs with their flexibility and constant questioning of their business model might have an advantage in the future. In an age where so many industries are being transformed, perhaps rethinking business models will be the most essential innovation.

Lack of Bank Loans Creates More Entrepreneurs

In China, a lack of loan-based funding for small companies plus high savings rate and liquidity in the market has brought about a massive VC/PE industry. According to the Ministry of Science and Technology of the PRC, the number of VC and PE in China reached 1775 by the end of 2015, compared to only 27 in 1995. A report released by PWC China estimated that the total investment volume in 2015 made by Chinese funds had a growth of 140% compared to that in 2014, while the global growth rate was only 18% during the same period.

Crowdfunding innovation via VC investment is nothing out of the ordinary in China. Most accomplished entrepreneurs in China have their own VC fund for tinkering with new ideas. On the corporate side, many companies use this type of innovation process extensively. Entrepreneurs and corporations invest in promising technologies that innovate related industries or that innovate technologies related to their core business. Apple's and Google's early investments into startups are often quoted in this book as great examples that serve as inspirations and models for local companies. Some company owners use their personal networks to build ecosystems that have a specific purpose, one often invisible to outsiders. I am lucky enough to see some of them, and more often than not, they revolve around Face, Family, Food, and Fun, as these are the China consumer mega-stories.

China's Basic New Economy Understanding: Innovation Through Entrepreneurship

As our market in China has become so dynamic and prone to massive shifts, some corporations are now going a step further and trying to keep even their largest companies agile. Haier's approach to turning employees into entrepreneurs has recently gained many followers, including Suning, which now offers entrepreneurial programs for its staff.

In my view, these are all extremely relevant management innovations, and they will to some extent create a new knowledge base in China, in fact, one born for the market here. All this activity will aim at driving product and service innovations. So, in Western terms, we are currently in a pre-phase where capturing consumer behavior and needs will create product innovations, as we understand them in a Western sense. My bet is that, given all these factors, the best innovations—except for heavily research-based innovations, e.g., pharma—will not come from research labs, but from tens of thousands of micro-entrepreneurs in China getting funded and supported by the first generation entrepreneurs' investment and support. Besides the argument about investment returns, the feeling I sense more and more from my circle of large enterprise owners is "I want to do something for the/my industry and create a legacy"—a very different picture than what often ends up in the media, namely stories of big companies simply getting bigger.

What could accelerate consumer product innovation—again, I'm not in a position to judge lab-driven or complex scientific innovations—is a crowdsourcing process, one that could accelerate even faster if foreign brand knowledge and some technical knowledge that foreign companies have accumulated through years of experience in product development could successfully be combined with the "local" free entrepreneur spirit. We've seen some examples here of companies that have acquired foreign product brands or have entered into cooperation with foreign brands to develop them on the local market (like Modern Media/TCL/Wanda). I have seen how successful this can be, especially when manufacturing and product development comes here to China—with advantages like being ahead of consumer evolution and achieving more efficient distribution.

As I am writing this, I am also exploring many new directions in my company—including some roads where we're not 100% sure where they end. While the ideas are plentiful, and the needs are often clear, bigger companies find it more difficult to incubate ideas into turnkey products or services with benefits fine-tuned to the consumer. Chinese entrepreneurs often leave this incubation process to smaller entrepreneurs, with the goal of buying these companies once the product or service is ready to go to market at scale. What I have observed in the process is that in China there are all sorts of entrepreneurs that can be "used" for this process.

In my industry, we can find single-person marketers (often bloggers and key opinion leaders) who act as product innovators and are funded from VC or the entrepreneurial environment to make new products. The goal is often to kill two birds with one stone: to get the product idea and at the same time buy public opinion through the spokesperson. In comparison, I suppose Western markets don't tend to be so entrepreneurial.

Emerging Need for Factory Automation in China

Most companies here are or initially were manufacturers and have since become brands. While the considerations mentioned above focus on innovation at the front-end of the business (i.e., on new products or how to market them), China has a massive need for innovation when it comes to manufacturing processes, one that stems from a shift towards automation. In the past, like when I ran my manufacturing business in China, the best processes were semi-manual—in other words, machine-supported manual labor. There were two reasons for this: (1) Machines were indeed more expensive than labor. (2) Machines can break down—and repairs and service used to be difficult and expensive in China, so back then, the more machines you used, the more risk of possible downtime (and losing customers) you faced and the higher your costs. Now the game has changed very quickly, as labor costs have risen dramatically in China, while products have become more complex, requiring specific manufacturing technologies, processes, and know-how. It's those areas that China needs to be competitive in and the reason why brands that have evolved from a manufacturing background acquire assets like robotic technologies (like Midea's acquisition of Kuka, a German robotics manufacturer, in 2016) or formulas and formulation experience (I see many small acquisitions in the cosmetics or skincare sector) and so on.

Clearly, innovation on the Chinese factory floor is imminent. It's partly happening through the import of know-how (for instance acquisition and licensing) and it's also happening through domestic innovation (a subject that this book does not deal with) sponsored by the government, private companies, a highly active VC community, and an incubation community. As China has caught up at a larger scale in this process, we will soon see a new wave of better products from China in areas we aren't yet accustomed to (we know China can build Apple phones or Sony TV sets). These products will be Made FOR China. The entrepreneurs that will provide them are here for sure.

To sum up: China certainly can innovate, but perhaps not (yet) in sectors that Westerns may call innovations right now. Most entrepreneurs have to focus innovations first to capture and cover the large market and outrun their competitors, followed by a need to improve the manufacturing base. We are now in a stage where small entrepreneurship is experiencing a surge in China. Together with innovation happening in real-time with the consumer on the market, combined with more overseas expertise coming in through acquisition or foreign investment, innovation is bound to take off and create new products and services, most likely together with Global China Brands.

Going Global

So, when and how will Chinese companies go global? This is another question I'm frequently asked. First of all, some have already done so, as you can see from many companies discussed here. Second, going global does not necessarily mean bringing their brands overseas. As you have gathered from reading this book, there are various ways for Chinese companies to go global. My observation from the interviews is that most companies have a clear view as to what they need in order to be successful on the world's future largest consumer market (China), and they are finding quiet ways to get to that know-how through acquisition, learning, or cooperation—which means Chinese companies' money is going global, not necessarily their brands. This is where engagement with China Inc. is likely most promising right now, either through cooperation or M&A.

Chinese Consumers Are Driving Change

That takes us back to the starting point, namely, how consumers are driving change in China, and how this is moving companies to evolve. I'd like to briefly summarize the trends that are most promising for those companies planning to do business here or with Chinese consumers.

It's simple: What are the themes that Chinese customers—GenRed, GenRise, GenPC, and GenMobile (or, if you prefer, GenX/Y/Z) care most about? Those are the themes that Chinese companies will follow, and the ones where we Westerners can engage with them when it comes to doing business not in but WITH China, wherever on Earth we do it.

In my company, a retail and e-tail business in China, we are busy figuring out what customers want all the time and to some extent I have the luxury of thinking more broadly; since retailers can sell anything, we are not bound by selling a specific brand or product all the time. So, I also have the luxury of being able to question "what consumers want" all the time. In attempting to categorize the trends that arise out of the specific needs for GenRed to GenMobile, with this book I have sought to categorize the most common themes into Face, Family, Food, and Fun, so as to explain the needs of Chinese consumers and the context of the companies in China that cater to or will cater to those needs.

We do a great deal of research at my company when it comes to what young consumers, the GenMobile and the very young consumers, buy, as we need some head start when it comes to designing the future. I always thought we would see a major shift when it comes to the trend, but—to be honest—I consistently see Face, Family, Food, and Fun topping the charts in our market studies. However, when it comes to young Chinese consumers, I find the following traits quite significant:

Young consumers are less brand-conscious—their preferences shift all the time, and they want products and services that they feel suit them at this moment; further, they don't mind frequently redefining what they need.

Young consumers increasingly want high-quality products and premium items, and they understand what that means from their inner circle of friends and social media.

For young consumers, markets are borderless, which means full transparency as to what's available around the globe, and they find ways to try the products they want, even if they aren't available in their home country.

I find local companies—initially busy with building their core businesses—generally understand these factors well, and they try to cater as much as possible to young consumers' common needs as described above. In most of the interviews here, company owners talked about these young consumers and trying to meet their needs. Digital commerce in connection with these trends appears to be one of the biggest business trends/opportunities in today's China.

I find the borderless market aspect relevant. Regardless of the recent political chatter about trade wars and new borders, China as a consumer market, or—

perhaps more correctly—the Chinese consumers as a global opportunity, is now one of the best growth opportunities on the planet. For Westerners, it's no longer about "deciphering China" or "doing business in China," but more about finding a role that will allow them to benefit from the Chinese consumer directly or indirectly (i.e., by cooperating with leading Chinese companies).

In closing, let me say a few words about "global China"—doing business with Chinese companies inside and outside China. There are a variety of ways for businesses to engage with China in connection with the evolving consumer.

As the Chinese consumer evolves both in terms of numbers (with increasing incomes) and in varied needs, through the consumer generations described here, there are many opportunities in every link of the value chain and not always limited by borders. Be it upstream (agriculture/dairy like Yili), in manufacturing technologies (TCL/Haier/Kuka), in distribution or brand management (Grace Vineyard/Hai Di Lao/Toread), or even on the ground in chain store development (Daphne/Gil Wonton/Yonghui), opportunities can be found, as the entire country is undergoing an upgrading process. Also, the challenges Chinese companies face today, e.g., cost explosion, productivity, and branding experience, are stages that Western companies have in a sense already gone through and could thus help companies here to quickly accelerate their progress.

With this book, I hope I have succeeded in sharing a more accurate insight into how some of the leading Chinese companies in the consumer sector think, triggered by the dynamics of the different consumer generations we now face in China. If so, that would be a respectable achievement. On top of that I was hoping to pass along a few thoughts how to market in China and/or with Chinese consumers. If the "4F" themes gave readers new ideas on how to engage with Chinese consumers anywhere in the value chain—perhaps by working with Chinese entrepreneurs like those introduced here to participate in the vast market for Chinese consumers globally—that would be an even greater achievement; Face, Family, Food, and Fun are sure to keep the Chinese consumer market churning for a long time to come.